# The POLITICS *of* HAPPINESS

# The POLITICS of HAPPINESS

WHAT GOVERNMENT CAN LEARN FROM
THE NEW RESEARCH ON WELL-BEING

**DEREK BOK**

PRINCETON UNIVERSITY PRESS

PRINCETON AND OXFORD

Copyright © 2010 by Princeton University Press

Published by Princeton University Press, 41 William Street, Princeton, New Jersey 08540

In the United Kingdom: Princeton University Press, 6 Oxford Street, Woodstock, Oxfordshire OX20 1TW

press.princeton.edu

Fourth printing, and first paperback printing, 2011
Paperback ISBN 978-0-691-15256-1

The Library of Congress has cataloged the cloth edition of this book as follows

Bok, Derek Curtis.
  The politics of happiness : what government can learn from the new research on well-being / Derek Bok.
       p.    cm.
  Includes index.
  ISBN 978-0-691-14489-4 (hardcover : alk. paper)  1. Well-being—United States.  2. Well-being—Research—United States.  3. Quality of life—United States.  4. Quality of life—Research—United States.
5. Happiness—United States.  6. Happiness—Research—United States.
7. United States—Social policy—1993–  I. Title.
  HN60.B63 2010
  306.0973—dc22                                          2009030872

British Library Cataloging-in-Publication Data is available

This book has been composed in Sabon and Scala Sans LF

Printed on acid-free paper. ∞

Printed in the United States of America

10 9 8 7 6 5

# CONTENTS

## ACKNOWLEDGMENTS

Many people have helped me write this book. Among them are a number of student research assistants who guided me to useful readings in the various fields of policy I wanted to discuss. All of them gave valuable assistance, but three deserve special mention. Andrew Nicol prepared an exceptionally valuable set of readings in philosophy. Chris Robert shared with me his firsthand experience observing the work of the government of Bhutan in implementing its official goal of increasing Gross National Happiness. Jason Marisam displayed a remarkable ability to survey a wide variety of policy issues and immediately produce an analysis filled with issues to explore and policy options to consider.

Other friends and colleagues kindly read individual chapters and gave me useful comments. Among these valuable critics were Mary Jo Bane, Dick Easterlin, Dan Gilbert, David King, John Helliwell, Steve Hyman, Michael McPherson, Mark Moore, David Nathan, Theda Skocpol, Julie Wilson, and Dick Zeckhauser. James Shulman and Elena Zinchenko were kind enough to read the entire manuscript and offer helpful suggestions, as did the three anonymous readers selected by the Princeton University Press. Kim Hastings also earned my gratitude for an outstanding copyediting job that significantly improved the final manuscript.

In addition, I owe particular thanks to Connie Higgins, who brought me countless books and articles and prepared more drafts and revisions of drafts than she or I could possibly remember.

Finally, as always, I owe a special debt to my wife, Sissela, who read and reread every chapter with meticulous care and attention to detail. By some quirk of fate, it happened that she too was writing a book on happiness, though from a perspective very different from my own. The conversations that grew out of our mutuality of interests helped deepen my understanding of the subject and make the writing of this book a special joy.

*The* POLITICS *of* HAPPINESS

# INTRODUCTION

Deep in the Himalayas, wedged between India and China, sits the tiny Buddhist nation of Bhutan, a land marked by tall mountains, deep forests, and glacier-fed rivers and streams. All but inaccessible to foreign visitors, Bhutan was virtually unknown to the outside world until the 1960s. Its poverty, illiteracy, and infant mortality ranked among the worst of all nations. In 1972, however, something unusual happened in this remote country that caught the attention of people around the globe. A new king, Jigme Singye Wanchuk, declared that from this point forward "Gross National Happiness" rather than Gross National Product would be his nation's principal yardstick for measuring progress. Speaking of Bhutan's five-year development plans, he declared: "If, at the end of the plan period, our people are not happier than they were before, we should know that our plans have failed."[1]

The details of Bhutan's new policy are not yet fully worked out, but the following "Four Pillars" of Gross National Happiness summarize the main components.[2]

*Good governance and democratization*: Although the people of Bhutan seemed more than pleased with their ruler, King Wanchuk concluded that democracy offered the surest guarantee of happiness over the long run. Against considerable opposition from his subjects, the popular monarch gradually moved his country toward democracy by insisting on shedding his royal powers in favor of an elected assembly, an executive council of ministers chosen by the assembly, and a separate system of courts. His son, who has now succeeded him, seems determined to continue the process of democratization. Under the current king's leadership, Bhutan introduced a new constitution and held its first national election in 2008 to choose the members of its legislature.

*Stable and equitable socioeconomic development*: Economic growth is actively encouraged, since many Bhutanese are still very poor. But the government has deliberately refrained from maximizing immediate growth in order to maintain a slower, steadier expansion over the long run. Officials believe that the fruits of this development should be shared equitably. While the exact meaning of this principle remains unclear, it has already meant free and universal education (through the ninth grade, as of now) and free medical care for all.

*Environmental protection*: Economic growth has been repeatedly sacrificed to allow a series of restrictions to protect the environment and preserve its natural beauty for future generations. For example, tourism is strictly limited, plastic bags are officially forbidden, tobacco trade is prohibited (though compliance is far from perfect), and tax incentives and reduced import duties have been used to favor eco-friendly products and technologies. To prevent deforestation, the government has promoted electric stoves, set aside vast areas as national parks, and decreed that a minimum of 60 percent of Bhutan's total land area must be reserved for forests.

*Preservation of culture*: The government not only seeks to retain distinctive elements of Bhutan's traditional culture but also tries to promote such values as voluntarism and service to others, tolerance, cooperation, and a harmonious balance between family, work, and leisure.

Rather than leave these objectives in the form of general guiding principles, government officials have now produced 72 indicators for measuring progress, and the central government has been reorganized to ensure that all policies are designed with these indicators in mind. Much progress has already occurred. Gross per capita income now substantially exceeds that of India, average life expectancy has risen from 43 years in 1982 to 66 years today, and infant mortality has fallen from 163 deaths per 100,000 births to 40. New schools and clinics have sprung up throughout the country, and literacy has increased from 10 percent in 1982 to 66 percent at present. According to the latest World Bank Survey, the quality of governance does not yet approach the standards of most Western nations, but it has improved steadily and now ranks well above that of India and China, and far above that of Nepal.[3]

Notwithstanding these accomplishments, all is not perfect in Bhutan by any means. Different goals sometimes conflict with one another, requiring difficult trade-offs. In order to promote objectives of health, environment, and equity, the government has chosen to restrict individual freedom by such measures as prohibitions on smoking and private medical practice along with compulsory dress codes and strict architectural requirements for the design of new buildings. Despite the government's desire to preserve Bhutan's Buddhist culture, the introduction of television and the Internet poses a threat to traditional values. As young people leave the countryside for the excitement of the city, unemployment in the capital is high, theft is rising, and drug use is said to be a growing problem.

Even more troubling has been the treatment of the substantial Nepalese minority.[4] In the name of cultural unity, the government imposed regulations on dress in the 1980s and banned the teaching of Nepalese in schools. When angry protests ensued, more than 100,000 Nepalese were forced to leave the country and now live in refugee camps in Nepal. Those who remain are supposed to have papers to prove their citizenship, no easy matter in a country where illiteracy is still common and documentation often spotty. Anyone who cannot supply the necessary proof is barred from obtaining a business license, attending college, or working in the government. Apparently, then, despite the goals of tolerance and equity, some people are more equal than others, presumably at considerable cost to the latter's happiness.

All in all, however, the record of Bhutan remains impressive.[5] Whether or not one agrees with every policy decision of the government, the progress to date appears to be substantial, and the seriousness of the enterprise is undeniable. The sheer utopian audacity of a country that commits itself to making happiness the centerpiece of national policy is enough to compel a respectful interest.

Bhutan is still the only nation to formally adopt the people's happiness as its principal goal, but the idea has begun to capture the attention of other governments as well. President Nicolas Sarkozy of France has announced an initiative to measure well-being throughout the country as a result of evidence that French people are experiencing increasing difficulty in their daily lives.[6] In Britain, the prime minister's strategy unit has prepared a study paper on the implications of happiness research for public policy, while David Cameron, Britain's Conservative Party leader, has declared that "we should be thinking not just about what is good for putting money in people's pockets but what is good for putting joy in people's hearts."[7] Britain, China, and Australia are all considering the use of official happiness indexes in addition to the conventional economic measures of prosperity and growth.

What accounts for this recent upsurge of interest? After all, instituting happiness as a national goal is not a new idea. In fact, the idea of happiness as a goal of public policy reached its high watermark in the eighteenth century. A whole series of political theorists—Cesare Beccaria, Claude-Adrien Helvétius, and Francis Hutcheson, among others—proposed the promotion of happiness and the avoidance of pain as the proper aim of personal and public morality.[8] The French Constitution of June 24, 1793, even declared: "Le but de la société est le bonheur commun" (The goal of society is general happiness).[9] In the United States, Jefferson famously included the pursuit of happiness in the Declaration of Independence, and more than half the states inserted the phrase in their constitutions.

One writer, Jeremy Bentham, gained enduring fame through his pronouncement that the overriding aim of government should be to secure the greatest happiness of the greatest number of people by maximizing pleasures and minimizing pain.[10] In his more optimistic passages, he wrote about a science of happiness, a "felicific calculus" by which governments could measure the expected pleasures and pains resulting from policy proposals and choose the one that would produce the greatest net happiness.[11]

Bentham's dream of a science of happiness attracted much interest at the time and still finds a place in any anthology of political theory. He remains a key figure in the rise of utilitarianism with its familiar tools of policy-making such as cost-benefit analysis. Yet his hope of reducing policy-making to a process of mathematical calculation soon came to naught. Neither he nor his supporters could explain how to measure the intensity and duration of pleasures and pains let alone how to aggregate the myriad sensations experienced by millions of citizens in order to determine the net effect of legislative proposals. As a result, his felicific calculus remained for many decades a subject suitable only for abstract discussions by political scientists and philosophers and their students.

In the last 35 years, however, psychologists and economists in growing numbers have tried to overcome the problems of measuring happiness by the simple device of asking people directly how pleasant or disagreeable they find particular activities throughout their day or by inquiring how satisfied ("very," "fairly," "not at all," etc.) they are overall with the lives they are leading.[12] By analyzing the answers, investigators have arrived at a number of conclusions about which activities and experiences contribute to feelings of happiness or unhappiness and which are most responsible for the differences among people in the satisfaction they feel about their lives.

Among these findings, four are especially thought-provoking, since they depart in intriguing ways from conventional wisdom. The first conclusion, reported by economist Richard Easterlin and several other investigators here and abroad, is that average levels of happiness in the United States have risen very little if at all over the past 50 years despite substantial growth in per capita incomes.[13] Although rich people, as a whole, are happier than poor people and average levels of well-being are almost invariably higher in wealthy nations than in poorer countries, the percentages of Americans who declare themselves "very happy," "pretty happy," or "not too happy" are almost exactly the same as they were half a century ago.

The second discovery of psychologists (including the Nobel Prize–winning Daniel Kahneman) is that people are often surprisingly bad judges of what will make them happy.[14] In particular, they seem unable to predict the duration of the happiness or unhappiness brought on by many common events or changes in their lives. Instead, they attach too much importance to the immediate effects of a happy or unhappy experience without realizing how quickly they will adapt and grow used to what has occurred. Thus, they move to California for the weather only to find themselves no happier than they were before. They buy an attractive new car but cease to experience any added satisfaction after a few weeks. When asked what would make the greatest positive difference in their lives, Americans are likely to reply: "more money." As previously noted, however, decades of increasing prosperity do not seem to have made people happier. Instead, Americans seem to be stuck on a hedonic treadmill. As incomes rise, people soon grow used to their higher standard of living and feel they need even more money to lead a good life.[15]

The third finding, by Professors Alberto Alesina, Rafael Di Tella, and Robert MacCulloch, is that the growing inequality of incomes in the United States over the past 35 years has not made Americans more dissatisfied.[16] Those with below-average incomes, who would presumably be most adversely affected, turn out to be no less content with their lot than they were several decades earlier when incomes were more evenly distributed. The only identifiable group of people who seem perceptibly upset by increasing inequality are well-to-do Americans. These conclusions have gained support from a Dutch scholar, Ruut Veenhoven, who has studied differences in happiness between richer and poorer citizens in Western countries. By his calculations, *rising inequality of incomes* in several of the advanced economies of North America and Western Europe has been accompanied by a slight but perceptible *narrowing of national differences in happiness*.[17]

Veenhoven has also studied government efforts to help working-class families and other vulnerable groups and has arrived at a fourth unexpected result. In a provocative study of the effects of social welfare programs—including public pensions, health care systems, and unemployment insurance—Veenhoven found no correlation between the percentage of gross national income that governments devoted to such purposes and the happiness or health or longevity of the populations involved.[18] True, some of the most generous welfare states, such as Sweden and Denmark, are among the happiest countries in the world, but so are Iceland and Switzerland, where the percentage of national income devoted to welfare programs is only one-third as large.

In one respect, Veenhoven's findings should be reassuring to persons of all political persuasions. If happiness in the United States were distributed as unequally as incomes, the country might have been consumed long since by seething social unrest. Still, his conclusions on the effects of social legislation must be discomfiting to liberals who have fought for years for redistributive programs that would help the sick and needy. Although conservatives have long maintained that social legislation often fails to help its intended beneficiaries, Veenhoven himself is no conservative. Instead, he declares himself a scholar of liberal leanings who undertook his studies expecting to demonstrate the human costs of cutting back European welfare programs in order to compete in a global economy.

Findings such as those just described raise questions about several widely held beliefs with respect to the proper goals and priorities of government. If happiness has changed so little over decades of increasing prosperity, does it make much sense for public officials to attach such importance to economic growth as a measure of the nation's progress? If people are such poor judges of what will give them lasting satisfaction, should conservatives continue to extol the virtues of free markets and consumer choice in promoting the welfare of the population? At the same time, if poor Americans are undisturbed by the growth of inequality in recent years, should liberals worry so much about the distribution of income in America and press so strongly for progressive taxes and expensive government programs to benefit the sick, the needy, and the unemployed?

Before we cast aside the conventional wisdom, however, and start looking to happiness scholars for guidance, we need to think seriously about several questions:

- What, exactly, have these investigators discovered?
- How valid and reliable are their findings? How do they make their measurements and how do we know they are accurate?
- Even if psychologists can measure the happiness of a population accurately and identify the conditions of life that affect it, should

lawmakers pay attention to such findings if they run counter to what most voters *think* they want?

- Is happiness too private, too self-indulgent, too insubstantial a condition to be a suitable goal for an entire nation or society? If it *is* an appropriate goal, should it be the *only* guide to public policy, as Bentham claimed, or are there other objectives that political leaders should pursue?

- And finally, if lawmakers did decide to pay heed to the emerging knowledge about happiness, what changes in public policy might one expect as a result?

The pages that follow attempt to answer these questions.

# 1

## WHAT INVESTIGATORS HAVE DISCOVERED

Although empirical research on happiness hardly existed before 1970, it has since become a boom industry. Mounds of evidence have accumulated on how happy people claim to be in different countries, how their levels of contentment vary from one subgroup of the population to another, and what conditions or experiences are most closely related to the way people feel about their lives.* Several thousand articles have now been published on the subject. Books on how to be happy fill entire shelves in Borders and Barnes & Noble. International conferences abound. There is even a scholarly journal devoted exclusively to the topic.

*Happiness* is a large word encompassing many shadings of feeling and emotion. No single definition can do full justice to all that it embraces. The dean of American happiness scholars, Ed Diener of the University of Illinois, does his best to respond by offering the following comprehensive definition: "a person is said to have high [well-being or happiness] if she or he experiences life satisfaction and frequent joy, and only infrequently experiences unpleasant emotions such as sadness or anger. Contrariwise, a person is said to have low [well-being or happiness] if she or he is dissatisfied

---

*Some authors who write on the subject speak of *happiness*, others of *well-being* or *subjective well-being*, still others of *satisfaction with life*. These terms have slightly different meanings. *Happiness* seems to refer to one's immediate feelings and impressions while *satisfaction* connotes a more cognitive appraisal of one's life as a whole. However, investigators find that groups of people respond quite similarly whether they are asked how happy or how satisfied they feel about their lives.[1] As a result, researchers tend to use the terms interchangeably. I do likewise throughout this book, while noting the occasional cases in which the precise words used make a meaningful difference in people's responses.

with life, experiences little joy and affection, and frequently feels unpleasant emotions such as anger or anxiety."[2]

Most of the empirical research to date is based on surveys that ask individuals how happy or how satisfied they are with their lives. But that is not the only method used. As we will discover shortly, investigators can also ask people how they felt at various specific times during the day—at work, playing with children, cleaning up the yard, or socializing with friends. Although the latter technique yields valuable results, the former method is far more commonly used and therefore accounts for the findings discussed hereafter except where otherwise indicated.

## The Relation of Income to Happiness

Investigators have examined a long list of factors in an effort to determine their effect on well-being. Among them, income has been studied most intensively, possibly because so many people believe that a bit more money would be the change in their lives most likely to bring them greater happiness. As it happens, however, the effects of money turn out to be a great deal more complicated.

One finding is clear. At any moment in time, average levels of happiness in the United States are higher as one moves up the income scale. (See table 1.)

Similarly, global surveys show that differences in average happiness among nations are highly correlated with differences in their

TABLE 1
Levels of Satisfaction by Income Quartiles (1975 to 1992)

|  | Top quarter | Second quarter | Third quarter | Bottom quarter |
|---|---|---|---|---|
| Very happy | 40.78% | 34.80% | 29.46% | 24.07% |
| Pretty happy | 53.14% | 56.22% | 58.02% | 56.04% |
| Not too happy | 6.08% | 8.98% | 12.52% | 19.88% |

The figures above are taken from Rafael Di Tella, Robert J. MacCulloch, and Andrew J. Oswald, "The Macroeconomics of Happiness," 85 *Review of Economics and Statistics* (2003), p. 809, table 1.

average per capita incomes.[3] With only a few exceptions, wealthier countries have happier populations than poorer nations.

These findings seem to reflect what economists have long assumed: that income plays a major role in people's happiness. Surprisingly, however, longitudinal studies that trace the happiness of a sample of people in prosperous nations over long periods of time show that most people's satisfaction with life tends to change very little with the rise and fall of their income as they progress through their careers and eventually retire.[4] More puzzling still, as pointed out in the introduction, a number of studies have found that average levels of satisfaction with life have not risen appreciably in the United States over the past 50 years, even though real per capita incomes have grown a great deal during this period.[5]

Much controversy has arisen over how to reconcile these findings. Why haven't rising levels of prosperity raised the reported levels of happiness if people with higher incomes tend to be happier than those with less money? Analysts have advanced several theories to explain the seeming paradox.

One explanation could be that richer people are happier, not because higher incomes make them so but because happier workers are more successful and earn more money. There is something to this argument. One study, for example, found that students who were identified as happier when they entered college earned 30 percent more by the time they were 40 years old than classmates who were rated less satisfied as freshmen.[6] It is doubtful, however, that this explanation can account for more than part of the gap in well-being between rich and poor Americans.

Another possibility is that income growth has indeed brought greater happiness but the effects have been nullified by other trends in the society that have depressed well-being, such as increased levels of divorce, crime, drug use, unemployment, and the like. On first glance, this theory seems promising. As it happens, however, scholars who have tried to account for all the known trends that might affect happiness other than economic growth have concluded that the positive trends are potent enough that the net effect should have been to *increase* happiness even more instead of holding it back.[7]

Other analysts have pointed out that the economic growth experienced in the United States since 1975 has largely gone to the wealthiest 20 percent of the population. Since only this small minority have benefited, it is arguably not surprising that the average happiness of the population as a whole has failed to rise.[8] This explanation too seems initially plausible. One problem with it, though, is that the distribution of happiness between rich and poor has *not* grown more unequal in the past 30 years, suggesting that even the fortunate fifth who have seen their incomes rise have not become happier as a result.[9] Another awkward fact is that levels of happiness in the United States appear to have stagnated, not merely since the 1970s but over a considerably longer period.[10] In fact, well-being reportedly declined slightly from the mid-1950s through the 1960s, even though incomes were growing smartly during this period for all segments of the population. Finally, this theory does not explain why happiness has failed to rise during the last 20 years in several other well-to-do countries, such as Belgium, Switzerland, Norway, and Austria, where the fruits of growing prosperity have been more evenly distributed throughout the population than in the United States.

A fourth possible explanation is that satisfaction with one's financial situation depends in large part on how one's income compares with the incomes of others.[11] Thus, some investigators have found that the effects on happiness of a change in income are influenced significantly by what is happening to the incomes of one's friends, co-workers, and neighbors, especially those with whom one socializes.[12] As a result, any satisfaction people gain from a boost in their income tends to be eroded significantly if incomes all around them are rising just as fast. It follows that when prosperity is increasing throughout the nation as a whole, the average level of happiness will not rise correspondingly.

The positive effects of rising standards of living can also dissipate as people get used to higher incomes and begin to aspire to even greater riches.[13] For example, in 1975, at a time of stagnating incomes, 74 percent of Americans said that "our family income is high enough to satisfy our most important needs." By 1999, although per capita incomes had risen substantially, only

61 percent made the same claim.[14] Similarly, although the median estimate of the income Americans felt they needed to "fulfill all of [their] dreams" was approximately $50,000 in 1987, the necessary amount rose to $90,000 (in constant dollars) by 1996.[15] Observing these trends, analysts have described the pursuit of financial goals as a treadmill in which people's aspirations are forever beyond their reach, leaving them perpetually unsatisfied.

Rising aspirations and adaptation to higher living standards may account for the failure of happiness to rise in America over the past 50 years, but they do not explain how richer people came to have higher average levels of happiness than poorer people in the first place. Some light may be thrown on this question by yet another theory. Perhaps the added happiness of wealthier groups in the society does not come about primarily from money per se or from the goods that money can buy but from the subtler rewards that tend to accompany greater wealth. One such benefit might be the satisfaction that comes from feeling more successful or having a higher status than people of lesser means. A second benefit could be the greater challenge, independence, and intrinsic interest associated with the kinds of jobs that persons with higher incomes tend to hold. Since the hierarchies that account for these added satisfactions have always existed and will presumably persist regardless of how much or how little a nation's standard of living rises, one should not be surprised if the overall level and distribution of happiness are unaffected by growth. Whether per capita national incomes increase, stagnate, or decline, there will always be people at the top enjoying more interesting jobs, recognition, and freedom of action as well as people lower down the ladder whose work is more routine and who must endure the petty frustrations and disappointments of being less valued and more subordinate than those at higher levels in the social and economic hierarchy.

Until recently, scholars debated the merits of the various theories just described. Many of them accepted the conclusion that economic growth increased well-being substantially only in relatively poor nations where most people had too little to meet even their basic needs. According to this theory, once a country achieved a per capita income of $10,000–$15,000 per year, further growth yielded little if any increase in happiness. In 2007, however, Angus Deaton analyzed the results of the recent Gallup World Survey and concluded that if one compared percentage increases in per capita income, rather than absolute dollar increases, and if one disregarded the former Soviet bloc countries, which had gone through exceptional change and turbulence after the collapse of Communism, a given percentage increase in Gross National Product brought at least as great a boost in well-being in prosperous countries as it did in poorer nations.[16] A subsequent analysis by Betsey Stevenson and Justin Wolfers reached the same conclusion.[17] If this finding holds, the seeming paradox disappears and no longer needs to be explained.

Deaton's conclusion, however, is by no means generally accepted, at least not yet. Much previous research contradicts it, and even experts who agree that economic growth brings greater happiness in prosperous countries often find that the rate of increase is very slight. The European happiness scholar Ruut Veenhoven, for example, claims that if happiness in the United States continued to rise at the rate of the past 40 years, it would take 167 years to gain a single point on a ten-point scale of well-being.[18] Other analysts who have studied the recent Gallup data, including Stevenson and Wolfers, still concede that well-being has risen very little in the United States over the past half century.[19] Thus, although the Gallup results have provoked a lively debate, they have not yet produced a consensus that explains the underlying puzzle.

What does this controversy mean for the countless individuals who set great store by achieving financial success? Annual surveys of college freshmen across America over the past 35 years have consistently found that over 70 percent of these students feel that making a lot of money is a "very important goal."[20] Could they be making a serious mistake and might they ultimately find that financial success brings no added happiness in its wake?

Certainly, those who climb to the highest levels of the financial ladder tend to be significantly happier than those who remain on the lower rungs. Regardless of how little they come to relish their opulent lifestyles and however fleeting their enjoyment of vacation homes, expensive cars, and other luxuries that poor people cannot afford, they can at least savor the subtler satisfactions of worldly success. Their jobs tend to be more interesting, they have more control over how they spend their time, and they are more likely to give orders than to receive them. The mere fact that they have succeeded in what they set out to achieve should make them more satisfied with their lives. These considerations might seem to justify placing a high priority on financial success.

Yet psychologists report that those who attach great importance to achieving wealth tend to suffer above-average unhappiness and disappointment.[21] One can think of several reasons why. Presumably, many of those who are preoccupied with becoming rich will fail to realize their ambitions and feel acutely disappointed as a result. Even those who succeed may become so preoccupied with money that they neglect the human relationships that affect their happiness. In fact, researchers have found that the more people care about becoming rich, the less satisfaction they tend to derive from their family life.[22] Finally, those who do achieve some financial success are likely to find much of their added happiness short-lived. As previously explained, people grow used to the extra possessions that higher incomes allow; luxuries turn into necessities and aspirations rise, leaving them no more satisfied with life than before.

How to reconcile these conflicting observations is not entirely clear. Probably, the happiest people among the well-to-do tend to be those who were never too preoccupied with financial success but prospered by working hard at what interested them most while managing not to sacrifice family and friendships along the way. In addition, one group of researchers has discovered that many who care a lot about making money and do succeed in becoming rich gain a satisfaction from their accomplishment that offsets any loss of well-being they experience from sacrifices made in other aspects of their lives.[23] Even so, however, not all who aspire to great wealth will succeed. At the very least, therefore, the findings of psychologists convey a warning that being preoccupied with getting rich carries a substantial risk of leaving one unhappy and disappointed in the end.

If the search for wealth yields such uncertain rewards, why do so many people try so hard to achieve it? One can only guess at the answer. Perhaps the concern with money and possessions took root in much earlier times when most people were poor enough that added income was essential to overcome genuine privation and want. Perhaps material desires continue to be nurtured and reinforced by constant advertising and vivid media portrayals of the possessions and lifestyles of wealthy people. It is also possible that in an ambiguous world where genuine success is often hard to define, people seize on income, salary, possessions, profits, sales, and market shares as tangible measures of what they have achieved in life and what they might strive to accomplish in the future. Many Americans might even find it difficult to muster much ambition or see much meaning in their lives if they did not have money and the things that it can buy to spur them on.

## Other Sources of Happiness

Financial success is not the only prominent aspect of life that seems to contribute less to happiness than most people suppose. Demographic differences also have relatively little impact, at least in the United States. Age does not count for a great deal.[24] For most people, apparently, well-being declines slightly from their youth until they are about 40 and then improves very gradually until they reach their early 70s (assuming one controls for variations in health).[25] As for gender, white women were a bit more satisfied than white men for many years, but their level of contentment has declined in recent decades and has now dipped slightly below that of men.[26] Why the happiness of white women should have declined is something of a mystery, since the opportunities for a career that they have long sought have become far greater than they were in earlier decades. Perhaps these possibilities have raised aspirations to a level that is hard to fulfill, or perhaps conflicts between work and family have proved difficult to reconcile. No one seems to know for sure.

As of now, race turns out to be the only prominent demographic factor that correlates strongly with happiness.[27] Blacks continue to be considerably less satisfied with their lives than whites, although the gap has been cut in half over the last 30 years and seems to grow smaller with age. Interestingly, unlike their white counterparts, black women have kept pace with black men and have not grown unhappier during this period.

Several familiar lifestyle choices also have surprisingly little effect on well-being. Moving to warmer climates does not help. Likewise, hours spent watching television or going to the movies do not make much positive difference and yield less satisfaction than exercising, gardening, or playing sports.[28] Other experiences, such as a good meal at a restaurant or an exciting day at the ballpark may bring a momentary surge of happiness, but the effects rarely last very long.

What aspects of life *are* associated with lasting happiness? Using surveys that ask people how satisfied they are with their lives, researchers have found that six factors (apart from inherited temperament) account for most of the variation in people's well-being: marriage, social relationships, employment, perceived health, religion, and the quality of government.

Repeated surveys have found that married couples are more satisfied with their lives than individuals who are single, divorced, separated, or cohabiting but unwed.[29] People who are married tend to live longer and are less likely to become depressed, commit suicide, or experience health problems than persons who are divorced or separated.[30] Apparently, a close conjugal relationship acts as a buffer against adversity and helps the immune system protect against illness.

As several scholars have pointed out, however, one should not immediately jump to the conclusion that marriage *causes* added happiness. Those who marry might be happier to begin with, and their cheerful disposition could presumably contribute to a successful union. Further research has indeed confirmed that the causation runs both ways. People who marry, at least if they are below the age of 30, are happier on average than those who stay single. But studies of people before and after they get married also show that marriage and the courtship leading up to marriage often produce a significant increase in well-being.[31]

While researchers agree that marriage can give a substantial boost to happiness, there is disagreement over how long such feelings last. A few investigators have found that marriage increases happiness for extended periods, but most report that the sense of well-being tends to return to prenuptial levels within two or three years.[32] Of course, as in all such studies, the results merely reflect tendencies. They presumably include many couples who continue to gain added happiness from their marriage for decades along with many others who encounter difficulties early on that sour the quality of their relationship. Eventually, researchers may throw a clearer light on such variations by undertaking studies that reveal the varying reactions over time of different subgroups included in the overall averages.*

Whatever marriage brings, longitudinal studies suggest that its termination—whether from divorce, separation, or the death of a spouse—leads to a sharp loss of happiness for many people.[33] To be sure, most divorced couples recover quickly and almost all recover eventually. A divorce preceded by intense conflict can even leave both partners happier than they were before the breakup occurred.** By most estimates, however, a divorce or separation is associated with an average decline in happiness (estimated at 5 points on a 100-point scale for a divorce and 8 points for a separation, according to some analysts), and the effect often lasts for the best part of a

---

*One team of researchers using a new statistical technique on a longitudinal eight-year survey of German couples has managed to trace the varying effects of marriage on different groups. The largest group (79.6 percent), which also had the highest average level of happiness, experienced almost no change in well-being from four years prior to marriage to four years after. The next largest group (9.1 percent) began to decline in happiness four years before marrying but then grew steadily happier for four years thereafter. Another group (6.0 percent) grew happier until one year prior to marriage and then became unhappier at an accelerating rate for the next five years. Finally, a small group (5.2 percent), which was by far the least happy four years prior to marriage, became steadily happier thereafter, reaching a level equal to that of the largest, happiest group in the first and second years of marriage before declining slightly in the final two years of the study period. Anthony D. Mancini, George A. Bonanno, and Andrew E. Clark, "Stepping Off the Hedonic Treadmill: Latent Class Analyses of Individual Differences in Response to Major Life Events" (unpublished draft, 2009).

**The same research team cited in the previous text note also traced the average happiness of several groups over an eight-year period from four years prior to divorce through four years thereafter. Once again, the happiest and largest group (71.8 percent) was not significantly affected either before or after divorce. The next largest group (19.1 percent) grew significantly less happy during the two years prior to divorce and continued to grow less happy for another two years thereafter while still not recovering significantly in the final two years. The third, and initially least happy group (9.1 percent), began to grow happier three years prior to divorce and grew steadily happier for the next five years before declining slightly in the final two years.

decade.[34] Such long-lasting distress is unusual, since people seem to adapt in a matter of months to most of the setbacks in their lives.[35]

The effects of having children are more complicated. Most married couples (and even some who are not married) are anxious to have children, to the point that many who cannot do so naturally employ complicated procedures, such as in vitro fertilization or artificial insemination, in order to have a child. Yet researchers have come to mixed results concerning the actual effects of parenthood on happiness. One investigator has found that couples that deliberately choose to be childless are just as happy as couples that make the opposite choice.[36] Other researchers have reported that couples that do have children experience higher levels of tension, depression, and emotional distress than couples without children.[37] Harvard psychologist Daniel Gilbert cites several other studies showing that the happiness of couples declines after the birth of children and does not rise again until their offspring leave home.[38] Thereafter, although it is widely believed that parents gain added happiness as their children grow up and have children of their own, at least one study has found that parents with grown children are no happier on average than persons of a similar age who are childless.[39]

Not all investigators agree with these conclusions, and there are surely many parents whose children are a source of joy throughout life.[40] Moreover, whatever parents feel while their children are alive, surveys find that most people consider the death of a child the worst thing that could befall them, and investigators have confirmed that such a loss, especially if it happens unexpectedly, does tend to bring deep and prolonged grief to both parents.[41] All in all, then, the effects of having children are not entirely clear, although the weight of the evidence suggests that parenthood often fails to increase well-being significantly, let alone bring as much happiness to most parents as popular opinion would suggest.

Social relations apart from family do seem to add a lot to well-being. Both shy introverts and bounding extroverts report feeling happier when they are with other people than when they are alone; and, several researchers have concluded that human relationships and connections of all kinds contribute more to happiness than anything else.[42] Close friends certainly matter, especially one's closest friend (though seldom to the same extent as a spouse in a successful marriage).[43] Like a good marriage, a network of friends can evidently act as a buffer against misfortune or depression and even strengthen the immune system to protect against illness.

Organizations and social groups are another source of human contact that adds to well-being. Some researchers have found that merely attending monthly club meetings or volunteering once a month is associated with a change in well-being equivalent to a doubling of income.[44] What is less clear is how the causation runs. Do more group memberships (or more friends) increase happiness or do happier people tend to belong to more groups and have more friends? Once again, the answer seems to be that both tendencies exist. As with marriage, most people who have many friends and social connections are happier to begin with, but it is also true that most individuals tend to be happier when they are with other people than when they are alone.

Another relationship that would seem to matter is employment. There is still disagreement, however, on how much job satisfaction tends to affect satisfaction with life. Most earlier researchers concluded that feelings about one's job had only a slight relationship with one's overall well-being, but several later studies have found the correlation to be considerably stronger.[45] One must again ask which way the causation runs, and once more the evidence suggests both that satisfaction with one's job makes people happier and that happier people tend to gain more enjoyment from their work.[46]

A recent paper by John Helliwell, Haifang Huang, and Robert Putnam reports that trust in management is the aspect of work with the greatest effect on happiness, far outstripping pay in this regard.[47] Interestingly, Helliwell and his colleagues find that such trust is significantly lower in unionized plants, presumably because less trusting employees are more likely to join a union and because many unions try to build loyalty and solidarity among their members by emphasizing management's shortcomings and questioning its motives.

While disagreement remains over just how important job satisfaction is to one's overall well-being, there is no difference of opinion on the effects of losing one's job, whether from a mass layoff or for cause.[48] By all accounts, those who are let go tend to suffer prolonged distress. Their average decline in happiness is substantial—approximately 6 points on a scale of 100, according to some estimates—and they are more likely to commit suicide, experience depression, or succumb to drugs or alcohol abuse.[49] Part of their distress may come from the sharp drop in income, but the larger part seems to result from a loss of self-esteem and a fear of losing the respect of others. As a result, generous unemployment benefits have limited effects in relieving the pain.[50] Even those who are laid off and then find other jobs with substantially similar rates of pay often fail to fully recover their previous level of well-being.*

Still another condition closely linked with happiness is how people feel about their health. A drop of 20 percent in self-evaluations of health is associated with a substantial decline in happiness averaging 6 points on a scale of 100.[51] Surprisingly, however, doctors' assessments of health turn out to be only modestly correlated with the opinions of their patients and to have a rather weak association with the latter's happiness.[52] Self-reported health seems to have a greater effect on happiness than the results of medical tests would suggest because it incorporates other conditions such as stress, social isolation, or depression that often have no obvious physical symptoms. In addition, self-reports reflect the remarkable ability of most people to adapt quickly to many forms of illness and disability. Even individuals who have lost a limb or become quadriplegic seem to regain much of their former satisfaction with life within a year.[53] Only a few afflictions resist adaptation and take a grave and lasting toll on happiness. Chronic pain is one; depression is a second; the onset of a fatal disease such as AIDS or cancer is a third.

Religion provides another source of lasting happiness for many people. Americans with a deep religious faith tend to have better health and longer lives and are also less likely to commit crimes, get divorced, or kill themselves.[54] In part, the benefit comes from joining a community of fellow worshippers and participating

---

*Richard E. Lucas, Andrew E. Clark, Yannis Georgellis, and Ed Diener, "Unemployment Alters the Set Point for Life Satisfaction," 15 *Psychological Science* (2004), p. 18. Some of the discomfort from losing a job can be alleviated by the realization that others are in the same boat. Apparently, misery loves company. Thus, unhappiness among employees who have been laid off tends to diminish somewhat if the general level of unemployment in the community is high or even if other members of the family are also out of work.

together in church activities. But a strong belief in God appears to have independent effects, at least in the United States, and is accompanied—according to one writer, Richard Layard—by an average gain of 3.5 points on a 100-point scale of happiness.[55]

The importance of religious belief suggests another possible source of happiness, namely, a sense that one's life and work have a purpose and meaning that make them seem worthwhile. Researchers have yet to confirm this supposition definitively, but at least two studies of groups that chose to change their lifestyle to achieve personal values such as "environmental friendliness" and "voluntary simplicity" found that both experienced higher levels of well-being.[56] Conversely, common sense suggests that a lack of meaning and purpose in what one does should make one's existence seem pointless, diminish one's sense of self-worth, and eventually rob daily life of much of its intrinsic interest.

Another interesting finding is that volunteering or performing acts of kindness contributes significantly to happiness.[57] In one recent experiment, for example, two groups of subjects were given a sum of money and instructed to spend it all in the next 24 hours.[58] One randomly selected group was asked to spend the money on themselves; the second was told to spend it on others in need. When the subjects were tested a day or two later, those who gave to others were significantly happier than those who spent the money on themselves. Investigators have reached a similar result in studying individuals who devote substantial amounts of time to volunteer activities to help others. It is not immediately obvious whether happy people volunteer more or volunteering makes people happier. Research that follows people over time suggests that both influences are at work.[59]

Finally, there is much evidence that the quality of one's government is strongly associated with happiness. Living in a democracy with guarantees of freedom is particularly important. The positive effects are not immediate; for example, most of the countries in the Soviet bloc experienced sharply increased unhappiness in the first turbulent years after their abrupt shift away from Communism.[60] As conditions become more settled, however—provided the quality of government is reasonably good—the benefits of democracy are increasingly appreciated, and satisfaction eventually rises. In this regard, it is noteworthy that almost all the countries in the world that rank highest in overall satisfaction with life have been successful democracies for more than 80 years.[61]

Various aspects of government are associated with happiness. Economic freedom matters greatly in less developed countries, while personal freedom plays a particularly important role in wealthier countries such as the United States.[62] Other significant correlates include observance of the rule of law, efficient government agencies, a low level of violence and corruption, a high degree of trust in public officials (especially the police), and responsive encounters by citizens with public agencies and officials.* According to a World Values study, tolerance of minority groups—whether defined by race, religion, gender, or sexual orientation—is likewise associated with greater happiness, not merely for the groups directly affected but for the entire population.[63]

Together, the several factors described in this chapter have a great deal to do with how content people are with their lives. Their combined effect explains most of the variance among advanced nations in their overall level of well-being. It is these aspects of life, therefore, that command most of our attention in the chapters that follow.

## Comparing Nations

Much of the research on happiness has involved other countries besides the United States. Investigators sometimes use this data to compare nations according to the overall level of their population's

---

*John F. Helliwell and Haifang Huang, "How's Your Government? International Evidence Linking Good Government and Well-Being" (unpublished paper, 2006). It is not entirely clear, however, in which direction the causation runs. Do good, democratic governments contribute to happiness or do happy people help sustain democracy and improve the quality of government? One scholar has found that both effects are true but that the more potent influence consists of the effects happy people have on the quality of their government. Ronald Inglehart, "Democracy and Happiness: What Causes What?" (paper presented at Notre Dame Conference on New Directions in the Study of Happiness, October 22–24, 2006).

TABLE 2
Comparative Survey: Average Satisfaction with Life

| Country | Life evaluation |
|---|---|
| 1. Denmark | 8.02 |
| 2. Finland | 7.67 |
| 3. Switzerland | 7.47 |
| 4. Netherlands | 7.46 |
| 5. Norway | 7.42 |
| 6. Sweden | 7.38 |
| 7. Australia | 7.36 |
| 8. Canada | 7.33 |
| 9. New Zealand | 7.31 |
| 10. Belgium | 7.26 |
| *** | |
| 15. United States | 7.11 |

See Raksha Arora, "A Well-Being Report Card for President Sarkozy" (January 17, 2008), p. 2, http://www.gallup.com/poll/103795/WellBeing-Report-Card-President-Sarkozy.aspx.

satisfaction with life. Although the rankings vary, the recent Gallup surveys of happiness in more than 130 countries offer a reasonably representative example of the many tabulations that have been made. Table 2 gives the scores of the United States along with those of the ten nations with the highest levels of satisfaction, using an 11-point scale (0–10) with 5 being the midpoint between extreme satisfaction (10) and total dissatisfaction (0). Another intriguing formulation, presented in table 3, compares the total lifetime well-being in each country by combining the average satisfaction with life, or subjective well-being (SWB), and the average life expectancy in each country. (Only the ten highest-scoring countries, together with the United States, are shown.)

There are many other lists of this sort. The Scandinavian countries are pretty consistently near the top, along with the Netherlands and Switzerland. The United States usually falls somewhat further down the list, but tends to lie somewhere in or close to the upper third of all advanced industrialized countries.

The most encouraging finding to emerge from comparative research is that so many people around the globe claim to be "very"

TABLE 3
Comparative Survey: Quality Life Years

| Country | SWB × Life expectancy |
|---|---|
| 1. Switzerland | 63.0 |
| 2. Iceland | 61.8 |
| 3. Costa Rica | 60.8 |
| 4. Canada | 60.6 |
| 5. Denmark | 59.9 |
| 6. Sweden | 59.9 |
| 7. Ireland | 58.4 |
| 8. Netherlands | 58.3 |
| 9. Norway | 57.5 |
| 10. Finland | 57.1 |
| * * * | |
| 13. United States | 56.9 |

Ruut Veenhoven, "Apparent Quality of Life in Nations: How Long and Happy People Live," 71 *Social Indicators Research* (2005), p. 61.

or "fairly" satisfied with their lives. Contrary to the assertions of several prominent psychoanalysts, such as Sigmund Freud and Jacques Lacan, who denied that human beings could be happy, empirical studies show that most people consider themselves at least fairly content not only in the United States but in almost all advanced industrial nations.[64] In fact, when people rate their happiness or satisfaction with life on some sort of numerical scale, few national populations anywhere in the world report averages below the midpoint.* Even in the slums of Calcutta, most residents claim to be more happy than not, and the same is presumably true of many other destitute communities.[65] Only in a small number of nations—chiefly, former members of the Soviet bloc, such as Georgia and Bulgaria, and a few nations wracked by poverty,

*This is not so true of responses to the somewhat different question of where respondents would place themselves on a scale of 0–10 where 0 represents the worst possible life and 10 the best possible life. This question tends to elicit comparisons with all other human beings in the world and results in lower average scores. In the 2007 Gallup World Poll, where the scale just described was used, 42 percent of the nations surveyed recorded average scores below the midpoint.

violence, and unrest, such as Zimbabwe and Haiti—are majorities of the entire population either somewhat or very unhappy with their lives.

It would be heartening if these results meant that conditions are reasonably satisfactory for human beings almost everywhere. However, in a world where billions of people live at the subsistence level with inadequate diets, primitive health care, and deplorable sanitation, such a conclusion seems highly implausible. It is more likely that most people have a natural tendency to be happy that exists even in trying circumstances due to their remarkable ability to adapt to differing environments. Perhaps the instinctive desire of most human beings to seek out pleasurable experiences and avoid unpleasant ones helps tip the balance of their lives in a positive direction. It is also possible that individuals tend to have an optimistic bias in judging their own happiness by focusing on only a few aspects of their experience that are mainly pleasant rather than unpleasant.[66]

By and large, national levels of satisfaction do not change much from year to year, but there are exceptions. Most striking are the figures derived from nations within the old Soviet bloc, including Russia.[67] Average well-being in these countries began to decline before the collapse of Communism, and the decline continued for several years thereafter as output fell, unemployment rose, and the social safety net unraveled. When conditions began to improve in the mid-1990s, many of these countries started to turn around and achieve rising levels of happiness, although they still lag behind the levels they recorded in the early 1980s and fall even farther below the average well-being in Western Europe and North America.

In Western Europe, average levels of reported satisfaction in most countries have been relatively stable over the last few decades.[68] The most striking exceptions have occurred in the percentage of national populations declaring themselves "very satisfied" with their lives.[69] For example, from 1975 to 2005, the percentage of people feeling "very satisfied" in Denmark rose from 44 to 66. In Belgium the percentage feeling "very satisfied" plummeted from 38 to 15 in 2002 before rebounding to 32 in 2005. In Luxembourg, the percentage rose from 32 to almost 49.

On examining these comparative levels of happiness, some readers may wonder whether there is much to be gained from inquiring into the prospects for improving well-being in the United States through government policies. After all, Americans already seem to have achieved a high degree of happiness—not the very highest, to be sure, but high enough to place us among the most contented nations of the world. Much of whatever dissatisfaction remains may be very hard for any government to cure, since national levels of well-being seem quite stable in most countries. As a result, it is fair to ask whether trying to boost our score by a few tenths of a point would be worth making serious efforts.

In thinking about this question, one must remember that even small percentage increases in a country as populous as the United States represent large numbers of people. According to most surveys, more than 10 percent of Americans are "not too happy."[70] Although this percentage seems modest, it amounts to more than 30 million people. Even if much of what troubles them lies beyond the reach of government, merely helping a small fraction would improve the lives of millions. Similarly, only about one-third of Americans claim to be very happy—a figure at least 30 percentage points below the level achieved by Denmark. Thirty percentage points amount to approximately 90 million people, more than enough to justify a serious look at ways to try to improve the quality of their lives.

## Experience Sampling

Most of the findings described up to now are derived from surveys asking people how satisfied they are with their lives. Other researchers, however, have used a different approach—called experience sampling—by asking individuals about their feelings at various points in the day. Consistent with the research on how happy or satisfied people are with their lives, a major study using experience sampling found that respondents were usually happy in what they were doing and reported negative feelings only 34 percent of the time.[71]

TABLE 4
The Effect of Specific Activities on Happiness

| | Hours spent (per day) | Effect of activity on happiness (on a scale from 1 to 5) |
|---|---|---|
| Intimate relations | 0.2 | 4.74 |
| Socializing after work | 1.2 | 4.12 |
| Dinner | 0.8 | 3.96 |
| Relaxing | 2.2 | 3.91 |
| Lunch | 0.5 | 3.91 |
| Exercising | 0.2 | 3.82 |
| Praying | 0.5 | 3.76 |
| Socializing at work | 1.1 | 3.75 |
| Watching TV | 2.2 | 3.62 |
| Phone at home | 0.9 | 3.49 |
| Napping | 0.9 | 3.27 |
| Cooking | 1.1 | 3.24 |
| Shopping | 0.4 | 3.21 |
| Housework | 1.1 | 2.96 |
| Child care | 1.1 | 2.95 |
| Evening commute | 0.6 | 2.78 |
| Working | 6.9 | 2.65 |
| Morning commute | 0.4 | 2.03 |

Daniel Kahneman, Alan B. Krueger, David Schkade, Norbert Schwarz, and Arthur A. Stone, "Toward National Well-Being Accounts," 94 *American Economic Review* (2004), p. 429.

Experience sampling provides direct evidence of the varying degrees of satisfaction associated with different kinds of activities in a normal day. Table 4 records the results obtained from one such investigation in 2004.

On most matters, the results obtained by this technique are consistent with those derived by asking people to evaluate their lives. Using experience sampling, however, the effects of several conditions, such as marriage, divorce, performance of government, and the like, are much more muted than those obtained by asking people how happy they are with their lives. In particular, differences in income are associated with much smaller differences in happiness than those obtained by comparing the average satisfaction with life of rich and poor people. Having a bad night's sleep affects well-being the next day far more than having little money.[72]

With respect to a few conditions of life, experience sampling and retrospective evaluations of life actually yield conflicting answers. For example, in evaluating their lives, the French regularly report levels of satisfaction that are well below those of Americans. However, Daniel Kahneman and his colleagues estimate that if French people were asked to record their feelings while engaged in specific activities throughout the day, their replies would be as positive as those of Americans.[73] Why this should be remains unclear. It could be because the two types of surveys measure somewhat different things. Or it could be that individuals in different cultures vary in their willingness to tell an interviewer that they are very satisfied with their lives.

Experience sampling and life satisfaction surveys also differ occasionally in the responses to particular events. For example, people who are divorced report feeling significantly less satisfied with their lives than those who remain married. Yet experience sampling finds that divorced spouses actually feel slightly happier than their still-married counterparts.[74] This result may come about because people tend to focus on being alone when they think about divorce in reflecting on their lives but overlook the added satisfaction they can derive from being able to spend less time on household duties and more time with friends and other people.

The most striking result from experience sampling is that almost all of the most pleasurable activities of the day take place outside of work—having sex, being with family, seeing friends, and so forth. The less pleasant aspects of the day involve activities associated with one's job, including commuting. (Other tasks that seem like work, such as child care and household chores, also receive low ratings.) To be sure, some careers can be absorbing and satisfying even when they involve long hours and considerable stress. Overall, in fact, most people consider their jobs to be more pleasant than unpleasant. But in the course of the normal workday, employees often experience tedium or excessive pressure. Such feelings seem to have become more pronounced in recent decades. From 1955 to 1991, the percentage of Americans who considered nonworking activities preferable to hours spent at work climbed from 49 percent to 68 percent, while the percentage preferring time at work to leisure hours dropped from 38 percent to 18 percent.[75]

These findings diverge somewhat from those derived from studies that ask employees how satisfied they are with their jobs. There, the replies tend to be more positive, presumably because of the influence of factors such as pay, job security, benefits, and the like that do not have much effect on moment-to-moment feelings while at work. Nevertheless, most polls show a decline in job satisfaction, especially surveys that inquire more deeply into the subject.[76] For example, the Conference Board (which is supported by industry) has reported a drop in the proportion of employees who are satisfied with their jobs from 61 percent in 1987 to only 47 percent in 2006.[77]

## The Benefits of Happiness

The previous discussion has touched on a long list of findings. Some are surprising and others troubling. Taken as a whole, however, the research has come to one strikingly reassuring conclusion. By and large, the experiences and conditions associated with people's happiness are almost all ones that most Americans approve of heartily: strong marriages, close friendships, acts of charity and community service, feelings of good health, religious faith, and a stable democracy with a responsive, effective, accountable government. It is equally gratifying to find that lasting happiness helps to strengthen social bonds and promote the welfare of others. If this were not so, if satisfaction came from taking advantage of others and being insensitive to their needs, happiness could hardly be an attractive goal for a society to pursue. As it is, the findings of researchers offer the appealing prospect of a world in which the happiest people tend to do more for others and to gain satisfaction by doing so.

The most serious obstacle to achieving such a world is that people do not always understand what will give them lasting satisfaction and consequently fail to act accordingly. Under these circumstances, must elected officials in a democratic government simply accept the impressions of the majority, however misguided they may be? If not, how can public policy create the conditions and encourage the behavior that will bring their constituents greater happiness? These are among the questions that the rest of this book tries to answer. Before discussing them, however, we need to take a closer look at the body of work described in this chapter. Many readers will understandably be skeptical of information gained by having fallible researchers ask questions of fallible human beings. Since the value of the research is only as great as the accuracy of its findings, it is necessary to pause and consider how much weight one can prudently put on results derived in this way.

# 2

## THE RELIABILITY OF RESEARCH ON HAPPINESS

Can anyone claim to measure something so elusive, so intangible, so changeable as happiness? Jeremy Bentham certainly thought so. To him, measuring happiness and unhappiness was a simple matter of "account and calculation, of profit and loss, just as for money."[1] In later life, however, he began to have doubts about whether the calculations were as simple as he had originally thought. Could someone's varied experiences, pleasures, and pains actually be combined by some mechanical process? And did we really know how to compare one person's happiness (or unhappiness) with another's? "You might as well pretend," he later wrote, "to add 20 apples to 20 pears."[2]

### Modern Methods of Measuring Happiness

As pointed out in the preceding chapter, researchers have used two methods to overcome the problems that stymied Bentham. Of the two, experience sampling asks the simplest questions and elicits answers that are least subject to the weaknesses and distortions of memory or judgment. However, the method is expensive, and it is difficult to find enough people who are willing to be called repeatedly and badgered about their feelings. As a result, researchers often use a simpler variation called the day-reconstruction method in which they ask subjects to recall the various things they did on the preceding day and describe their mood during each activity. Although this approach relies on memory, the remembered events are very recent, and experiments have confirmed that the answers people give are very similar to those obtained by repeatedly calling each subject.[3]

Investigators who inquire more broadly about how satisfied people are with their lives ask their subjects to respond with varying degrees of precision. One widely used survey simply inquires whether respondents are "very happy," "fairly happy," or "not too happy." Other investigators ask people to make more exact estimates by evaluating their satisfaction with life on a scale of 1–7 or 0–10 ranging from extreme dissatisfaction to total satisfaction.

However precisely the question is phrased, the answers people give in describing their overall satisfaction with life represent a composite of reactions to a host of particular actions and events that could be harvested with greater accuracy through the use of experience sampling. Yet asking individuals to sum up their feelings about their lives elicits more than just adding up responses to a long list of particular experiences. It calls for a more thoughtful effort to recognize what is more important and less important in a vast jumble of happenings and often includes interpretations and evaluations that do not occur to people at the moment they are asked to record their reactions to activities in their daily lives.[4]

For example, many experiences seem more valuable thinking back on one's life than they did at the moment they occurred. In retrospect, people often attach great positive value to their battle with cancer, their ability to survive the challenge of Marine boot camp, or their successful climb to the top of a high mountain even though these episodes may have seemed very difficult and unpleasant at the time. Artists who lose themselves in their work may have no sense of being particularly happy while painting a picture yet count the experience as very satisfying when they pause to reflect on their lives. Similarly, one's immediate feelings while working in a factory or behind a desk are part of the experience of being employed but so are other factors, such as one's salary, one's sense of having done a job well, or the degree of respect one receives from friends and neighbors by holding a responsible position. Considerations of status and self-esteem probably help explain why large majorities of men and women say they would continue working if they won a lottery, even though many would presumably rate their time on the job quite low compared to other daily activities if they were asked to record their feelings at specific moments in the working day. It is no wonder, then, that the two methods of measuring happiness sometimes arrive at different or even conflicting results.

The choice of which method policy-makers should prefer depends on the purpose for which the answers will be used. Experience sampling is especially helpful for detecting activities that consistently elicit feelings of happiness or dissatisfaction. The immediate reactions to particular experiences by large numbers of people allow researchers to construct a scale of activities from the most to the least pleasant. The results have obvious relevance to lawmakers. Reducing the time spent on less pleasant pursuits, such as household chores, while increasing the time available for more satisfying activities, such as socializing with friends or being with one's family, is likely to add to happiness. Shifting the allocation of time toward activities that are widely considered unpleasant will normally have the opposite effect.

Asking individuals how satisfied they are with their lives elicits a more comprehensive and complex evaluation. It evokes impressions arising from the general condition of one's life such as feelings of success and failure that are not necessarily reflected in the immediate reactions to specific daily activities. Together with experience sampling, therefore, it can help to give a more complete understanding of a person's well-being. It would be hard to consider happy someone who felt distressed or bored or anxious at most times of a normal day. But it would be just as difficult to regard as happy a person who felt dissatisfied and disappointed with life as a whole. As a result, if governments ever did decide to make use of research on happiness, they would be well advised to pay attention both to studies that record the immediate sensations people experience in the course of a typical day *and* to reports that reflect people's judgment about the quality of their lives overall.[5]

Even these two measures combined may not fully capture all of the subtle feelings and emotional shadings that can enter into feelings as broad as "happiness" or "satisfaction with life." Nevertheless, in the absence of any practical way to disentangle all of the different threads and assign to each its proper weight, the methods just described provide the closest approximation of well-being that investigators are currently able to achieve.

## The Accuracy of Retrospective Evaluation

For better or for worse, retrospective evaluation (asking people how happy or satisfied they are with their lives) has been much more widely used than experience sampling by investigators who have done research on happiness. It is, therefore, the method that offers the most to public officials, at least for the time being. Admittedly, however, people can easily succumb to lapses of memory or biases of one sort or another in evaluating anything as complicated as their own lives. As a result, public officials must consider whether answers received by this technique are accurate enough for use in making policy decisions.

In thinking about this question, it is important to distinguish between *inaccurate* and *unreasonable* responses. For example, investigators have found that Olympic silver medalists tend to be less satisfied than the bronze medalists they defeated. Apparently, silver medalists fret about how they might have won it all while bronze medalists are delighted simply to have earned an Olympic medal.[6] Some observers may consider the silver medalists unreasonable, but there is no cause to doubt the accuracy or truthfulness of their responses.

Inaccurate answers are those that do not truly represent how respondents feel or how they would normally feel under similar circumstances. Such answers may be either unreliable or invalid. If the responses someone gives to the same question differ markedly from one period to another, it is a sign that the answers are not reliable. Such variations can arise for a number of reasons.[7] The sequence of questions can significantly alter how respondents answer. If they are asked how satisfied they are with their lives and the inquiry is immediately preceded by a question about recent visits to the dentist, people are likely to give unreliably low estimates of their well-being because their minds are still focused on memories of the dental chair. Transitory moods can also cause respondents to give unreliable answers. For example, people describing their level of satisfaction on September 12, 2001, could easily give more pessimistic evaluations than they would normally give because of the shock and sorrow brought on by the terrorist attack on the World Trade Center. Even less dramatic events and circumstances can affect responses in this way—a rainy day, a headache, the breakup of a romance.

To the extent that such transient conditions affect only a single respondent, no great harm is done to the reliability of a large survey, since random influences of this kind will tend to cancel themselves out. It is possible, however, that circumstances that affect one person's answers will affect all or most of the other respondents in the same way. For example, an event as drastic as the attack on the World Trade Center might have an influence on many of the replies to a survey administered the next day.

Researchers are usually sophisticated enough to avoid problems of the latter sort. Still, people may be subject to pervasive influences of a permanent kind that consistently affect the accuracy (or validity) of even the largest and best-designed surveys. For example, it is possible that people have a persistent tendency to exaggerate their degree of happiness in responding to a researcher.[8] If so, the results will not be an accurate reflection of their true feelings. (Of course, if the tendency does not vary in intensity over time, it may still not affect the usefulness of *trends* in happiness or even distort conclusions about the relative importance of the various factors that enter into self-assessments of overall happiness.)

Some analysts worry that biases of this kind may not exist to the same degree in different cultures. Thus, a greater reluctance in countries such as France to express satisfaction about one's life to strangers could account for the fact that the French score below Americans in their average overall happiness even though neither direct sampling methods nor objective evidence gives reason to suspect that the two populations actually feel any differently about their lives.[9] Conversely, an opposite bias may account for the fact that people in Latin America claim to be happier than conditions in their countries would lead one to expect. Because of the possibility of such cultural differences, efforts to compare the average levels of well-being of different countries should be treated with considerable caution. For purposes of domestic policy, however, this problem has little significance, since international comparisons are seldom relevant to the choices about domestic policy that public officials have to make.

Efforts to estimate one's satisfaction with life can also be invalid because of certain common misapprehensions people have in making such judgments. For example, experiments have shown that most people do a poor job of predicting the effect of many events and circumstances because they focus on their immediate reaction and do not take account of how quickly they will adapt to the change in question. Moreover, since no one can remember everything in one's life, individuals typically make judgments based on only a few of the countless experiences they have had and thus may overlook events that would seem to be important enough to affect their overall evaluation. These distortions are usually random enough that they are canceled out in surveys involving many subjects. Moreover, even if a persistent, widespread bias exists (such as a pervasive tendency to remember more happy than unhappy experiences), the responses can still be an accurate reflection of how the respondents feel, whether or not they seem unduly optimistic or pessimistic to an outside observer. And in the last analysis, it is the satisfaction individuals feel about their own lives, not the judgment of some outsider about how they ought to feel, that matters most in measuring people's happiness.

Two authors have recently argued that happiness is simply too complex a state of mind for individuals to evaluate, so that the answers given to surveys of well-being cannot be relied upon for making policy decisions.[10] The example the authors use to prove their point involves the responses given by those who have suffered serious permanent injuries. Such persons typically adapt surprisingly quickly and claim to be quite happy after only a few months. The same people, however, if asked what they would give up to be restored to their previous condition often state that they would willingly sacrifice years of their life.

While these answers may seem contradictory, the contradiction is more apparent than real. Researchers have long recognized that those who suffer serious injuries do not fully regain their previous level of well-being but remain significantly less happy than before. At the same time, the estimates people provide of how many years they would give up to have their health restored are likely to be exaggerated, since those who claim that they would willingly shorten their lives would probably feel quite differently when the time finally came to live up to their bargain.* As a result, the sacrifice that seriously injured people would actually make to regain their previous condition may not be inconsistent with the loss of satisfaction they feel because of their disability.

Aware of doubts such as those just described and mindful of the difficulty of combining the myriad experiences and sensations entering into any estimate of one's satisfaction with life, happiness scholars have gone to considerable lengths to test the accuracy of their findings. Most of these efforts have involved checking the results against independent evidence of well-being. These checks have tended to support the results of the surveys. For example, evaluations of subjective well-being turn out to correlate with the consensus opinion of friends and relatives about how happy the subjects of the survey seem to be.[11] Other tests have established that people who describe themselves as happy tend to smile more often and more genuinely than those who declare themselves less content.[12] Brain scans have even shown that subjects who call themselves happy activate more frequently a part of the brain that neuroscientists have associated with pleasurable sensations.[13]

Still other studies have shown that people who claim to be happy are more likely to experience positive outcomes and less likely to experience unfavorable events. Thus, individuals who are very satisfied with their lives turn out to be less prone than dissatisfied people to commit suicide or to experience psychiatric problems.[14] They are also more likely to live a long life, have happy marriages, remain employed, and enjoy good health.[15]

Even if the responses to a survey are reasonably accurate, policymakers must exercise care in interpreting the results. For example, it is easy to confuse causation and correlation. As mentioned in the

*The same authors also indicate that self-assessments of happiness are inaccurate because many experiences in life turn out to have value that is not fully appreciated at the time the experience takes place. This point is undoubtedly correct in the case of responses given to investigators using the experience sampling technique. As mentioned earlier, however, the subtler feelings that can be lost in people's immediate reaction to events are much more likely to enter into the evaluations people make when asked how satisfied they are with their lives. That is an important reason why combining both methods of exploring happiness can give a more complete picture of happiness than either one alone.

preceding chapter, the fact that happiness is significantly correlated with marriage (or some other condition) does not necessarily mean that marriages *cause* happiness. Sometimes the causation will run in the opposite direction. Often, causation runs in both directions, and the relative importance of each must be teased out by studying people's experience over time or by using other methods of analysis.

It is also possible that neither happiness nor the other condition being studied is causally related to the other even though the two are highly correlated. Instead, some third factor may be responsible. For example, if poorer people are less happy than their richer compatriots, the cause may not be lower incomes but the fact that people with lower incomes tend to have less interesting work with less authority and freedom of action. Investigators can try to take account of this possibility by controlling for status differences in jobs and other factors that might conceivably be responsible, but it is always possible that they will overlook the real cause.

All in all, however, careful researchers seem to measure happiness or dissatisfaction with enough accuracy to make the results useful for policy-makers. It is true that a variety of transitory influences can affect people's judgments about how happy or satisfied they are. Most of the time, however, these distortions are sufficiently random to cancel themselves out in surveys involving substantial numbers of people. As time goes on and more and more important findings are confirmed by other surveys conducted by other investigators using other subjects, the results should be accurate enough to be helpful to government officials.

In the end, the relevant question in making policy is not whether self-evaluations of well-being are perfect but whether they are at least as accurate as the best alternative ways of gauging people's preferences, opinions, and needs. In this regard, the findings of researchers investigating happiness are likely to be more accurate than the methods lawmakers typically use, such as talking to voters and reading mail from constituents. Such methods are obviously vulnerable to all the ways in which vocal minorities and well-organized interest groups can cause some voices and opinions to speak more loudly than others. Opinion polls asking people to state their priorities or list their concerns are not much better. Psychologists such as Daniel Gilbert have shown experimentally that people thinking about their needs and desires frequently err by failing to appreciate how quickly they will adapt to most changes in their lives.[16] They continue to feel that a bit more money would resolve their troubles and bring happiness to their lives despite a number of studies showing that the pleasure of extra income soon fades. They focus too much on some particular aspect of a new experience, such as a warmer climate or a larger television screen, and ignore other aspects that will have a contrary effect. Conversely, they fail to anticipate how quickly they will adapt to many of life's misfortunes and hence often have exaggerated fears.

Opinion polls are not the only questionable statistics commonly used in Washington. Official unemployment figures do not count the number of people who would like to work but have given up trying. Poverty statistics continue to be cited widely even though the official figures are based on evidence of income that differs greatly from available information about the value of goods and services actually consumed by low-income Americans. The Gross Domestic Product is likewise a very crude way of estimating welfare.[17] It measures output rather than consumption. It excludes many activities that benefit society, such as caring for children in the home, while including others that are actually harmful or useless, such as the manufacture of cigarettes. Moreover, a nation's total production of goods and services is at best a means to other ends and often a dubious means at that. In contrast, happiness, or satisfaction with life, can lay claim to being not merely an end in itself but the end most people consider more important than any other. In light of these weaknesses, the results of happiness studies seem, if anything, more reliable than many familiar statistics and other types of evidence that legislators and administration officials routinely use in making policy.

If there is any special weakness in the research on happiness, it is that the subject is still quite new. While hundreds of studies have been carried out, many possible sources of happiness and distress are still unexplored. Moreover, most studies merely show correlations between well-being and other factors at a single point in time so that the direction of causation is often unclear. Varying definitions of happiness and differing methods of inquiry can make it difficult to compare studies, while significant findings have not always been replicated and tested enough to warrant a high degree of confidence in their accuracy. For these reasons, though old verities are periodically questioned and new discoveries made in every field of inquiry, a subject developed as recently as happiness research is bound to be less stable and more prone to controversy than most. Findings that seem definite and settled at any given moment are more likely to be challenged and qualified than the established tenets of older areas of inquiry. The dispute about whether rising incomes increase well-being offers a typical illustration. Over time, however, as more studies accumulate, more findings are confirmed, and existing disagreements are resolved, current uncertainties should diminish.

## Further Reservations

Philosophers have raised additional questions of a more speculative nature about the definition of happiness used by current researchers. For example, a woman may consider herself happy because she feels she has a secure, well-paying job with a bright future and a husband who loves her. Suppose, however, that she is actually about to lose her job for poor performance and that her husband has many clandestine love affairs of which she is unaware. Can we say that this woman is truly happy? According to some philosophers, the correct answer is no; individuals can only give a proper account of their well-being if they base their opinions on an accurate perception of the relevant facts.[18]

On first impression, this point of view is hard to comprehend. However mistaken the woman may be about the underlying facts, there is no reason to doubt that she is giving an accurate view of her feelings of satisfaction at the time psychologists put the question. To deny this runs quickly into a host of awkward problems. Many Christians gain happiness from their belief in the existence of heaven. It would surely be far-fetched to insist that they can be truly happy only if their belief in heaven turns out to be accurate. What philosophers must mean, then, is not that the woman does not in fact feel happy but that a happiness built on false perceptions of reality is simply not worth having.

Whatever one thinks about this point of view, it is not likely to have much effect on happiness surveys. Estimates of well-being are usually based on a number of different factors—marriage, children, financial circumstances, health, friends, and the like. Some individuals may be grossly in error about an important element of their lives, but they will normally be few in number. Even fewer people will be seriously mistaken about *several* important matters. Moreover, not all will err in the same direction so that the mistaken happiness of some will be neutralized by the unfounded distress of others. Rarely, if ever, therefore, will such errors affect the research findings that interest lawmakers.

Several philosophers have raised another doubt about the usefulness of judgments people make in evaluating their own lives. To these writers, such appraisals can be truly valid only if they accord with logic and sound judgment. For example, the philosopher John Rawls has defined happiness as success in achieving a *rational* life-plan, while Joseph Raz avers that well-being consists of the successful pursuit of "*valuable* activities" (italics supplied).[19]

The relevance of such definitions for policy-making depends on the way in which the test of rationality or value is applied. If lawmakers agree that their object is to further the well-being of their constituents but consider the particular proposal before them to be a poorly reasoned means to that end, they can certainly reject such a proposal as irrational and unwise. But if they use rationality or value as a device to impose their own views on how people *ought* to live their lives instead of trying to maximize the happiness experienced by their constituents, the situation is quite different. Philosophers can try to persuade their readers of the proper aims and elements of a worthwhile life, but legislators have a more restricted mandate. Their responsibility is to promote the well-being experienced by their constituents, not to impose their own values by deciding what kinds of happiness (or other goals) their constituents *ought* to seek. When lawmakers have ignored this principle—for example, by outlawing the consumption of liquor or by criminalizing homosexual relations—the results have often been unfortunate.

## Are the Results of Happiness Research Accurate Enough for Policy-Makers to Use?

Analysts looking at the research on well-being have pointed to some genuine problems with the methods used to measure something as complicated and subjective as happiness. Such criticisms are useful and can sometimes lead to helpful improvements. Where skeptics err is when they use these imperfections to reject self-evaluations entirely even though the results are reasonably accurate and better than any available alternative. Having dismissed the findings, the critics can then feel free to substitute whatever alternative conclusion happens to suit their favorite theory or political preference. Thus, in the tradition of Freud and Lacan, the psychoanalyst Slavoj Zizek insists that talk of happiness is "inherently hypocritical" and that those who consider themselves happy are simply deluding themselves.[20] In contrast, libertarian Will Wilkinson suggests that it is our misguided tendency to compare ourselves with fortunate neighbors and friends instead of with our grandparents that confuses us so that "we simply don't realize how good we feel," and how much our free market economy has improved our condition over that of earlier generations.[21] Policy-makers should resist the temptation to follow these examples by seizing on every possible imperfection in the methods of measuring happiness to justify more questionable conclusions derived from voter surveys, the arguments of favored lobbyists, or some preferred ideology or unsubstantiated hunch about what people "really" want.

Of course, at this early stage of happiness studies, the weight that policy-makers give to this research should ultimately depend on the nature of the choices they are making. A prudent legislator might not wish to rely on such findings in weighing choices that will entail major changes in the existing order or disrupt the lives of many people in the hope of greater gains for others. Decisions of this kind require a degree of certainty that a young field such as happiness studies may not yet be mature enough to provide. Similarly, in making decisions that would entail large new expenditures on novel programs that purport to increase well-being, lawmakers may gain useful insights and intriguing possibilities from the relevant research but still wish to postpone a final decision pending further research to determine whether the available findings hold up under criticism and replication. When choosing how best to deploy limited funds among a series of plausible opportunities, however, research suggesting that some options will tend to produce greater satisfaction than others may well be of greater help in setting priorities than any other evidence available.

At the very least, the field of happiness studies seems to have enough promise to warrant a closer look at its usefulness to policymakers. Yet some critics will still question whether happiness is an appropriate goal for democratic governments to pursue. Such arguments must be dealt with before undertaking to consider the practical implications of the recent research.

# 3

## SHOULD POLICY-MAKERS USE HAPPINESS RESEARCH?

There are powerful arguments for making happiness a focal point for government policy. Its overriding importance to human beings has been affirmed by influential thinkers from Socrates to John Locke to Sigmund Freud. According to opinion surveys, happiness usually ranks at the top of the goals people hope to achieve, a high regard that should surely count for something in a democratic state.[1] What's more, as indicated in chapter 1, the way to lasting happiness seems to include acts of civic engagement, kindness, and other behaviors far more beneficial to society than an endless pursuit of momentary pleasures and trivial pursuits. In turn, people with high levels of well-being are more likely to be healthy, happily married, effective in their jobs, and civic-minded, generous, and tolerant citizens.[2] If both the causes and effects of happiness are so worthwhile, why wouldn't any sensible government want to shape its policies to help its citizens achieve higher levels of well-being?

### Is Happiness a Proper Aim of Public Policy?

Despite the arguments just noted, not everyone will agree that governments should devote themselves to promoting happiness. Some readers undoubtedly have other ends they consider more important. They may attach greater value to fulfilling their highest potential, or to leading a virtuous life, or to dedicating themselves wholeheartedly to God or the welfare of others.

Although these goals may seem appealing, legislators would make a serious mistake if they proclaimed a particular virtue, or religious faith, or some other value of their own choosing as the proper end of government. In a democracy, political leaders are representatives of the citizenry; they are elected to promote the welfare of the people, not to impose their own conception of an exemplary life. Even a goal as laudable as virtue is a dubious aim to insist on for others. As Immanuel Kant once wrote: "What are the ends which are at the same time duties? They are these: one's own perfection and the happiness of others."[3] In much the same way, politicians (and philosophers) may choose whatever goals they wish for themselves; they may even try to persuade people to adopt them. What they should not do is to use the power of the state to demand that their constituents accept such values (except to the extent necessary to protect the legitimate rights and interests of others).

Some who would agree with this conclusion, however, may still balk at choosing happiness as the proper goal for governments to pursue. Almost 200 years ago, Benjamin Constant maintained that *liberty* is the only appropriate objective for the state. As for happiness, he declared, "Let [government officials] confine themselves to being just. We shall assume the responsibility of being happy for ourselves."[4] Of course, Constant wrote these words before the era of modern Western democracy at a time when governments were much less likely than they are today to act in the best interest of the people. Yet even now, many libertarians would restrict the activities of government to protecting individual liberty by defending the nation against its enemies and enforcing such rules as are necessary to ensure that no one acts in ways that unfairly interfere with the personal freedoms and property rights of others.

Many of those who share this view believe that governments are almost always run by fallible politicians who frequently act to please the special interest groups that help them cling to office. With leaders such as these, they maintain, better to restrict the powers of government and give individuals a maximum of freedom to pursue happiness in their own way by their own initiative, guided by the invisible hand of the market.

Political scientists differ among themselves on whether governments with limited ambitions do a better job than welfare states in promoting the well-being of the people.[5] For purposes of this discussion, however, the answer hardly matters. In seeking to restrict the powers of government, libertarians who doubt the ability of public officials to promote well-being are not claiming that happiness is an inappropriate aim for policy-makers to pursue. They are merely insisting that private ordering is a surer way to achieve this goal.

Proponents of limited government may worry nonetheless that a nation that actively promotes happiness will eventually become a "nanny state" that does so much to protect its citizens from the vicissitudes of life that people will lose their self-reliance and cease to grow strong by having to meet challenges and overcome adversity by themselves.[6] Once again, however, those who hold this view are not really disputing the importance of happiness; they simply disagree with welfare statists over how best to help human beings achieve a fulfilling life. The argument is partly one of time horizons. Those who favor a welfare state wish to alleviate some of the familiar hazards of life, while those who emphasize self-reliance claim that citizens will flourish more in the long run if they learn to fend for themselves and gain the confidence, pride, and self-respect that come through overcoming challenges by their own efforts. This too is a respectable argument, but it is an argument over how best to achieve well-being, not about whether well-being itself is an appropriate aim for governments.

Some libertarians may go further, however, and insist that freedom is so important in its own right that it ought to be the sole aim of government. As Jan Narveson has put it in *The Libertarian Idea*, "The only relevant consideration in political matters is individual liberty."[7]

On reflection, this is a difficult argument to accept or even to understand. Happiness scholars agree that both political and economic freedom contribute significantly to a satisfying life. As a result, freedom is surely an important aim of government. Disagreements arise only when libertarians claim that freedom is the only source of well-being that the state should promote. As the findings summarized in chapter 1 make clear, happiness has many sources and individual liberty may not even be the most important. As a result, those who insist on freedom as the "only relevant consideration" must either define freedom so broadly as to make it virtually indistinguishable from well-being or claim some intrinsic value in freedom that is not only independent of well-being but so important that it overrides all other aims of policy. What this value might be is hard to fathom. Those who insist on it would apparently do away with many, if not most, existing laws, including programs such as Social Security and Medicare that enjoy overwhelming public support in all leading democracies and contribute greatly to well-being. Apart from other objections, such a position is clearly impractical and unrealistic in a modern democracy.

Although the libertarian critique may not offer a convincing argument against the use of happiness as a goal of public policy, it does convey a valuable note of caution. The findings of researchers conceal a great deal of individual variation. Not everyone defines happiness in the same way. Not everyone achieves happiness in the same way. Lawmakers must take care, therefore, not to use the research to impose some monolithic recipe for well-being on all its citizens.

Of course, the government may require everyone to pay taxes in order to support measures enacted to promote the general welfare; even libertarians will accept a tax for such basic functions as national defense and law enforcement. Government can also provide incentives in order to encourage people to make choices that tend to increase their well-being, as it does by imposing taxes on cigarettes and liquor or by creating tax incentives to contribute to private pensions. It can educate in an effort to persuade the public to make better choices, as it does by sponsoring premarital counseling or ads to give up smoking. However, using rules and requirements to impose happiness by fiat is another matter. It would be clearly inappropriate to force citizens to change their behavior by requiring them to join a church or engage in community service on the basis of research showing that these activities tend to be accompanied by greater well-being. The Declaration of Independence proclaims a universal right to pursue happiness; it does not suggest that everyone must pursue it in the same way. In a few instances, governments have imposed such rules: compulsory schooling, seat-belt laws, and social security taxes are all prominent examples. One need not be a libertarian, however, to recognize that measures of this kind should be viewed with great caution and enacted only when there is clear and convincing evidence that they will truly increase well-being.

The British author Aldous Huxley sounded yet another cautionary note in response to the idea of making happiness a goal of public policy. Huxley's novel *Brave New World* describes a society whose leaders have pushed the idea of happiness to the extreme of dispensing masses of feel-good pills to everyone along with endless amusements, such as a form of motion pictures ("feelies") that give audiences the sensation of actually experiencing all manner of fantasies and delights instead of merely seeing them on a screen.[8] From this programmed world, all sources of discomfort have been systematically removed; even aging has been replaced with enduring youth while conditioning has erased all envy over social status. The leaders of this society see to it that everything runs smoothly and pride themselves on the universal feeling of contentment and social stability they have helped to engineer.

Into this society comes a young man from one of the remote reservations set aside for survivors from much older civilizations. Welcomed as an object of curiosity, this youth—nicknamed "the Savage"—surprises his hosts by rejecting their utopia. One of their officials, Mustapha Mond, asks him:

> "Don't you want to be comfortable?"
> "I don't want comfort," the Savage replies. "I want God, I want poetry, I want real danger, I want freedom, I want goodness, I want sin."
> "In fact," Mond observes, "you're claiming the right to be unhappy."
> "All right, then," says the Savage, "I'm claiming the right to be unhappy."[9]

Thereafter, the Savage retreats to a remote lighthouse and eventually kills himself after he is discovered by hordes of curiosity seekers and hounded to distraction.

*Brave New World* makes a forceful argument that even if happiness is a legitimate goal of public policy, not every form of pleasure is desirable, nor is every means of achieving universal happiness acceptable. Secretly injecting some euphoric substance into the water supply might create a form of happiness, but such a scheme would surely be resisted because of the underhanded means employed. Dispensing free marijuana could also produce a state of widespread contentment, but it is a contentment that most people would reject, either because it gives a form of happiness that is not worth having or because a society made happy in this way would be highly vulnerable to eventual decay and disaster.

At the same time, while Huxley presents a picture of society that is chilling to most readers, it is an extreme example that hardly bears much resemblance to conditions in the United States, either now or in the foreseeable future. The mindless hedonism in his dystopia is not at all similar to the happiness described by contemporary researchers. Nor does government pose the greatest threat of tranquilizing the public with superficial pleasures. The nearest approximation to *Brave New World* in America today is not the product of official policies but arises from the overuse of Prozac and other antidepressants prescribed by private doctors and from the flourishing trade in drugs that persists in spite of government efforts to suppress it.[10] If anything else threatens to lull the American people into passivity, it is products of the market such as television, iPods, and computer games rather than policies of the state.

Still another argument against making happiness a goal of public policy proceeds along quite different lines. The fear is not that governments might try to produce a form of mindless happiness by artificial means. Rather, the worry is that public officials could succeed so well in promoting genuine happiness by legitimate means that people would no longer experience the kinds of setbacks and misfortunes that have spurred exceptional individuals to great achievements and helped countless others gain insights that enlarged their understanding and enriched their lives. Worries of this kind have prompted some authors to question making happiness a goal on the ground that dissatisfaction and melancholy are the indispensable spurs to creativity and human progress.[11]

While this criticism has a romantic appeal, its basic premise is suspect. One can certainly think of some remarkably creative people, such as Schopenhauer, Nietzsche, and Beethoven, who suffered serious misfortunes and seem to have had distinctly melancholic dispositions. Whether their distress contributed to their achievements, however, is not so clear. Moreover, leaving aside such exceptional individuals, a careful analysis of many empirical studies has revealed that happiness tends to promote rather than retard original thinking while also helping employees perform more effectively in a wide variety of jobs.[12] Overall, then, there is little scientific basis for the claim that a society with high levels of well-being would eventually lose its dynamism and creativity.

There *is* evidence, however, that people who achieve the highest levels of well-being—the happiest 10–12 percent—do not succeed as well in some endeavors as those who are slightly less happy.[13] The happiest do better at establishing close personal relationships and are the most likely to volunteer and help others. But they are not as likely to earn very high incomes or become active participants in politics as others who are also happy but somewhat less so. Apparently, individuals who reach the very highest level of happiness do not possess the nagging sense of unfulfilled ambition that drives others to work exceptionally hard for worldly success.

One may agree or disagree over the need to preserve such intense ambition for money, power, and fame, but the question has little practical significance in judging whether lawmakers should actively promote the happiness of the people. No government seeking to increase well-being is likely to succeed to a degree sufficient to dull the ambitions and energies of its people. Most of the policies that legislators can pursue will consist of efforts to mitigate sources of prolonged unhappiness such as unemployment, mental illness, or lack of adequate health care. Such measures are important but are hardly calculated to lift people to the highest level of happiness. The same is true of other policy initiatives such as efforts to improve the quality of government, or to encourage people to be more civically active, or to strengthen the bonds of marriage and family. Whatever it takes to achieve complete happiness appears to exist within individuals and not within the powers of public officials.

There are too many pitfalls and setbacks in human lives that are beyond the reach of the state and too much unhappiness rooted in genetic sources that are not susceptible to manipulation by official policies. As science advances, perhaps, the time may conceivably come when governments can help everyone achieve a state of perfect contentment, but that day still seems far in the future.

The point just made suggests one final argument against the use of happiness as a goal of public policy. Far from worrying about the consequences of achieving universal contentment, some skeptics wonder whether government policy can do anything at all to produce lasting happiness. Samuel Johnson declared centuries ago: "How small, of all that human hearts endure, that part which laws or kings can cause or cure."[14] More recently, Johnson's observation gained scientific support from two psychologists, David Lykken and Auke Tellegen, who wrote that up to 80 percent of the variation in happiness is fixed genetically and cannot be altered significantly by human intervention.[15] In their view, while particular events, such as winning a lottery or losing a loved one, may bring initial pleasure or pain, most individuals will quickly adapt and return to a fixed, genetically determined state of well-being. The authors based this conclusion on studies of identical twins who showed remarkably similar levels of happiness even though they had been reared apart by different families. These findings led the authors to conclude their analysis with the cryptic statement that "trying to be happier is as futile as trying to be taller."[16]

Since this study appeared in 1996, other investigators have responded with a flurry of contrary arguments. While everyone agrees that genes play an important role in forming the disposition to happiness, there is now compelling evidence that human interventions, including the actions of government, can also have substantial effects. For example, there have been large shifts in levels of well-being in a number of countries. As pointed out in the last chapter, the percentage of Danes indicating that they were "very satisfied" with their lives increased markedly over a 20-year period, while the percentage of Belgians fell substantially.[17] Another telling example comes from the contrasting trends in well-being in East and West Germany following the destruction of the Berlin Wall and the subsequent reunification of the two countries.[18] While average levels of satisfaction in West Germany remained essentially unchanged, massive efforts to integrate the poorer East with the prosperous West eventually helped cut the percentage of East Germans with low levels of well-being from 28 to 15 and raise the percentage of highly satisfied people from 38 to 54.[19] Other Soviet bloc countries also weathered several years of declining satisfaction after the fall of the Berlin Wall and then experienced steadily increasing happiness as their standard of living started to improve. Fluctuations as substantial as these could hardly have resulted from some sudden change in the genetic makeup of the populations involved.

Evidence from individual lives also tends to refute any notion that people have a genetically fixed level of happiness to which they rapidly return after experiencing brief surges of satisfaction or distress. As mentioned in chapter 1, while individuals adapt remarkably quickly to many pieces of good fortune and misfortune, some events, such as unemployment or divorce, can leave a residue of unhappiness that lasts for years. Conversely, marriage gives some couples a lasting boost in well-being. More generally, after analyzing a large sample of people over a 17-year period, Frank Fujita and Ed Diener reported that levels of happiness among a substantial fraction of the participants during the first five years of the study changed significantly by the last five years.[20]

In light of all the evidence, the consensus of researchers today is that heredity probably accounts at most for 50 percent of one's happiness level but that the other 50 percent is determined by events and circumstances and deliberate choices. Moreover, it may not even be useful to make such clear-cut divisions between genetic and environmental influences on behavior. Some genetically based conditions that affect well-being are treatable by human intervention. The obvious example is clinical depression, which brings acute unhappiness but is often controllable by drugs, psychotherapy, or a combination of the two. Moreover, hereditary influences are only tendencies; they may be realized or not, depending on whether one experiences or avoids the circumstances that tend to bring them into being.[21]

The critical point to emerge from this discussion is not that heredity is unimportant, but that ample room remains to affect well-being through human intervention. The acts and policies of government are one means by which well-being may be influenced. In this regard, it is worth noting that the countries with the highest levels of happiness are almost all countries that have long enjoyed stable democracies, while the lowest levels of well-being in the world occur in nations such as Zimbabwe, Haiti, or Angola that have been marked by instability, violence, or oppression brought about in no small part by government policies.

## Should Happiness Be the Only Goal of Public Policy?

If the well-being of the public is an appropriate, important, and feasible goal for lawmakers to pursue, should they go further, as Bentham proposed, and look upon the happiness of their constituents as the *only* legitimate aim of public policy? Were Bentham alive to defend his case, he might point out that happiness is a capacious enough objective to gather virtually any other plausible aim of government under its banner. Making the United States secure against its potential enemies, for example, clearly furthers the well-being of Americans by reinforcing feelings of security and minimizing the risk of being attacked and possibly subjugated by a hostile power. Protecting individual liberty also promotes happiness, since researchers have found a strong association between national levels of well-being and the freedoms that go with democratic government.

There are limits, however, to this line of reasoning. For one thing, it is not clear that *all* worthwhile government actions can be accurately described as policies that add to people's satisfaction. While Americans overwhelmingly support the First Amendment in principle, large majorities have long disapproved of allowing well-known Nazis or Communists to appear on radio or television.[22] As a result, permitting such people to speak may be fundamental to free speech, but the net effect on the public's happiness is anybody's guess. The same is true of other basic Constitutional liberties that have been construed by judges in controversial ways, such as outlawing prayer in schools or requiring that students be bused to achieve racial integration.

In the last analysis, some acts of government are required and others prohibited under our Constitution regardless of what researchers tell us about their effects on the public's happiness. Judges do not outlaw segregated schools or protect newspaper editorials merely to make people happy. Nor do they seem to care whether allowing the Ku Klux Klan to march in Skokie, Illinois, or banning racial covenants that exclude blacks from white neighborhoods will produce a net increase in people's satisfaction with their lives. Utilitarians may try to explain these results by arguing that allowing such a march to take place or prohibiting restrictive covenants will actually increase people's happiness in the long run. But that is not why judges make these rulings, nor is it clear how they would go about making such a determination. Instead, it seems safer simply to conclude that both cases involve principles of free speech and equal rights for individuals and minorities, principles that must be upheld whatever the effects on happiness.

Several influential philosophers have raised another persuasive reason for honoring aims other than happiness as a basis for making policy. Because human beings have such remarkable power to adapt, people may come to feel satisfied even when they are living under plainly unsatisfactory, unjustified conditions. Amartya Sen has put the argument very clearly.

> A person who has had a life of misfortune, with very little opportunities and rather little hope, may be more easily reconciled to deprivations than others reared in more fortunate and affluent circumstances. . . . The hopeless beggar, the precarious landless labourer, the dominated housewife, the hardened unemployed or the over-exhausted coolie may all take pleasures in small mercies, and manage to suppress intense suffering for the necessity of continuing survival, but it would be ethically deeply mistaken to attach a correspondingly small value to the loss of their well-being because of this survival strategy.[23]

If happiness were the sole end of public policy, lawmakers might be inclined not to worry about "the hopeless beggar," "the landless labourer," or "the hardened unemployed," provided such individuals were truly as happy as others who enjoyed more comfortable lives. But such a single-minded concern with happiness would lead to unsettling results. Imprisoning a man for a crime he didn't commit shouldn't be excused just because he has come to enjoy the routine of prison life. Immoral practices, such as slavery, cannot be justified by a rigorous study showing that slaves are as satisfied as a control group of free individuals with comparable education, intelligence, and ethnic background. Instead, there must be other values beside happiness that can condemn particular policies regardless of their effect on the feelings of those affected.

This point might seem to represent a very narrow exception, since slaves and innocent prisoners are not often found in great numbers in advanced democratic societies. But Sen's point could be used to question the treatment of larger groups, such as those in poverty or near poverty. Even if it could be shown that almost all low-income families had adapted to their condition in life and achieved a surprising degree of happiness, that would not necessarily mean that policy-makers had no reason to help them. Obviously, if it could be shown that their economic condition was clearly unfair (e.g., because they had been cheated by their employer), the ends of justice could still require an effort on the part of the government to come to their assistance however well they had adjusted to their fate.

At the same time, examples such as those just discussed cannot justify a broad legislative disregard for reliable evidence of their constituents' happiness. In a democracy, citizens should be the judges of their own well-being unless their feelings conflict with clear and generally accepted principles of justice. The fact that legislators happen to have different values or subscribe to different theories or ideologies should not be a sufficient reason to ignore the feelings of their constituents. Otherwise, those in authority would assume too great a license to impose their own views about what is best for the human beings they represent. Rather, slavery, false imprisonment, and fraud should be regarded as special cases involving basic principles of fairness that are so widely accepted that they compel government intervention regardless of the feelings of the victims.

Committed Benthamites may try to explain away even these exceptions by arguing that Americans are ultimately happier knowing that no person in this country can be wrongly imprisoned, defrauded, or enslaved. Such claims may be difficult to prove, however, and hence have little practical value in guiding policy-makers. In any case, judges will not be much interested in empirical evidence on the feelings of the public (or those of slaves or innocent prisoners, for that matter). Under our Constitution and our basic understanding of justice, slavery, fraud, and punishment for a crime not committed are clearly unjust, and the feelings of those enslaved, defrauded, or improperly imprisoned cannot alter that conclusion.

In summary, then, there are good reasons to conclude that happiness can be only one aim of government, albeit a very important one. Upholding civil liberties and equal opportunity are others. Still others include the various Constitutional and legal safeguards that protect the government from trying to promote well-being by manipulative or unjust means.* Once additional ends of this kind are recognized, of course, the enterprise of government will become more complicated, since different ends can sometimes conflict with one another. Even so, complexity is hardly a reason for refusing to accept policy objectives that are otherwise worth having.

## Should Lawmakers Use Research on Happiness in Making Policy?

Although the happiness of the people may be an important goal for public officials to pursue, that does not automatically justify the use of research on well-being to help guide policy decisions. Clearly, such research must be sufficiently valid and reliable to warrant its use in making decisions that will affect people's lives.

---

*The safeguards referred to in this paragraph help counter the frequent argument against utilitarianism that societies committed solely to maximizing happiness leave open the possibility that majorities can exploit minorities and thereby achieve greater overall well-being. The need for such safeguards is aptly illustrated by pointing to the shabby treatment of the Nepalese minority in Bhutan despite the professed commitment to Gross National Happiness as the goal of public policy. Utilitarians may respond by arguing that rules protecting minorities will enhance overall well-being. Indeed, Ronald Inglehart and his collaborators have found, using his World Values Survey in various European countries, that greater tolerance of gays and other minorities increases national happiness. Ronald Inglehart, Roberto Foa, Christopher Peterson, and Christian Welzel, "Development, Freedom, and Rising Happiness: A Global Perspective (1981–2007)," 3 *Perspectives on Psychological Science* (2008), p. 271. Whether or not Inglehart is right, however, there can be no guarantee that minority rights will be respected without Constitutional safeguards.

The discussion in chapter 2 has sought to address that issue, pointing out that competently executed empirical studies of well-being are at least as reliable and valid as many findings that have long been used routinely in considering legislation. There is an additional issue to be resolved, however, before one can feel completely comfortable recommending the use of this body of work in deciding policy questions.

Happiness research is most interesting when its results challenge conventional wisdom about what people want instead of simply affirming what everyone has always assumed would improve well-being. Thus, studies that cast doubt on whether happiness increases as a result of expanding incomes are likely to attract more attention than findings that most people are happier under democratic rule. However, even if researchers can show conclusively that widely held views about achieving happiness are mistaken, one may still question whether legislators should allow such findings to influence their decisions. In a democracy, shouldn't elected officials try to carry out the will of the people? If large majorities feel that rising prosperity is the surest way to increase their happiness, should lawmakers disregard their opinions just because researchers have concluded that other policies will do more to enhance satisfaction with life?

This question raises the longstanding problem of what duly elected representatives owe to their constituents in a democracy. Is it simply to reflect the wishes of those they represent? Or are lawmakers elected to use their best judgment of what their constituents need? This issue is still debated just as it was when Edmund Burke wrote his famous letter to constituents in 1774, declaring that his proper role as an elected member of Parliament was to use his best judgment and not simply follow the wishes of the voters in his district.[24]

On reflection, neither alternative seems feasible under all circumstances. If legislators never felt bound to follow constituent opinion, they might not remain in office for long and their citizens might suffer from some very unpopular laws. Yet if lawmakers always felt obliged to follow the wishes of those who elected them, compromise would frequently be impossible and the legislature might arrive at some unfortunate decisions on issues where the public was either misinformed or gripped by momentary passion.

In practice, there are so many different interests in an electoral district and it is so difficult to assign them appropriate weights that representatives are often at a loss to know what "following constituent opinion" means. Not surprisingly, then, most American legislators proceed pragmatically. On questions about which a large majority of constituents feel strongly, lawmakers are likely to accede to popular sentiment, if only to avoid being thrown out at the next election. On other issues, where voters are closely divided or have no strong opinion one way or the other, legislators tend to exercise a good deal of discretion in deciding how best to serve the interests of their constituents.

In the latter case, using happiness research to inform decisions seems an eminently defensible way of enlightening legislative discretion. In doing so, lawmakers are not ignoring the interests of their constituents by catering to powerful interest groups. Nor are they expressing their own private views about what voters ought to value. Rather, they are relying on persuasive evidence of what *will* make constituents happy instead of accepting what people mistakenly *think* will promote their well-being. Most voters would probably prefer to be happy rather than have their representative mechanically accept their mistaken impressions of how to reach this goal. If so, it would seem entirely proper for lawmakers to heed the counsel of research—assuming that the investigations are carefully done—and choose the policy that will actually give satisfaction to their constituents.

Naturally, there are limits to the use of research in such situations. If voters are so committed to their mistaken views that ignoring them would endanger reelection, a legislator will feel obliged to follow their wishes. In this sense, citizens still exert some ultimate control over the use of happiness research to inform the discretion of elected representatives.

## The Practical Uses and Limitations of Happiness Research

Although happiness research has overcome some of the problems Bentham experienced in seeking to apply his "felicific calculus," the earlier discussion has shown that it cannot remove all need for judgment and turn policy-making into a purely mechanical science. For one thing, if happiness is only one of several aims of government, albeit a very important one, conflicts will arise between happiness and competing goals. These conflicts require a weighing of values rather than a demonstration of facts, and no amount of empirical research can provide a conclusive answer.

There are plenty of other reasons why research on happiness cannot reduce policy-making to a science. Since no one can predict all the consequences of a major piece of legislation such as health care reform, it is impossible to give policy-makers a reliable and complete account of the effects of such proposals on happiness. Other, smaller acts of government involve benefits that are not sufficiently tangible or substantial to be calculated exactly, let alone have a measurable effect on people's well-being. For example, legislative decisions whether to provide funds for another aircraft carrier or a new weapon system may have a bearing on national security, but their significance will not be apparent enough to ordinary citizens to affect their happiness one way or the other.

Other kinds of legislative proposals may raise questions of judgment that are not susceptible to resolution by empirical means. Take the case of laws affecting those who are not citizens of the United States. What weight should American policy-makers attach to the happiness of civilians in Iraq? Of illegal immigrants? Of unborn fetuses? Of animals? These questions involve values rather than facts alone, and nothing psychologists can measure will give a definitive answer.

The problem of value judgments is not restricted to cases involving noncitizens. For example, consider a proposal for a major hike in cigarette taxes. Researchers find that those who stop smoking rather than pay the tax will be happier for having summoned the willpower to end a habit that is expensive and injurious to their health.[25] Smokers who do not quit will be less happy because of having to pay a higher price. Psychologists can estimate the impact on both groups. But should a legislature attach equal importance to the feelings of those who can and those who cannot muster the determination to give up such a dangerous habit? Again, this is not a question psychologists can answer.

Although the limitations just noted are substantial, happiness research can still have many uses. One of the most promising involves helping governments choose priorities. For example, existing research suggests that lawmakers will be well advised to pay more attention to important sources of persistent unhappiness, such as mental illness and chronic pain. To pick another example, findings that senior citizens are, if anything, more satisfied with their lives than younger Americans may help policy-makers decide to give a higher priority to improving the lot of younger Americans through measures such as more affordable child care or higher-quality preschool education than to raising Social Security benefits.[26]

Many legislative proposals involve recurring opportunities to raise or lower a tax, a subsidy, or some other benefit or burden. In time, researchers may be able to make before and after measurements that will give lawmakers better estimates of the net effects of further changes in these laws on the well-being of those affected. The examples just described involving cigarette taxes and retirement benefits help illustrate what is possible.

Finally, happiness research may be able to throw light on possible institutional changes in government itself. A striking example comes from the work of Bruno Frey and Alois Stutzer, who have compared the happiness of citizens in the different cantons of their native Switzerland.[27] Surprisingly, they find significant variations in happiness according to the extent of direct democracy (initiatives, referenda, citizen assemblies) in each canton. The more direct democracy, the greater the happiness. Moreover, the positive effects are largely confined to citizens (rather than foreign residents), suggesting that it is the opportunity to participate, more than the results achieved by direct democracy, that increases happiness.

As it happens, Frey and Stutzer's findings have been challenged by other Swiss scholars so that the results may still be too uncertain for policy-makers to use.[28] Even so, their work suggests a fruitful area for research in America. With 50 different states, possessing varying government processes and responsibilities, researchers in the United States should have many promising opportunities to explore the effects of direct democracy and other institutional arrangements on the satisfaction of citizens.

To conclude, although there are limits to the value of happiness research in making policy decisions, investigators can now publish findings about the well-being of populations that are far more useful to policy-makers than anything Bentham and his contemporaries could produce. In doing so, researchers have challenged traditional assumptions, raised important questions, and offered the prospect of improving many of the judgments that public officials make in devising programs to better the human condition.

The task that remains is to illustrate the potential uses of this research by discussing some specific steps that a government could take to achieve higher levels of happiness. The research summarized in chapter 1 suggests a variety of possibilities that lawmakers might consider—among them, educational reforms that could prepare young people to live fuller, more satisfying lives; measures to remove the anxiety of having no health insurance; and stronger efforts to relieve the lasting distress of mental illness and unemployment. It would require too much time and space to discuss all the legislative possibilities and analyze their potential contributions to happiness. What follows, then, in the remainder of this book is not a complete account of every measure a government might take to promote happiness but an analysis of several fields of policy in which research either suggests promising opportunities for intervention or raises especially challenging questions.

# 4

## THE QUESTION OF GROWTH

The most provocative issue raised by the new research on happiness is whether Americans are wise to place such a high priority on increasing and sustaining economic growth. In claiming that the added possessions people crave do not necessarily bring lasting happiness, investigators have not only attacked a major aim of government policy; they have called into question a central premise of economics—namely, that consumers are the best judge of their own welfare so that one can reasonably assume that a rising per capita Gross National Product will provide a corresponding increase in well-being. The implications of this critique are profound. If it turns out to be true that rising incomes have failed to make Americans happier, as much of the recent research suggests, what is the point of working such long hours and risking environmental disaster in order to keep on doubling and redoubling our Gross Domestic Product?

The constant expansion of goods and services has become so basic to the American way of life that it is hard even to imagine what the consequences would be if Americans came to believe that it added little or nothing to their well-being. Economic growth is now the most influential single measure of our national vitality and progress. Quarterly reports on the changes in our Gross Domestic Product (GDP) are widely publicized everywhere. The trends they record are the principal measure for comparing America's progress with that of other countries. The chairman of the Federal Reserve periodically appears before Congressional committees to report on the prospects for faster or slower growth. Policy proposals in Congress live or die on the basis of their estimated effects on the rate of economic expansion.

Much the same is true in other countries as well. Around the globe, as historian John R. McNeil has observed, "the overarching priority of economic growth was easily the most important idea of the twentieth century."[1] Even the Swedes, widely known for their "third way" of organizing society, grew restive and dissatisfied when their economy slowed in the 1960s and '70s and per capita income slipped from near the top of the Western European nations to slightly below the average.

For all its prominence, however, the primacy of growth as a goal for government is a relatively recent phenomenon.[2] In the United States, growth became the principal aim of economic policy only after World War II, replacing a longstanding preoccupation with taming the business cycle and avoiding mass unemployment. As predictions of an immediate postwar recession proved unfounded, doubts about the prospects for continuing prosperity gave way to optimism. In the late 1940s, under the chairmanship of Leon Keyserling, the Council of Economic Advisers repeatedly emphasized growth in its annual reports on the economy. After President Eisenhower's more cautious economic policies, marked by an abiding concern over inflation, John F. Kennedy made expansion an important part of his campaign to "get America moving again."

Putting growth at the center of government policy was politically attractive, since it offered something of value to a variety of powerful groups. For business, it promised new markets, increased sales, and larger profits. For labor, it meant more jobs at higher wages with added fringe benefits. Lawmakers on both sides of the aisle saw it as a way to pay for the programs they favored without having to raise taxes.

From the beginning, however, informed observers understood that growth had its limits. With memories of the Great Depression still vivid, lawmakers and other public officials recognized the danger of provoking inflation and eventual recession if their zeal for promoting economic expansion overheated the economy. In the corridors of Washington and the halls of academe, experts debated how to balance increased production against the need to keep prices stable through judicious fiscal and monetary policies.

Beginning in the 1950s, new voices began to be heard express-ing concern that continued growth was using up finite natural resources, polluting the air and water, and destroying the ozone layer. These worries were later joined by ominous predictions that greenhouse gases could eventually raise global temperatures, melt the polar ice caps, flood coastal areas, and provoke fierce storms and droughts to threaten humankind and all living things.

Most of those who shared these ecological concerns did not urge an end to growth. They simply called for measures to curb its harm-ful side effects and thus allow a more prudent expansion, one that could continue indefinitely without doing irreparable damage to the environment. Just as policy-makers needed to prevent inflation in the near term by taking care not to "overheat" the economy, so also were they urged to avoid the kind of uninhibited growth that could eventually do irreparable harm to the environment and thus diminish the quality of life for unborn generations.

In recent years, these concerns have intensified as scientists have confirmed the existence of global warming and documented the immense damage it will cause if the buildup of greenhouse gases continues unchecked. Stronger measures will be necessary to avoid this danger than were called for to deal with lead, sulfur dioxide, chlorofluorocarbons, and other pollutants. Still, according to most experts, the worst effects of warming can be avoided without dras-tic reductions in the rate of economic growth if the necessary ac-tions are taken soon.[3] As a result, continuous expansion remains at the core of domestic policy—subject only to the need to act prudently now to avoid dire consequences later on.

## The Controversy over Growth

Although a growthless economy seems unimaginable today, it has not always been thus. In the mid-nineteenth century, John Stuart Mill looked forward approvingly to a stationary state "where economic growth and ceaseless economic striving would end with the realiza-tion of abundance."[4] As late as the 1920s and '30s, prominent fig-ures echoed this thought. Franklin Roosevelt declared in 1932 that "our industrial plant is built. . . . Our last frontier has long since been reached. . . . Our task now is not . . . producing more goods. It is the soberer, less dramatic business of administering resources and plants already in hand . . . of adapting economic organizations to the service of the people."[5] The best-remembered essay on the future of growth came from John Maynard Keynes, the most influential economist of the twentieth century: "The time is not far off when the economic problem will take the back seat where it belongs, and the heart will be occupied . . . by the real problems—the problems of life and human relations, of creation and behavior and religion. [Then], man will be faced with his permanent problem—how to use his freedom from pressing economic cares, how to occupy the leisure, which science and compound interest will have won for him, to live wisely, and agreeably, and well."[6]

Today, no political leader, no aspirant to high public office, no orthodox economist would dare to make statements such as those just quoted. Continuing growth is now an established part of the nation's economic orthodoxy. According to Gregory Mankiw, Harvard economist and former head of George W. Bush's Council of Economic Advisers: "Because most people would prefer to receive higher incomes and enjoy higher expenditures, GDP per person seems a natural measure of the economic well-being of the average individual."[7] Added Lawrence Summers, then secretary of the Treasury and currently head of the White House Economic Council, we "cannot and will not accept any 'speed limit' on American economic growth. It is the task of the economic policy to grow the economy as rapidly, sustainably, and inclusively as possible."[8] Apparently, then, the idea of growth has shifted from a means to desired ends to an end in itself, an end with no foreseeable end in sight.

Not everyone has accepted the gospel of continuous growth. From outside the mainstream, a few dedicated environmentalists, such as Gus Speth and Bill McKibben, continue to warn against continuous expansion.[9] In their eyes, the rising tide of goods and services is ruining the environment, creating urban sprawl, choking our highways with cars, and threatening to inflict grave hardships on future generations. Far from increasing happiness, argues social critic Juliet Schor, our fixation on growth leads to rising levels of stress and insecurity together with longer hours of work that keep individuals from more rewarding pursuits.[10]

The research on happiness has added fuel to the debate about growth. Writers such as McKibben, Speth, and Schor have eagerly seized on Richard Easterlin's claim that happiness in the United States has not increased over the past half century despite the massive growth in our Gross Domestic Product. As explained in chapter 1, however, Easterlin's findings have not gone unchallenged. Other researchers, citing new Gallup surveys, have argued strongly that growth continues to have large positive effects on well-being even in the richest countries, thus lending support to those who preach the gospel of endless expansion.[11] As yet, this debate has not arrived at a generally accepted conclusion.

However the controversy is ultimately resolved, the attacks by environmentalists and their allies, and the use they have made of some of the research on happiness, have prompted several mainstream social scientists to respond. One economist, for example, Stanley Lebergott, has brushed aside suggestions that the public is no happier than it was 50 years ago, arguing that few if any Americans would willingly return to the conditions of the 1950s when people had to make do without computers, the Internet, color television, and countless other things that make life better today.[12]

Lebergott may be right, but his point does not dispose of the surveys showing that Americans are no more content with their lives than they were in 1950. As Americans adapt and yesterday's luxuries turn into today's necessities, people are naturally unwilling to give them up, but that does not mean that they are any happier than they were before the process began. Neither does it suggest that the products they yearn for in the future will bring them any greater pleasure. What, then, is the justification for future economic growth? Are there persuasive arguments for continuing expansion if the lasting satisfactions that will supposedly result turn out to be illusory? Mill and Keynes would have clearly had doubts. If there are reasons to the contrary, Lebergott has not supplied them.

Other writers have tried to justify continued expansion on the ground that growth should not stop or even slow very much so long as millions remain in poverty. This is a convincing argument for the governments of poor nations, but it is much less persuasive for the United States. True, there are many Americans who experience hunger and have no place to sleep other than a park bench or a homeless shelter. Even so, the United States is more than rich enough to deal with these problems appropriately without continuing to grow. What is lacking is political will, not a dearth of goods and services.

Most Americans today who are officially classified as poor are neither hungry nor homeless but own television sets, refrigerators, automobiles, and cell phones—possessions beyond the imagination of poor families in the 1930s. Indeed, according to Nobel economist Robert Fogel, those who currently occupy the bottom 10 percent of the income scale often enjoy a standard of living exceeding all but the top 10 percent of those living in 1900.[13] Yet they are still considered poor and elicit much the same concern from sympathetic fellow citizens as their needy counterparts a century ago. However much the economy grows, there will always be some who have much less than others and will continue to seem poor to those with vastly greater resources. Poverty has now become relative; it is a problem of income distribution that will not be solved merely by continued growth. The fact that so many millions remain officially poor in the world's most prosperous economy makes the point very sharply.

A more substantial defense of economic growth has recently been made by economist Benjamin Friedman.[14] His principal argument is that growth has moral value, since rising incomes nurture the empathy and optimism in the public that are needed to preserve social solidarity and permit more generous policies to help the poor and disadvantaged. In his words, "economic growth—meaning a rising standard of living for the clear majority of citizens—more often than not fosters greater opportunity, tolerance of diversity, social mobility, commitment to fairness, and dedication to democracy. . . . When living standards stagnate, or decline, most societies make little if any progress toward any of these goals."[15]

Friedman acknowledges that his theory does not always fit the facts. The greatest period of progressive reform in modern American history occurred during the Great Depression, hardly a time of ebullient growth. In Friedman's view, however, the 1930s are a rare exception created by a crisis of truly unusual proportions. To buttress his case, he marshals a wealth of evidence from different times and countries. In particular, he points to the postwar experience in the United States where major advances in civil rights and social legislation took place in the 1960s at the height of a long period of widely shared prosperity, only to diminish sharply after 1973 when the incomes of most Americans stopped increasing.

Friedman concedes that other influences beside growth help build tolerance, generosity, and civic spirit. But it is far from clear that growth has even been a "powerful force," as he contends. Years before the growth rate slowed, support for social programs to help poor people and minorities had begun to fade as a consequence of urban riots, a rising tide of out-of-wedlock births, mounting drug use, protests over Vietnam, and suspicions that the Great Society reforms were not working. Similarly, the conservative mood that grew so strong in the 1980s had less to do with stagnating incomes than with the rising influence of Christian fundamentalists and other groups that were not upset as much by the sluggish economy as by the attack on traditional values marked by court rulings on matters such as prayer in the schools, busing, abortion, and gay marriage.

Other scraps of evidence raise similar doubts about the effect of growth and stagnation on attitudes toward civic responsibility, racial minorities, and the plight of the needy. The steep decline in trust and confidence in government, along with the substantial drop in voting rates, did not occur during a time of stagnant incomes but in the growth years of the 1960s and early 1970s.[16] Charitable giving (as a percentage of personal income) fluctuated in ways quite independent of trends in the Gross Domestic Product, falling amid the widespread prosperity of the late 1950s and 1960s, rising again in the 1980s, and declining slightly during the renewed growth of the 1990s.[17] In the case of racial tolerance, attitudes did not harden in the decades after 1973, when incomes were flat for most Americans; they continued to improve.[18] By 1997, over 75 percent of the public (and more than 70 percent of every age group, region, and income segment in the United States) still felt that "it was no time to let up" on "efforts to assure equality among the races."[19] As for the needy, notwithstanding almost two decades in which median incomes failed to rise, 65 percent of the public in 1991 still believed that America should be doing more to help the poor.[20] During the presidency of Ronald Reagan, despite his efforts to roll back the welfare state, large majorities continued to feel that most existing programs of social protection should be maintained or even strengthened.[21]

Whatever the doubts about the effects of growth on people's empathy, tolerance, and generosity, Friedman mentions another, more compelling reason why costly government programs for the poor and the needy are more likely to emerge during periods of rising prosperity. However generous and open-minded Americans are in principle, they are chronically opposed to raising taxes for almost any reason. As a result, Congress can pass costly spending programs much more easily in periods of growth when revenues are rising and new levies are not needed. In periods of slow growth (barring an exceptional crisis such as the Great Depression), new initiatives for needy groups are much harder to enact because the necessary funds would either require new taxes or come at the expense of other programs. Neither alternative has much chance of success in the United States.

These tendencies make a no-growth society in America highly problematic.[22] Almost everyone would agree that there are *some* government programs that bring real benefits and therefore deserve to grow. The most determined opponents of growth would probably favor extending health insurance to every American, providing better schooling in the inner cities, expanding Head Start, and offering quality child care to all needy parents. Informed voters would probably acknowledge that health care costs for programs such as Medicare and Medicaid will have to continue rising faster than the cost of living because of persistent increases in the elderly population and the mounting costs of medical technology. Most people would also support increased funding for biomedical research to encourage discoveries that will prolong human life and bring relief to sufferers from cancer, AIDS, Alzheimer's, and other debilitating diseases.

In addition to these investments, many Americans might insist on increased government outlays for research on the ground that discovering new knowledge is a powerful end in itself, a virtual "manifest destiny" to discover more and more about ourselves, our planet, and our universe. Even committed environmentalists might support increased research, since the best chance of avoiding ecological disasters may come through hydrogen-powered automobiles, safer nuclear power, or other advances that demand the kind of technological innovation that requires heavy investments in new knowledge. Finally, however much opponents of growth may protest, large majorities of Americans will doubtless want to keep spending more on defense as long as other major powers continue to improve their military capabilities and terrorist activities require expensive efforts to counter the threat.

In a stationary or near-stationary economy, where would the government find the funds to pay for all these expensive needs? What programs or economic sectors would be trimmed to offset the added costs? In theory, of course, it is easy for any citizen to identify appropriations to cut in order to free up resources for worthy causes. Agricultural supports, dubious subsidies such as the ethanol program, and pork barrel projects would be high on many people's lists. As a practical matter, however, it is doubtful that much additional money would be forthcoming from these sources, since almost all are stoutly defended by powerful vested interests. If growth came to an end, it is only realistic to suppose either that the funds needed for worthy purposes would not be appropriated at all or that they would come, at least in part, by sacrificing outlays for other worthwhile causes that have only weak political support.

Even if there were no need to fund new programs or to provide for selective areas of growth, the end of expansion would intensify the struggle for advantage. While corporate managers, entrepreneurs, salesmen, and countless others would still strive to increase their business, success in a stationary economy would be much harder to achieve. Any gain would have to come at the expense of someone else. Merely keeping from losing ground would require unremitting vigilance and struggle. Under such conditions, companies would be sorely tempted to use political influence, deception, or even illegal acts in order to get ahead. If black markets and other forms of petty corruption flourished even in World War II, how much more prevalent would they be in less patriotic times? More and more controls and regulations would be required to curb such behavior. In this unruly, politicized environment, success would not necessarily come to the deserving, and everyone would have to endure increased red tape, intrusive oversight, and bureaucratic error.

Halting growth in the United States could also have severe repercussions for vulnerable populations in other parts of the globe. America is such a major market for other nations that stopping expansion or even slowing it severely could easily throw the world into recession. Inflicting such hardship on countries struggling to escape from poverty is not a prospect that should appeal to many environmentalists and other opponents of growth.

There is also little reason to believe that many countries would agree to follow America's lead in stopping growth. India, China, and other developing nations with per capita incomes far below ours would surely be reluctant to do so. Many nations would have to continue growing simply to keep up with their mounting populations. Hence, serious environmental threats would remain regardless of what the United States chose to do.

In addition to these global issues, severe practical problems would arise in trying to manage the transition to a stationary or near-stationary economy without creating serious economic disruption and unemployment. Of course, the government could simply prohibit any increases in the production of goods and services, with appropriate exceptions for health care, scientific research, and other priority items. But this solution hardly deserves serious consideration. Officials would have to impose more and more intrusive regulations to enforce such a ban while relying on the vagaries of the political process to determine which activities merited exceptions in the public interest. As the experience of the Soviet Union made clear, prolonged efforts by a central authority to manage a complex economy by decree are almost certain to be impractical and ultimately disastrous economically, politically, and administratively. To impose such a solution in the name of happiness would be an especially ironic misadventure.

The more obvious way to stop growth would be to proceed indirectly by such means as increased taxes and diminished incentives for saving, investment, and corporate research. In practice, however, these tools are blunt instruments whose precise effects cannot always be predicted. In the effort to halt growth, public officials could easily tip the country into a depression, causing widespread unemployment and consequent distress here and abroad.

Problems of implementation would not end after the initial effort to bring growth to a halt. As productivity continued to increase, ever fewer workers would be needed to produce the same per capita quantity of goods and services. In principle, growing unemployment could be avoided by reducing the maximum hours of work per week below the 40-hour limit currently mandated by the Fair Labor Standards Act (FLSA). But the FLSA is an even blunter tool than monetary policy. It is very hard to predict the effects of a given reduction in working hours. Analysts still do not agree on how many additional jobs, if any, were created by the French decrees in 2001 and 2004 that cut the workweek from 40 to 35 hours.[23] Moreover, even if one could forecast how many new jobs would result from a given reduction, it is most unlikely that they would be the right kinds of jobs or in the right locations to absorb the surplus labor created by a stationary economy.

Aside from these problems of implementation, any program to abandon growth must confront one last and especially forbidding obstacle. Whatever the adverse effects of growth and however false its promises of greater happiness turn out to be, the vast majority of Americans support it and continue to feel that a bit more money and a few more possessions are the key to future happiness. It is unrealistic to suppose that our democratic government could simply ignore these attitudes and alter the country's way of life by legislative decree. Even if further growth brings no added happiness, continuous expansion will remain an important goal until a majority of Americans are persuaded that the process no longer makes sense and should be modified or abandoned.

For the time being, any chance that Americans will turn their back on growth seems highly remote. It is not just that current attitudes are defended by powerful vested interests and reinforced by a continuous barrage of advertisements trumpeting the benefits of added consumption. As pointed out in chapter 1, an expanding economy does more for a great many Americans than merely bring them new material goods or satisfy manufactured desires. The larger market shares, the profit and production goals that growth entails, the rising incomes and the added possessions they provide are all ways of measuring success in life. As such, they elicit great energy, effort, and imagination. For enterprising people, growth can supply an excitement akin to what the American frontier evoked in earlier generations. For the consumer, possessions are a way of defining one's status and giving evidence of one's achievement. As a result, doing away with growth would diminish the challenge, motivation, and purpose in many people's lives without putting new forms of meaning in their place. One may deplore such incentives and wish for a nobler set of ambitions that would channel activity toward worthier ends. Yet the prospects for altering popular desires in this way are surely small in the foreseeable future. Such seismic changes are not undertaken lightly nor accomplished easily.

## Will Americans Ever Change Their Minds?

Could the government overcome the obstacles to stopping growth by offering people attractive benefits in return for only a gradual reduction in the rate of expansion? For example, could it try to slow the rate of growth by gradually reducing the hours of work? According to Daniel Kahneman's calculations (based on experience sampling), work is less satisfying for most people than most other activities in the day so that fewer hours on the job might increase well-being.[24] Creating more leisure time might seem an especially promising prospect for the United States, since the average full-time employee in this country works more hours per year than workers in almost any other advanced industrial nation. The best-educated Americans in the highest-paying executive and professional jobs, who could easily afford a more relaxed lifestyle, are now working longer hours than employees with less education and less remunerative jobs. Substantial numbers of successful young professionals hold "extreme" jobs in which they labor more than 70 hours per week with few if any vacations, presumably at some cost to their health and family.[25] Under these conditions, couldn't the government gain widespread support by shortening the workweek or by following Europe's example of mandating several weeks of paid vacation every year?

In fact, the case for reducing time on the job is not as simple as the preceding paragraph suggests. For one thing, the effects on growth of reducing hours of work are quite uncertain. For another, many people prefer to work long hours. Even most of the harried young professionals who work more than 70 hours per week say that they enjoy the hectic pace (although few wish to keep it up for more than a few years at most). According to Sylvia Hewlett and Carolyn Luce, two-thirds of the "extreme" professionals they surveyed claimed to love their jobs.[26] Many other families are struggling to make ends meet; there are always more things they want to buy than they can afford. For them, fewer hours will probably mean lower pay, and they will not welcome the trade-off.

There are also serious difficulties in enforcing limitations on work hours. Toward the bottom end of the pay scale, federal officials have a hard time checking conditions in the hundreds of thousands of small enterprises that employ a large fraction of lower-paid employees. At the high end of the market, where working hours are longest, it is often impractical to impose maximum limits. Trial lawyers, corporate executives, general practitioners, and many more are simply not engaged in the kinds of work that lend themselves to fixed hourly limits. That is doubtless one reason why the Fair Labor Standards Act has never attempted to cover them. The problems involved are harder than ever with the advent of modern means of communication. Faxes, cell phones, and Black-Berries have blurred the lines between work and leisure, leaving many professionals exposed to conference calls and urgent client demands at night, on weekends, and during vacations. The Internet has even allowed millions of Americans to work from their homes, making it all but impossible for officials to monitor the number of hours spent on the job.

Apart from these problems, it is not at all clear how much happiness would be gained even if the government could somehow succeed in reducing the workweek. Although there has been little reduction in the hours per week that Americans spend working, both men and women have more time for themselves today than they did in 1965.[27] Women are spending more hours in paid work, but have reduced by even more the time they give to minding their children and doing household chores. Men (except the most highly educated) are simply working less though devoting a few more hours per week helping out at home.

The net result is that leisure hours increased from 1965 to 2003 between 5.6 and 8 hours per week for men, depending on the definition of leisure used, and between 3.7 and 6.8 hours for women.[28] But how was the extra time actually spent? According to the most careful recent estimates, the added leisure was swallowed up by a jump of 7.4 hours per week watching television. At the same time, the number of hours per week devoted to reading dropped by 3.1, while the hours spent socializing with friends fell by 3.9.[29] The net effect of reducing the time spent on work-related activities, then, was not more hours devoted to pursuits such as reading and socializing that appear to bring considerable pleasure. Instead, the big gainer was a passive activity (television) that has been found to bring noticeably less satisfaction, according to Professor Kahneman's calculations.[30]

Once again, therefore, it turns out that the government will have a hard time making people happier so long as Americans lack a clearer understanding of the kinds of activities that will bring them lasting satisfaction. Just as with the pursuit of money and possessions, a legislature cannot require individuals to give up television in favor of socializing, exercising, and civic activities unless they choose to do so of their own accord. The successful use of leisure is much more likely to come about through education than by official decree.

Considering all the problems involved in drastically curtailing growth, it may not make much practical difference whether Professor Easterlin is right in claiming that happiness has not increased over the past 50 years or whether the analysts who disagree with him are correct. In either case, the problems with abandoning growth seem so formidable that it is hard to imagine government leaders agreeing to a major shift in this direction.

Are we condemned, then, to soldier on in an endless struggle to grow even if it should become clear that we will be no happier as a result? Not necessarily. In the longer run, predictions become very difficult, and almost anything is conceivable. For example, if environmentalists' worst fears come to pass, the consequences could provoke far-reaching changes that seem highly improbable today. As Milton Friedman observed, once a crisis occurs, "the politically impossible becomes politically inevitable."[31]

A very gradual shift in aspirations and values also seems possible over a long enough period to give the economy time to adjust to a much slower pace of economic growth. Already, 89 percent of Americans believe that "our society is much too materialistic," while 84 percent agree that "too much emphasis on money is a serious problem in our society."[32] Compared with other highly advanced countries such as Russia, Holland, and Japan, Americans are much more likely to feel constantly under stress, rushed for time, and without enough opportunity to be with family and friends.[33] A surprising number of people are even acting on their concerns. From 1990 to 1996, 19 percent of American adults reported having made a voluntary lifestyle change that reduced their earnings, such as working fewer hours or taking a less stressful job.[34] Studies suggest that those who cut back for environmental reasons or for some other principle they believe in tend to be just as happy, if not more so, than others with more conventional lifestyles.[35]

To be sure, such "downshifting" did not prevent Americans as a whole from buying more and more and going deeper into debt until the recession arrived in 2008. Still, the trends do suggest a greater willingness to question the wisdom of an endless pursuit of growth. The odds of an eventual transformation will almost certainly increase if researchers ever reach a firm consensus that continued growth is failing to make Americans any happier. Although it might take many decades for the public to accept the full import of such a finding, people usually come to terms with the facts eventually.

For the time being, lawmakers might consider making an effort at the margin to strike a somewhat different balance between expansion and well-being. Whatever research eventually shows concerning the effects of income and possessions on happiness, it surely does not suggest that money and the goods and services it buys are the dominant source of well-being. As a result, while continued growth may be needed in the foreseeable future, insisting on having the economy grow "as rapidly as possible" is harder to justify, especially when it becomes a reason for opposing sensible policies that could brighten the lives of large numbers of people. Congress can hardly have good reason to block such proposals as paid parental leave or stricter environmental rules merely because they might conceivably have some slight adverse effect on the economy. Nor should legislators claim that the country cannot afford measures, such as improving the quality of child care and preschool education or providing universal health care, even as they urge new tax cuts in the hope of inducing faster growth.

All of the reforms just mentioned have long since been adopted in other advanced industrial nations. Some of them will pay for themselves eventually, while others will turn out to have no demonstrable ill effects on the economy. To oppose them in the name of growth gives economic expansion a preferred position in the hierarchy of national priorities that seems hard to justify when doubt exists over whether it does much, if anything, to promote the well-being of the American people.

However the debate over growth and well-being is ultimately resolved, one thing is clear—and was already clear long before psychologists began to explore people's feelings about happiness. Rising standards of living are not the only source of satisfaction with life. In a country as prosperous as the United States, they may well not be the most important. As pointed out in chapter 1, many other conditions, ranging from human relationships to the quality of government, contribute to happiness—conditions that may provide opportunities for helpful policy initiatives. It is to these possibilities that we turn in the remaining chapters.

# 5

## WHAT TO DO ABOUT INEQUALITY

To liberals, inequality of income has long cast a dark shadow over America—"a stark challenge to American national life," in the words of James K. Galbraith.[1] These words seem truer than ever today. Income differences in the United States are unusually large and have widened steadily in the past few decades. From 1973 to 2000, the most affluent 20 percent of Americans increased their income by 61.6 percent, six times faster than the poorest 20 percent (10.3 percent). By the end of the century, the richest 1 percent claimed a share of the national income not equaled since the 1920s.

### Redistributing Income

The recent growth of inequality has provoked renewed interest in redistributing income by one means or another. Since the poorest people are the least happy and since added income is thought to yield diminishing increments of happiness the further one moves up the economic ladder, it is natural to suppose that if the government could somehow take money from the rich and give it to the poor, the net effect would be to increase well-being.

Available statistics on happiness lend some support to the liberal position. Granted, the General Social Survey reveals that an impressive 80 percent of Americans in the bottom quarter of the income scale were either "very happy" or "pretty happy" with their lives over the period from 1975 to 1992.[2] Still, almost 20 percent of this group were "not too happy," compared with only 6 percent of those in the most affluent quartile. Conversely, while almost 41 percent of the wealthiest quartile were "very happy," the same was true of only 24 percent of the poorest quartile.[3]

While these statistics suggest that well-to-do Americans are happier, on average, than poorer Americans, this fact alone does not prove that taking money from the rich and giving it to the poor would reduce the "happiness gap." Researchers have found that variations among nations in income inequality have no significant effect on average levels of well-being.[4] Moreover, although the tabulations are not strictly comparable, evidence from Western Europe does not suggest that happiness is more equally distributed than it is in the United States even though most European countries tend to have less income inequality and more generous social welfare programs. On the contrary, Eurobarometer surveys from 12 European nations from 1975 to 1992 reveal that the proportion of the population in the lowest income quartile who are "very satisfied" or "fairly satisfied" (73 percent) is several points below the percentage of Americans from the bottom quartile who are "very happy" or "fairly happy" (80 percent). Conversely, the proportion of low-income Europeans who are either "not very satisfied" or "not at all satisfied" (27 percent) is substantially greater than the proportion of Americans (20 percent) who are "not too happy."[5]

Moreover, while incomes in the United States and much of Western Europe have become less equal during the past 30 years, the distribution of happiness in these countries has moved perceptibly, albeit modestly, in the opposite direction.[6] Even in the United States, where inequality has increased especially rapidly, unhappiness has not increased among the poor, the very ones who ought to mind the most.[7]

Happiness researchers were not the first to discover that most lower-income Americans are untroubled by inequalities of income and disinclined to want to take from the rich and give to the poor. In the1980s, Jennifer Hochschild explored this subject in depth using extensive interviews with 28 working residents of New Haven, Connecticut.[8] As she concluded, "the surveys confirm our political and historical knowledge that most people with incomes below the mean do not believe in [redistributive] policies that appear, at first blush, to be in their self-interest."[9] Twenty years later, Katherine

Newman discovered much the same thing in her intensive study of fast-food workers in Harlem.[10]

The attitude of lower-income Americans toward income inequality seems to set the United States apart from Europe. Americans are much more likely to feel that financial and occupational success comes from ability and hard work rather than luck or family wealth and social position.[11] As Katherine Newman found in the course of interviewing her fast-food workers: "At each point [in 1993–1994, 1997, and 2001–2002] an overwhelming majority of respondents—from 72 to 88 percent—told us they believe in that quintessentially American dream that anyone, by dint of hard work, can succeed."[12] Opinion surveys show that Americans are twice as likely (60 percent) as Europeans (29 percent) to believe that the poor can get rich if they only try hard enough.[13] While most Europeans feel that where you end up is largely a matter of luck or other circumstances beyond your control, fewer than half of Americans agree.[14] Armed with these beliefs, lower-income Americans are less likely to blame society when inequality grows and more inclined to believe that persons of great wealth must deserve their good fortune.

If growing differences of income do not increase unhappiness, most of the reasons for urging large-scale redistribution to achieve more economic equality become much harder to sustain. For example, the most obvious reason for deploring income inequality is our instinctive sympathy for those who must make do with many fewer goods and services than they would like. It is not immediately clear, however, why growing inequality should elicit such compassion if lower-income Americans themselves have not become less happy.

Of course, there are undoubtedly individuals who suffer because they have too little money—families that cannot afford a decent breakfast for their children or people who are ill and lack the funds to pay for needed medication. These privations are real and cry out for attention. Yet simply shifting money from rich to poor is a clumsy way to proceed. A more generous, efficient food stamp program is a more economical and effective way of combating hunger than simply redistributing income in hopes that poor families will feed their children better. Similarly, a system of universal health insurance is far more likely to ensure proper medical care for all than merely leveling incomes. The better response to privation, then, is not a massive shifting of incomes but a set of programs specifically designed to overcome whatever suffering exists.

Another familiar argument against excessive income inequality is that it elicits envy on the part of those with lower incomes. According to this theory, "keeping up with the Joneses" is a familiar theme in America, and those who lack the income to live as their neighbors do must suffer distress as a result.

On reflection, even assuming that envy is a problem for governments to remove rather than a weakness for the envious to overcome, shifting money from the rich to the poor is unlikely to make much difference. Any conceivable redistribution will still leave substantial differences in wealth and income with plenty of room for envy among those who are so disposed. True, redistribution may make the differences smaller, but it is far from clear that larger income disparities cause greater envy than smaller (but still substantial) differences. Everyday experience suggests that most envy comes from observing advantages in the lifestyle and possessions enjoyed by friends and neighbors, not from observing the vastly greater wealth enjoyed by a Bill Gates or a Donald Trump. Were this not so, unhappiness should have increased as the wealthiest 1 percent grew ever richer than the rest of the country over the past 30 years. Yet that is precisely what did *not* occur. One would also have imagined that countries with smaller income differentials would tend to have higher average levels of happiness, but once again, this does not appear to be so.

Some writers have also argued that growing inequality erodes social cohesion, increases class tensions, and thereby threatens to fray the fabric of society.[15] If the widening gap between rich and poor has not produced unhappiness, however, it is hard to make out why class tensions should increase. Moreover, there is no accepted way to measure social solidarity in order to test this theory. It may be true, as Robert Putnam suggests, that social capital has declined in recent decades, causing civic participation and social ties of many kinds to weaken.[16] But it is far from clear that this trend has resulted from growing income inequality rather than from immigration, racial tensions, television, or a host of other possible causes. Interestingly, Putnam's exhaustive recent study of this subject, *Bowling Alone*, does not include inequality among the causes of dwindling social capital in America. The word does not even appear in the index.

Similar reservations apply to the argument that rising inequality lowers the self-respect of those with smaller incomes. If that were true, one would expect that poor people in countries with greater economic inequality would be especially unhappy. As previously noted, however, this does not appear to be the case, nor does it seem that growing inequality in the United States has caused increased unhappiness among lower-income Americans. To be sure, economic setbacks can occur that do diminish self-esteem; losing one's job is perhaps the most obvious example. But making incomes more equal will hardly do away with layoffs or remove their effects on well-being. Once again, other measures aimed more precisely at the underlying problem seem preferable.

Finally, it is facile to assume that redistribution will increase happiness just because the marginal utility of additional income may be greater for the poor than for the rich. As indicated in chapter 1, any incremental happiness for the poor is likely to erode as beneficiaries grow accustomed to their extra income and adjust their aspirations upward. That is surely one reason why the broad-based economic growth that benefited lower-income Americans in the 1950s and 1960s did not increase their well-being. Moreover, as researchers have discovered, taking money from one group creates much more distress than the added happiness gained by giving the same amount to another.[17] The net effect of redistribution, therefore, is far from obvious. If rising inequality after 1975 did not produce more unhappiness in the United States and if differences in income distribution in prosperous nations are not correlated with differences in their overall levels of happiness, it is unlikely that transferring money from rich to poor will bring a net increase in well-being.

## Income Inequality and Longevity

A different reason for opposing income inequality has arisen in another quarter. Several public health experts have argued forcefully that added income inequality in America has widened differences in longevity between rich and poor.[18] They also claim that states with greater inequalities of income tend to have larger differences in longevity than states with a more equal income distribution. If these conclusions could be proved convincingly, the case for redistribution would be strengthened. On closer analysis, however, the findings rest on shaky ground. Later and more careful studies have concluded that differences in longevity among the states do not result from varying levels of inequality but from other causes, such as differences in health insurance coverage and in the percentage of African Americans in the state population, that the earlier work did not take into account.[19] As Angus Deaton points out, "it is not true that income inequality itself is a major determinant of population health. There is no robust correlation between life expectancy and income inequality among the rich countries, and the correlation across the states and cities of the United States is almost certainly the result of something that is correlated with income inequality but that is not income inequality itself."[20]

Assuming Deaton is correct, it remains true that rich people tend to live longer than poor people. That fact alone might be a reason for narrowing differences in income if one could be sure that doing so would cause poor people to live longer. It is unlikely, however, that redistributing income, by itself, could accomplish much. Some of the causes of higher mortality among the poor result from differences in lifestyle, such as habits of exercise, diet, and drug and alcohol use, that would not disappear merely by redistributing income. Other causes are much subtler and seemingly unconnected with economic deprivation. For example, Oscar winners turn out to live a full four years longer than Oscar nominees who do not win, a curious fact that cannot be explained by differences in income.[21] Similarly, in a celebrated study of British civil servants, Michael Marmot discovered large differences in mortality between higher- and lower-level officials even though none of the officials surveyed were poor and all had access to the same system of health care.[22]

The evidence summarized thus far casts considerable doubt on compassionate or utilitarian arguments in favor of a large-scale redistribution of income in the United States. Although poor people undoubtedly endure plenty of disadvantages and hardships, there are several reasons why changes in income inequality seem to have so little effect on well-being. Part of the explanation for reduced levels of well-being among lower-income groups stems not from disparities in wealth but from differences in status, autonomy, and authority that will not go away by merely redistributing income. Such differences, for example, probably account for the variations in health and longevity that Professor Marmot discovered among British civil servants. Other sources of unhappiness among the poor are rooted in behavioral patterns—such as differences in diet, smoking, and alcohol use—that will not disappear with changes in income. Conversely, most of the things that higher incomes can buy will not bring lasting satisfaction because of adaptation and rising aspirations. And finally, the feelings of resentment, envy, and bitterness that many intellectuals fear will result from income inequality do not appear to be widely shared by those on the lower rungs of the economic ladder.

Nothing just said is intended to deny that there are pockets of hunger and other forms of suffering in America that require help on humanitarian grounds. Nor do these arguments imply that taxing the rich in order to pay for new programs is necessarily wrong or that all programs that disproportionately benefit the rich are justifiable. They most emphatically do not apply to other countries, especially less prosperous nations where attitudes of the population may differ from our own and added income for the poor may have quite different effects on well-being. The point made here is simply that it is better to analyze individual policies in the United States in terms of their capacity to solve specific problems rather than support them or attack them on the basis of broad generalizations about the effects of redistribution on well-being.

## Income Distribution and Justice

This conclusion will not satisfy liberal philosophers who have their own reasons for advocating a more equal division of income.[23] These writers do not necessarily assume that poor people are unhappy nor do they take note of the recent research suggesting that increased inequality has not made Americans less happy. They seldom base their claims for a proper distribution of wealth and income on empirical observations about happiness but argue instead from intuitive notions of justice—an instinctive sense that it is presumptively unfair for some people to have much more money than others because of their inherited abilities, or the wealth and advantages of their parents, or other factors for which they are not personally responsible. While these theorists may concede that *some* differences of income are justified to supply incentives that will increase the prosperity of all, most of them insist that much of the existing inequality in America cannot be defended on this or any other basis.

Philosophers who share this view disagree, however, about what distribution of income would be just. The most influential among them, John Rawls, argues that the fairest distribution would be one that people would agree to if they were about to enter the world without knowing what talents or advantages they would possess once they got there. As he sees it, the most likely consensus would be that everyone should enjoy the greatest and most equal liberty consistent with the rights of others and that differences in income would be justifiable only if they would improve the situation of even the poorest members of the society under conditions in which all people had an equal opportunity to advance according to their merits.[24]

Whether or not they fully accept Rawls's formulation, many liberal philosophers agree that incomes should be distributed in such a way that inequalities will result only from failings for which the individuals involved can be reasonably held responsible. They disagree, however, on which failings merit such treatment just as they tend to differ on whether compassion, self-respect, social solidarity, or simply an intuitive notion of what fairness demands is the decisive reason for their position.[25] These disagreements often result, at least in part, from further differences of opinion over which behaviors are genetically determined and which are the product of free will for which individuals can be held responsible. Thus, articles exist discussing questions such as whether those who spend their lives surfing in Hawaii are entitled to an equal share of income or whether society should pay extra to those who have compulsively expensive tastes.[26]

Philosophers are likewise not unanimous in claiming that justice requires greater equality of *income*. Some writers, such as Ronald Dworkin, argue for equality of initial resources.[27] Others, such as Martha Nussbaum and Amartya Sen, argue instead that one should try to equalize "capabilities," such as the possession of skills, freedom of action, and good health.[28] Not surprisingly, conservative writers reject all these proposals to redistribute incomes or equalize capabilities on the ground that they are unworkable, unrealistic, and insufficiently justified.

Whatever one thinks about the intellectual merits of the positions taken by liberal philosophers, it is hard to regard them as plausible measures for a democratic government to adopt. Most of the proposals call for massive shifts of income, causing consequences so disruptive and so impossible to anticipate, that they seem both impractical and unwise. At the very least, they require the most compelling justification. Yet the very fact that philosophers differ so much among themselves makes it hard to construct a convincing case. After all, if arguments for greater equality ultimately rest not on logic or empirical demonstration but on moral intuition, such wide disagreements over how to define the intuition and describe its practical applications gravely weaken its value to lawmakers.

As a practical guide to policy, moreover, the proposals of liberal philosophers also suffer from the disadvantage of differing profoundly from the prevailing beliefs of most Americans. For example, in a study soliciting opinions from both individuals and small discussion groups, one investigator found that only 4 percent of the individuals and none of the groups preferred Rawls's proposal that incomes should be equally distributed except where differences would bring about increased prosperity for the least well-to-do members.[29] Instead, a large majority favored a distributive scheme that would maximize the average income in the society subject to some sort of compassionate minimum of support for the poorest members. The next most popular scheme was to maximize average incomes *without* a minimum floor, leaving the poor to rely on charity for survival.

There is nothing wrong, of course, with philosophers advancing unpopular proposals. New ideas often meet with public disfavor at the outset, and the job of intellectuals is to persuade people to change their minds. Until people are persuaded, however, it is hardly proper in a democracy for lawmakers to disregard strong public opposition and impose some radically different theory of distribution based on intuitive notions of justice that do not command a clear consensus among philosophers, let alone win approval even from those who will supposedly benefit as a result.

It is conceivable that new findings in the future will supply a more convincing reason for large-scale redistribution. For the time being, however, most arguments for achieving greater equality by redistributing income represent yet another example of the pervasive tendency to overemphasize money as the source of lasting happiness. With so little support from public opinion or empirical research, such proposals stand on even shakier ground than economic growth as a key to greater well-being. Before leaving this subject, however, we need to examine two other forms of equality, which may provide more compelling goals for public policy.

## Other Forms of Equality

In defining the conditions of a just society, John Rawls did not merely try to define a just distribution of income; he placed even greater emphasis on equal liberty, including full and equal political rights, and on equal opportunity for all to compete for positions in society and the economy on the basis of their ability, effort, and ambition.[30] Although the case for redistributing income may be unpersuasive, there are stronger reasons for reforms that would achieve more equal political rights and opportunities for advancement. In contrast to greater income equality, both of these other goals command very wide support not only from philosophers and political theorists but from the entire population as well.

*Political equality*: By almost universal agreement, each citizen should have an equal right to cast a ballot. The political process should be separated from the marketplace; there must be no poll taxes and no buying of votes. No one's vote should count more than others by virtue of superior wealth, wisdom, or education. In the age of John Stuart Mill, graduates of Oxford and Cambridge were granted two votes rather than one. No longer. Although some people have more knowledge of public affairs than others, political equality is now considered necessary because no one, however well informed, can be trusted to fully understand the concerns of others or to weigh their interests as perceptively and as sympathetically as those directly affected by the government's policies.

Although the goal of political equality receives overwhelming support as a matter of principle, it is realized only imperfectly in practice. Each citizen has an inalienable right to cast one vote (and only one vote), but that is not enough to protect the political process from the influence of money. In a large and complicated society, where few citizens fully understand the issues at stake and even fewer know the candidates personally, victory usually depends on having the funds and organization to reach the electorate with a constant stream of political messages written by paid advisers skilled in crafting such appeals. Huge sums are consequently needed to finance successful campaigns, especially those for national office. Individuals who can afford to make substantial political contributions or persuade others to give are eagerly pursued by candidates and often rewarded with special access to elected officials and influence over policy.

In this environment, lower-income groups operate at a distinct disadvantage. Members of the richest quartile of Americans are more than nine times as likely as members of the poorest quartile to make a contribution to a political campaign. In all, the poorest 20 percent of voters give barely 2 percent of the money raised, while the richest 3 percent contribute 35 percent.[31] According to the American Political Science Association, 95 percent of the donors who contribute substantial sums to political campaigns have incomes in excess of $100,000 per year.[32] In addition, poor people are far less organized and far less likely to vote, or even to communicate with lawmakers and other officials, than better-educated, wealthier citizens. Members of the richest quartile go to the polls in national elections at almost twice the rate of Americans in the poorest quartile and are roughly two and one-half times more likely to belong to a political organization.[33]

The differences just described have a pronounced effect on the influence wielded by different income groups on policy. According to a recent study of the U.S. Senate by political scientist Larry Bartels: "In almost every instance [of policy-making], senators appear to be considerably more responsive to the opinions of affluent constituents than to the opinions of middle-class constituents, while the opinions of constituents in the bottom third of the income distribution have *no* apparent statistical effect on their senators' roll call votes."[34] A task force on political equality appointed by the American Political Science Association reached a similar conclusion, finding that "government officials who design policy changes are more than twice as responsive to the preferences of the rich as to the preferences of the least affluent."[35] According to Professor Bartels, while lower rates of voting, communication with officials, and membership in political organizations may all help explain this result, the vastly greater contributions made by wealthy citizens to political campaigns provide the most plausible explanation for the lack of responsiveness by elected officials to low-income Americans.[36]

These findings leave the ideal of political equality in shambles. Superior resources and organization give certain groups of citizens much more power than others. Poor people are by far the most disadvantaged since they have neither the money nor the organization to have a significant effect on the decisions that affect their lives. The result is something of a vicious circle. As poor people realize how little effect they have on public policy, their interest in government and politicians wanes, and they vote and participate politically even less.

To some extent, of course, the poor themselves are responsible for their weakened state. If they would vote in numbers equaling or exceeding more affluent groups and if they could form strong unions and political parties (as is the case in Europe), their influence would doubtless grow. But it is difficult simply to blame the poor. Their low voting is partly their own doing but is also heavily influenced by the frequent unwillingness of candidates and their advisers to spend money campaigning or even advertising in poorer districts. Similarly, America's failure to develop strong working-class organizations has multiple causes, many of which are hardly the fault of the poor themselves.

Under these conditions, as Professor Bartels points out, "the economic order of the contemporary United States poses a clear and profound obstacle to realizing the democratic value of political equality."[37] The question is how to improve matters. Redistributing income is unlikely to do much to solve the problem. No conceivable redistribution will come close to overcoming the immense advantage that wealthier citizens have over lower-income groups in contributing to political candidates. Moreover, the relative weakness of the poor involves far more than money. Much of the effort of well-to-do people to influence policy stems from their position as owners or leaders of powerful organizations, positions that will not disappear by redistributing income. Conversely, much of the political weakness of low-income groups is rooted in a lack of organization and in a widespread apathy and cynicism toward politics and politicians forged from many decades of experience. Merely giving the poor more income, therefore, hardly guarantees that they will use the money effectively to counter the influence of powerful, affluent segments of the population.

A more promising approach would be to limit the influence of money and organization on elections by enacting measures to increase voting and change the ways campaigns are financed. The intricacies of campaign funding are sufficiently great that an adequate treatment of the subject would stray too far from the central themes of this book. Suffice it to say that though there are no ideal solutions, some methods of regulation are better than others and much superior to the status quo. Based on experience in states that have taken this route, replacing private donations to candidates and parties with full public financing of campaigns seems the best of several imperfect remedies. Once private donations are no longer made, and restrictions on gifts and other favors for politicians are strictly enforced, the strongest links between wealth and political influence will be severed.

The principal weakness of this approach is that privately funded "independent organizations"—operating without supervision or coordination from political parties or their nominees—can appear during election campaigns and advertise on their own account to assist or attack particular candidates. Such activities not only help perpetuate the unequal power of money in elections. They have the further disadvantage of taking much campaigning out of the hands of the candidates, who are accountable for what is said, and placing it in the hands of shadowy front organizations accountable to no one. Congress has attempted to limit the use of such ads within 60 days of an election. For the present, however, a majority of the Supreme Court interprets these restrictions very narrowly so that most political ads from interested groups are treated as constitutionally protected free speech.[38] Apparently, then, such appeals, often paid for by anonymous sources, command a greater importance in the eyes of the majority than the disproportionate political influence they give to well-organized segments of the population. So long as this view prevails, public funding of elections will still be worth having but it will not work perfectly. A fully effective program to blunt the effects of money in politics will have to wait until the Court changes its position to allow carefully defined restrictions that limit the ability of independent entities to sway elections and influence elected officials without preventing them from commenting on the issues.

Other rulings of the Court make it impossible to restrict the amount of money candidates can spend from their own private resources during an election campaign.[39] A recent Supreme Court ruling even struck down a state law granting extra public money to candidates if they were outspent by opponents who used their personal fortunes to fund their campaigns.[40] In the eyes of the majority, such provisions are impermissible infringements on free speech. The result, of course, is to give a marked advantage to candidates wealthy enough to contribute heavily to their election.

Political parties have responded by seeking out well-to-do members to run for office and often agreeing to sponsor candidates only if they pledge in advance to contribute a substantial sum to their own campaigns. It is hardly a surprise, therefore, that a large percentage of senators and governors are independently wealthy, making top elected officials less representative of the people they are supposed to serve.

Even if the Supreme Court were persuaded to change its mind, campaign finance reform would not fully succeed in achieving political equality. Lower-income Americans cannot expect to have an influence commensurate with their numbers so long as their voting rates continue to languish at levels barely half those of the well-to-do. Not surprisingly, researchers have found that states in which the voting rates of rich and poor are more nearly equal have social legislation and employment laws that are more favorable to lower-income citizens than those of other states where differences in turnout are greater.[41] It is no accident, then, that most European countries have old-age pensions, health care insurance, and other social welfare programs that are more generous than ours. Low-income citizens in these countries vote at rates that are as high or almost as high as those of more affluent segments of the population. With strong labor unions and workers' parties to mobilize members, they also have much more powerful advocates to plead their case to legislators and other public officials.

No known policy will cause the poor to vote as frequently as the rich. Holding elections on Sundays or making election days a holiday would probably increase turnouts, but there is no assurance that the added voters would come disproportionately from lower-income groups. Same-day registration would probably accomplish more, if only because it would make canvassing in poor neighborhoods more productive than it is when campaign workers must make separate efforts, first to persuade individuals to register, and then to make sure that they go to the polls on election day. Even if such reforms are enacted, however, it is unlikely that less affluent Americans will vote at rates close to those of the well-to-do unless more successful efforts are made to improve civic education in the public schools and organize poor and working-class neighborhoods.

Until then, carefully drafted rules for financing campaigns will help, but they will not bring complete political equality.

*Equality of opportunity*: The second important form of equality is equality of opportunity. Among the core values of our society is the goal of giving all Americans an equal chance to succeed according to their abilities and aspirations. Huge majorities of the public accept this principle and consider it fundamental to the American Dream.

Some philosophers criticize equality of opportunity as incoherent and unfair, pointing out that it means different things to different people and may actually accentuate the disadvantages of those with incurable disabilities, such as low intelligence or other genetic handicaps, for which they cannot be held responsible.[42] Such criticisms may have merit, but they are of little help in defining a set of practical steps to improve upon the status quo. On this score politicians have done better. Over the years, they have arrived at a rough-and-ready consensus on reducing a number of arbitrary barriers and handicaps that could otherwise keep deserving individuals from realizing their ambitions or enjoying benefits to which all members of the society should have access. This effort has resulted in a host of familiar laws and programs—among them free public education for all children; subsidized higher education; access for the handicapped; and antidiscrimination laws to protect racial minorities, women, gays, and members of religious groups. While many of these policies are imperfectly achieved, they have clearly done much to help all children develop according to their ability and to benefit all Americans by doing away with arbitrary obstacles and exclusions that could prevent them from living a fuller, more successful life.

Conceived of in this way, equality of opportunity does not reward those who are responsible for their own predicament. Nor does it force employers to hire unqualified people. On the contrary, it improves the performance of the economy and of all other organizations by helping to ensure that positions throughout society are filled according to people's ability to do the job.

Equal opportunity has many advantages. It enhances the possibilities for all people to achieve their full potential and thus contributes to a broader conception of well-being that embraces human flourishing and self-realization as well as happiness, a goal with roots in philosophy extending back at least to Aristotle.[43] Equal opportunity also has something in common with Amartya Sen's proposal to equalize capabilities rather than incomes and even goes partway in addressing his concern about using happiness as a guide to policy. As Professor Sen points out, it seems intolerable to condone conditions that are clearly harsh and unjust merely because those affected have adapted to their fate and accepted their predicament in good spirit.[44] At the same time, leaving it to legislators to decide when conditions are "unacceptable" or "unjust" affords an uncertain remedy at best. Equal opportunity offers a partial answer to this dilemma by giving everyone a more equal chance to become sufficiently educated and informed to resist exploitation and to defend themselves by appealing to the courts or to their political representatives when arbitrary restraints and disadvantages do occur.

As matters now stand, America is far from providing equal opportunities to all its citizens despite the overwhelming support for the underlying principle. Of course, some of the handicaps faced by poor children are largely beyond the power of policy-makers to correct—differences in IQ, for example, or inadequacies of child-rearing resulting from parental ignorance or indifference. Compared with youngsters from families in the lowest socioeconomic quartile, children from the highest quintile are four times as likely to have a computer in the home and have three times as many books. They are read to much more often, watch far less television, and are much more likely to visit libraries and museums. By the time they are three years old, they already have twice the vocabulary of children from low-income households.[45]

Overcoming such handicaps poses a formidable problem for any government. Still, not all sources of inequality are so resistant to change. At present, poor children also suffer from inadequate child care. Fewer than half of all children from families with incomes below $50,000 attend preschool and those that do are often enrolled in programs of inferior quality.[46] Inner-city schools continue to receive less money than suburban schools while suffering from substandard facilities and higher teacher turnover.[47] The high cost of college still tends to restrict access for many sons and daughters from less affluent homes.

Arbitrary disadvantages of this kind seem well within reach of public policy. Greater efforts could doubtless be made to reduce infant mortality, premature births, and physical handicaps through proper prenatal care for all expecting mothers. Much more could be done to provide higher-quality child care and preschool programs for all children. Governments could likewise do more to equalize opportunities in schooling by continuing to narrow the differences in budgets, teacher salaries, and teacher turnover that handicap schools in poorer communities.

Political leaders could also make college more affordable for lower-income families by lowering the economic barriers that have arisen as states have had to cut back on support for higher education to cope with rising Medicaid and other costs. According to former Princeton University president William Bowen, "the odds of getting into the pool of candidates for admission to a selective college or university are six times higher for a child from a high income family than for a child from a poor family."[48] Part of this disparity may result from the fact that children of wealthy parents have higher IQs than children from poor families. Yet even among young people who test in the top 25 percent of ability, only 44 percent of those whose families are in the lowest socioeconomic quartile attend a four-year college, compared with 80 percent of the high-scoring students from families in the top socioeconomic quartile.[49] Lawmakers could undoubtedly narrow this gap by improving college counseling in the high schools and by providing more generous scholarships for low-income students, including older, part-time students who now constitute a large share of the nation's undergraduate population.

The measures just noted would probably do more to reduce inequality of income than any top-down program of redistribution. According to Harvard economists Claudia Goldin and Lawrence Katz, an important reason for the growing gap between rich and poor over the past 30 years has been that too few children from lower-income families graduate from college and professional school.[50]

Would increased equality of opportunity (or greater political equality, for that matter) increase happiness? While any answer must be speculative, it is likely that such changes would lead to favorable legislation and further opportunities for advancement that would bring added satisfaction to many lower-income Americans. At the very least, greater opportunity and political influence would make expressions of well-being by the poor more convincing and less likely to merely reflect adaptations to conditions that are unjust and unacceptable.

In collaboration with George-Marios Angeletos, Alberto Alesina (the same scholar who found that growing inequality did not increase unhappiness) has shown empirically what common sense would suggest—namely, that "people enjoy great satisfaction when they know (or believe) that they live in a just world where hard work and good behavior pay off."[51] The exceptional tolerance of Americans for substantial inequality appears to rest in large part on their belief that rates of social mobility are unusually high in the United States and that anyone who works hard can get ahead in life. Yet this belief appears to rest on a misapprehension of the facts. Although differences of opinion still exist, most analysts have concluded that rates of economic mobility are no higher in the United States than in other advanced democratic nations and may actually be somewhat lower for poorer Americans.[52] Thus, Americans' tolerance for inequality stands on shaky ground. In a country that is marked by such large disparities of income, it is only prudent and fair to bring the facts of life into closer alignment with prevailing beliefs about mobility and opportunity. Creating greater equality of opportunity and political influence is the best way to achieve this result.

Ultimately, however, there is an even more powerful argument for making greater efforts to improve campaign finance laws and increase equality of opportunity. Unlike redistributing income, both equal opportunity and political equality are goals that Americans support overwhelmingly. Both rest on widely accepted principles of fairness that are worth achieving quite apart from their effect on well-being. As pointed out in chapter 3, happiness is not the only goal that political leaders should pursue. America will be a more just society if all its citizens have an equal voice in speaking to their government and an equal chance to succeed in life to the full extent of their efforts and abilities. That is reason enough to support measures that will bring the country closer to these ideals.

# 6

## THE THREAT OF FINANCIAL HARDSHIP

L ife is full of risks. Most of them stem from events that no one else can do much about—the end of a love affair, a rejected first novel, a failure to win a coveted promotion. But some common hazards can be minimized by legislation. Indeed, many acts of government—food and drug laws, for example, or speed limits—can be described as efforts to reduce risk. One frequently used device for this purpose is some sort of mechanism that spreads the cost of misfortune widely and thereby softens the blow to individual victims.[1] Compulsory unemployment and automobile insurance are familiar examples. Through their use, the government gives peace of mind to large numbers of people while saving many others from acute distress.

The economic crisis of 2007–2008 focused attention on a set of financial hazards that have persisted and increased in recent years, bringing mortgage foreclosures, bankruptcies, and other forms of economic hardship to millions of American families. Three risks are especially widespread: the possibility of having too little money for a satisfying retirement; the risk of falling ill without the means to pay for needed health care; and the threat of losing a job with the attendant loss of income and self-esteem. The worry and pain these risks have caused are sufficiently serious and long-lasting to warrant a search for policies that will bring relief and increased well-being.

### Retirement

Almost all older Americans enjoy at least a modicum of financial security in retirement. Virtually all will receive Social Security benefits, protected against inflation, for the rest of their lives. In addition, Medicare pays for many (though not all) of their health care costs. While retirees currently spend an even larger share of their income for health care than they did before Medicare was enacted, they are relieved of many medical expenses and can look to the government to defray a substantial portion of their mounting prescription drug costs. Senior citizens who are poor enough are covered by Medicaid for even more of their health care expenditures.

Compared with pensions in other advanced industrial nations, however, Social Security provides rather modest levels of support for retired Americans, many of whom have no other source of income.[2] The average retiree in the United States can expect monthly payments amounting to only 41 percent of preretirement income. Those who consistently worked for low wages can receive up to 56 percent while high earners receive a much lower proportion. Benefits rise, of course, if both husband and wife were employed for a sufficient length of time prior to retirement.

Because the payments are relatively low, it seems only prudent to save additional amounts for retirement, and most families do. The principal source of saving is through contributions to company pension plans. For many years, the vehicle of choice was a defined benefit plan in which workers contributed a stipulated amount in return for a commitment by their employer to pay them a steady retirement income for life that varied according to their years of service and prior earnings. In the last 20 years, however, more and more employers have changed their policies to shift some of the risks of retirement saving to their employees.[3] Instead of offering defined benefit plans, these companies have turned to defined contribution plans, most often in the form of so-called 401(k) accounts. Such plans set aside a fixed portion of employees' wages, usually with an added contribution from the employer, while giving workers a choice in determining how to invest the proceeds. Defined contribution plans give employees a chance to earn greater returns from the stock market, but also subject them to the risk that the market will be in decline at the time they retire and collect their pension. Moreover, unless employees use their 401(k) account to buy an annuity when they retire, they are not guaranteed an income for life and thus run the added risk of outliving their savings.

It is easy to spot the weaknesses in a retirement policy that sets universal support levels (Social Security) at relatively modest levels and relies on voluntary employment-based pension plans to cover additional needs. Only approximately half of all employees work for companies that offer any sort of plan, while 35 percent of all households have no member with pension coverage. The mix of public and private pensions has worked to the particular disadvantage of poorer families. Lower-paid workers are especially likely to lack coverage, while the wealthiest 20 percent of employees are virtually all included in a plan and capture well over half of the many tens of billions of dollars in federal tax subsidies that the government gives to encourage the growth of pension coverage.[4]

In this system where only some have a private pension, approximately 20 percent of retirees, most of them with modest prior earnings, have no source of funds other than their Social Security checks. Thirty percent rely on Social Security for over 90 percent of their income. Although official poverty rates for the elderly have declined sharply since 1960, roughly 10 percent of current retirees have low enough incomes to be officially classified as poor. Poverty is especially prevalent among elderly widows, many of whom used up their savings paying medical and nursing home expenses for their seriously ill husbands.

The various options allowed under 401(k) plans do give employees freedom of choice. It is questionable, however, whether employees have been making prudent decisions. Only 74 percent of eligible workers elect to join a plan and contribute toward a pension. Only 10 percent contribute the maximum allowable amount. Many employees do not roll their plans over when they change jobs but take the sum they have contributed and spend it on other things. Many others borrow against the plan to pay for more immediate needs. Most employees when they retire do not use their accumulated funds to purchase an annuity but assume the risk that they will outlive their pension savings and spend their remaining years with only their Social Security checks to sustain them.[5]

Despite the gaps and hazards associated with the current pension system, recent studies suggest that the situation of today's retirees is reasonably satisfactory overall.[6] Since they seldom have to support their children and no longer have job-related expenses, retirees can maintain their lifestyle with less income than they received while working. Experts often estimate that 75 percent of prior income is enough to achieve this result. With that in mind, one study of the economic condition of households that includes their savings, homes, and other assets has found that retired couples with private pensions have an average income of 79 percent of preretirement income while couples without a private pension can replace 62 percent.[7] An even more comprehensive analysis that included government services, subsidies, and tax benefits concluded that Americans over 65 are actually better off than younger generations.[8] A third study has found that very few current retirees were unpleasantly surprised by their income after retirement.[9] Seventy-five percent reported that they received about what they expected and fewer than 10 percent received less; the remaining 15 percent declared that they had higher incomes than they anticipated.[10] Even those who suffered a significant drop in income have often adjusted without much difficulty, both because they have lower expenses than when they were working and because they have more time to shop carefully and maintain an equivalent diet and lifestyle at lower cost.

However one chooses to describe their economic condition, retired Americans seem on the whole to be a remarkably contented lot. An impressive 60.1 percent find retirement "very satisfying," another 32.4 percent find it "moderately satisfying," and only 7.5 percent consider it "not at all satisfying."[11] Just over half of the elderly population find retirement to be better than their lives prior to retirement, and another 32.9 percent find it "about the same."[12]

These surveys suggest that Americans over 65 are feeling happier about their lives than the rest of the adult population, a conclusion supported by other studies showing that well-being for Americans in reasonably good health slowly rises after 30–40 years of age and continues to increase into their 70s.[13] Even the small minority who report that they are dissatisfied in retirement do not seem chiefly concerned about money. One of the few existing studies of well-being in retirement discovered that income matters much less than whether retirees left the workforce voluntarily or against their will.[14] Illness and the loss of a spouse also appear to have much greater effects on happiness than a low income. Apparently, then, money is not perceived as a major problem by the vast majority of currently retired Americans.

Whether these conditions will persist, however, is a matter of some dispute. By every indication, Social Security benefits will be worth less than in the past, if only because the age at which older workers can retire with full benefits is scheduled to rise from 65 to 67. While valued employees who enjoy good health will be able to continue working until they reach 67, one-third or more of all workers will probably have to stop before they planned to retire because they will fall ill or lose their job involuntarily. For them, Social Security payments are likely to be significantly less than anticipated. At the same time, contributions to Medicare (deducted automatically from Social Security checks) are projected to rise from 6.8 percent of Social Security payments to 10.2 percent by 2030.[15] Income taxes on benefits will also rise. Together, these changes will reduce the effective average replacement rate (Social Security checks minus deductions, chiefly for Medicare) from 39 percent of previous income to 30 percent by 2030.[16]

Out-of-pocket health care costs will also be growing steadily, and fewer retirees will have them paid for by their former employer, since more and more companies are ceasing to provide such coverage for their retired workers. In addition, an estimated 39 percent of persons aged 65 will require some nursing home care before they die, and 20 percent of them are likely to remain there for five years or more. These expenses are not covered by Medicare and are available under Medicaid only for those meeting strict tests of poverty.[17] At an average cost of $70,000 per year, nursing homes can quickly deplete whatever savings an average couple may have accumulated.

In addition to these problems, workers retiring after 2007 saw their 401(k) portfolios decline drastically with the plunge in the stock market. If the market does not recover for several years, as many economists predict, large numbers of employees could retire with much less money than they anticipated.

Today's employees can protect themselves against these problems by working more years before retirement. It is not clear, however, how many will actually do so.[18] Fifteen to 20 percent are estimated to be incapable of working for health reasons. Others are likely to have trouble finding a job, since many employers consider older workers less productive and more expensive to insure against illness. For whatever reason, more and more employees have been retiring early to the point that the average retirement age now stands at only 62 years. While lower Social Security checks and heavier debts may persuade some employees to work longer, it is difficult to guess how many.

For all these reasons, most future retirees are unlikely to replace as large a share of their previous incomes as retirees do now if they merely rely on the sources they have depended on in the past. Current employees are not at all certain that they are saving enough to make up the difference. Thirty-four percent in 2005 acknowledged that they were "not too confident" or "not at all confident" that they would have enough money for their "golden years."[19] Gallup polls painted an even more forbidding picture; a full 50–60 percent of respondents said that they were unprepared financially for their retirement.[20] With all that has happened to the economy since these polls were conducted, the figures must be considerably higher today.

According to some analysts, more than 60 percent of Americans aged 47–64 are not saving enough to produce a retirement income equal to 75 percent of prior earnings (a level many consider necessary to maintain their preretirement way of life).[21] Even before the stock market collapsed in 2007–2008, the average 401(k) (or IRA) account of 55- to 64-year-olds contained only $60,000, far less than retirees need to avoid a steep drop in their living standard, let alone pay for nursing homes or other unexpected expenses. Meanwhile, savings outside of pension plans have disappeared almost completely for the average employee; even home equity has been mortgaged away by many families. Observing these trends, many analysts worry that workers who retire in the future will face a much more difficult time than current retirees unless Congress takes major steps to shore up weaknesses in existing policies.

Some economists, however, have a radically different and more optimistic view of the future.[22] According to these writers, financial institutions grossly overstate the amount that current workers need to save in order to assure an adequate retirement. Either they fail to take account of all the ways retirees can lower expenses or they undervalue the assets the elderly can use to help pay their bills. According to one group of analysts, 88 percent of current employees are saving enough, or more than enough, for their later years, and most of the rest are saving close to what they will need.[23]

Most of the dissenting researchers have based their conclusions on the situation of workers who recently retired or were about to be retired. These retirees, however, are still within what analysts call the "golden age" of retirement; they do not have to contend with pushing back the Social Security retirement age from age 65 to 67 or the decline of defined benefit programs. Yet it is these developments, critics insist, that make the outlook for future retirees much bleaker than anything faced by their predecessors.[24]

Whether or not current employees are saving enough for their retirement, they have plenty of risks to cause them to worry about their welfare after they stop working. Will the stock market be depressed (or will their employer declare bankruptcy) and destroy much of the pension they have worked for over many years? Will they be among the 15 percent of elderly persons who are projected to incur out-of-pocket medical costs amounting to more than a quarter of their income? Will they outlive their retirement savings and spend their final years in penury? Will their spouse require extended nursing home care that will eat up almost all their nest egg before they can qualify for Medicaid? With such risks to consider, one would suppose that anxieties about retirement saving must be running high. However, the reality is more complicated. Psychologists point to several reasons why current employees may not be deeply concerned about their condition in retirement.[25] The benefits of good retirement planning are distant and speculative, while the cost of additional saving is immediate and often hard to bear. Moreover, most people instinctively resist thinking carefully about such morbid subjects as decrepitude and death. Until their mid-50s or beyond, they put off worrying about their retirement needs, and such thought as they occasionally give to the subject does not cause them great anxiety.

Eventually, of course, *some* older Americans will almost certainly suffer serious hardship after they retire, from unusual out-of-pocket medical costs, outliving their retirement savings, or some other reason. However large or small the percentage turns out to be, the number of unlucky retirees could easily amount to millions of people as the huge baby boom generation starts to retire. As a result, it is surely worth considering whether changes in policy might help reduce the number of current employees who eventually suffer economic hardship at a time in their lives when they can no longer do much about it.

## Illness and Health Care

Health care is one of the most spectacular failures of American social policy.*

Somehow, the United States has managed to spend far more per capita on health care than any other country on the planet while still allowing over 45 million people, including several million children, to remain uninsured. In addition, at least 29 million more Americans are thought to be underinsured.[26] These gaps in protection are primarily due to the government's decision many years ago to rely on health insurance supplied by employers willing to

---

*A recent Commonwealth Fund survey of patients and physicians in the United States and five other highly advanced democracies reveals America's weaknesses very clearly. Among many aspects of health care, the United States ranks first in only one: preventive care. In all other respects—quality of care, access to care, efficiency, equity, life expectancy at age 60, infant mortality, deaths preventable by proper care, among others—America ranks last or next to last among six nations: the United States, Britain, Canada, Germany, Australia, and New Zealand. Even in the use of information technology, where one might have thought this country would excel, America lags well behind most of the other nations in the survey. Karen Davis, Cathy Schoen, Stephen C. Schoenbaum, Michelle M. Doty, Alyssa L. Holmgren, Jennifer L. Kriss, and Katherine K. Shea, *Mirror, Mirror on the Wall: An International Update on the Comparative Performance of American Health Care* (May 2007).

provide such a benefit for their workers. As a result of this policy, the United States is the only advanced industrial nation that does not guarantee adequate health care for virtually all its citizens.

The principal reason why so many people are uninsured under our voluntary system is the high and rising cost of care. Since 1950, expenditures have risen more than tenfold in real dollars. With the baby boom generation nearing retirement and with the mounting cost of ever more sophisticated medical technologies, there is no relief in sight. More and more employers are either withdrawing entirely from giving health insurance to their employees or capping their costs by providing a lump sum and leaving it to their workers to buy insurance for themselves.

The risk of being uninsured falls most heavily on lower-wage employees who cannot afford insurance themselves and often work for small companies that find it especially hard to pay for coverage. According to a 1998 survey, 41 percent of employees earning less than $20,000 were uninsured compared to only 3 percent of those earning more than $60,000.[27]

Having no insurance does not leave individuals entirely without care. The uninsured can still seek help in hospital emergency rooms, and almost all do. Nevertheless, such care is far from optimal. Since the uninsured cannot get regular checkups or obtain proper preventive care for conditions such as high blood pressure, elevated cholesterol levels, cancer, diabetes, and other diseases, they tend to succumb more often to illness and to see a doctor only when their condition has deteriorated to the point that it is harder to treat. When they do go to a physician, they often cannot afford to follow up. In 1999, 49 percent of all uninsured persons reported that they went without needed care or failed to fill prescriptions for lack of money, and the numbers today are doubtless even larger.[28] An estimated 18,000 uninsured patients between the ages of 25 and 64 die unnecessarily every year for lack of adequate care.[29]

The lack of insurance coverage is not the only cause of distress for American families. The amounts most employees must contribute toward the cost of their health plan are substantial and regularly rise more rapidly than the earnings of the average family. Even families that are enrolled worry that some of the expenses they incur will not qualify for reimbursement under the terms of their policy. Nearly 40 percent of Americans in 2003 had out-of-pocket medical expenses that exceeded 10 percent of their income, while more than 30 percent had bills exceeding 20 percent.[30] It is little wonder, then, according to Harvard bankruptcy expert Elizabeth Warren and colleagues, that almost 20 percent of families in bankruptcy cite medical problems as a contributing cause.[31]

In contrast to retirement, the problems of paying for health care seem to weigh heavily on the minds of many working Americans. According to a Louis Harris poll in 2005, 34 percent of current employees admitted being "very worried" about not being able to pay their medical bills if they fell ill.[32] These anxieties are especially prevalent among lower-income Americans, who have the least capacity to pay for health expenses and are the most likely to be uninsured. Half of those with low incomes are "very worried" about paying for health care costs compared with only 21 percent of wealthier Americans.[33]

Such persistent concerns take a toll on well-being.[34] Unlike retirement, which seems remote to many employed Americans, the threat of illness is more immediate, capable of striking a family at any moment. Thus, when Congress enacted Medicare in the mid-1960s and gave universal health care coverage to the elderly, the mood of Americans over 65 improved significantly from being somewhat less happy than their younger fellow citizens to being somewhat more happy.[35] It is probable that the government could likewise increase well-being among younger Americans by bringing proper health care within the financial reach of everyone. As this book was being written, a new American president pledged to reform the health care system and greatly expand its coverage, but only time would tell whether he could succeed where so many previous reformers failed.

## Unemployment

Every year in the United States, several million employees lose their jobs. With increased global competition, the number of layoffs has been growing in recent decades, especially for male workers. Even in normal years of economic prosperity, at least 4.3 percent of the workforce are laid off annually, and some observers put the number considerably higher.[36] Corporate executives, pressed by investors to show short-term results, resort increasingly to cutting payrolls as a quick way to improve the bottom line and convince shareholders that they are determined to achieve results. As companies restructure, even white-collar and middle-management jobs that were once thought secure are now at risk of being eliminated.

One striking finding from the research on happiness is how painful and long-lasting the effects of losing a job can be. Although many displaced workers cope reasonably well with the shock of unemployment, researchers have found that laid-off workers have sharply greater risks of becoming depressed, committing suicide, or abusing drugs or alcohol.[37] Overall, the average level of well-being among those who lose their jobs is far below that of the employed and recovers only after several years.

Part of the distress comes from the loss of income. Employees who are laid off may receive federal unemployment insurance, but fewer than half of all workers in the United States are covered by the law, and benefits last for only 26 weeks unless extended by act of Congress. The number of workers who experience long-term unemployment has jumped several-fold in the last two decades, and many have had their benefits run out before they could find new employment. [38] In contrast to employees in other advanced industrial nations, most workers who lose their job in the United States also lose their health insurance. With their normal source of income cut off, two-thirds of laid-off workers cash out all or part of their 401(k) account (instead of transferring the accumulated funds to their next employer), thus risking financial hardship when they retire.[39]

Losing wages and benefits, however, is often easier to bear than the loss of self-esteem from feeling rejected and a failure to families, friends, and neighbors. Even unemployed workers who are lucky enough to receive generous jobless benefits will often feel wounded, and the pain can persist long after they find a new job.

Worse yet, many of those who suffer repeated bouts of unemployment lose the desire to work altogether, much like oft-jilted lovers who are afraid to risk another serious relationship.[40]

These hardships are commonly regarded as a painful but necessary cost of economic progress. Yet researchers have found that large-scale layoffs often fail to yield lasting benefits to investors while damaging employee trust and morale in ways that can diminish rather than improve efficiency.[41] The findings have been succinctly summarized by Harvard Business School professor Nitin Nohria and Don Sull.[42] As they point out, several well-known consulting firms have studied the long-term effects of layoffs in scores of large companies and found that most of them did not increase productivity, improve cash flows, or even reduce costs.

The United States does less than virtually any other advanced industrial nation to cushion the shock of unemployment. Compared with such countries, the United States gives proportionally fewer employees the right to receive advance notice before being laid off, and the requirements that exist are very poorly enforced.[43] Existing laws in the United States also fail to protect employees from unnecessary job loss by requiring employers to consider work-sharing arrangements or reduced hours so as to resort to layoffs only when other reasonable alternatives are impractical. Although jobless benefits are quite substantial for those lucky enough to receive them, eligibility requirements are highly restrictive and have become even more so in recent decades. As a result, the percentage of workers who are eligible to receive benefits has now sunk well below the levels of other advanced industrialized nations.[44]

Once employees are laid off, the government performs poorly in helping them find new jobs. The Federal Employment Service is notoriously weak. Only 10 percent of employees who come to the Service find work as a result, usually in low-paid, often temporary jobs.[45] Employers are not required by law to notify the Service of job vacancies, and fewer than one-third make use of it.

Congress has been active in providing training programs to help employees gain the skills to acquire new jobs. Scores of such programs have been created over the years. Even so, the United States still spends less on training than other industrialized nations and very few, if any, of the programs established have proved more than mildly helpful.[46]

As global competition has increased, American workers are increasingly worried that they may lose their jobs. The fraction who admit to being "frequently concerned about being laid off" rose from roughly one-tenth in 1980 to more than one-third in 2001.[47] Several studies have found that insecurity is now one of the principal causes of job dissatisfaction both in America and in Europe.[48]

Although there is little direct evidence of the effects of job insecurity on workers' well-being, researchers have found that persistent anxiety about almost anything tends to diminish happiness.[49] Several studies have shown that worry over losing one's job leads to a higher incidence of sleep disorders and depression along with declines in perceived health, all of which are important predictors of well-being.[50] Hence, the weight of the research seems to confirm what common sense suggests and the International Labor Office maintains: namely, that workers who are afraid of losing their jobs are likely to be less happy as a result.[51]

## Living on the Edge

The financial risks of retirement, illness, and unemployment have all become more serious in the past 35 years. Because average earnings for the great majority of Americans have risen very slowly in the past 35 years, many families have elected to preserve their lifestyle by depleting their savings and taking on debt. Lenders have been only too happy to oblige by offering a host of new opportunities for obtaining cash. Second mortgages and home equity loans rose from 4 percent of total mortgage debt in 1981 to 12 percent in 1991.[52] Home equity loans alone rose from $1 billion in 1981 to $132 billion ten years later.[53] More and more consumer goods could be purchased on the installment plan with interest costs often back-loaded to make the payments seem more manageable. The burgeoning credit card industry made it easy for individuals to carry substantial amounts of debt, typically at high rates of interest. Lenders allowed workers needing cash to borrow against their 401(k) retirement accounts.

Under these conditions, many families accumulated large debts and lived with a persistent fear of being unable to make ends meet and having to endure bankruptcy or foreclosure. With their homes fully mortgaged, both spouses working, and retirement savings already spent down, they had no margin of safety left. By 1995, hundreds of thousands of families were declaring bankruptcy every year. Mortgage foreclosures had already risen fivefold since the 1970s, even before the recent collapse of the housing market pushed the number well above two million in 2008 alone.

According to the National Opinion Research Center, of all the negative events that can happen to Americans, only the death of a child is considered more painful than declaring bankruptcy or losing one's home and having to live on the street.[54] It would be surprising, then, if the threat of financial disaster—whether from inadequate retirement savings, crushing medical bills, layoffs, or simply excessive debt—did not take a toll on the well-being and peace of mind of millions of American families. As a result, finding policies to minimize such risks offers an especially promising opportunity to help alleviate widespread anxiety and distress.

## The Issue of Personal Responsibility

The hardships just described have provoked a flurry of proposals for universal health insurance, restructuring mortgages, helping the unemployed, and more. Reform does not come easily, however. Throughout our history, efforts to protect individuals from risk have provoked dire warnings that personal responsibility will suffer and weaken the moral fiber of the nation.* Those who make

---

*Some opponents of protective legislation may cite Ruut Veenhoven's study, mentioned in the introduction, which found that countries with more extensive safety nets do not have higher levels of well-being than nations offering much more modest protection. "Well-Being in the Welfare State: Level Not Higher; Distribution Not More Equitable," 2 *Journal of Comparative Policy Analysis: Research and Practice* (2000), p. 91. This study certainly suggests that one should not automatically assume that larger social welfare programs will

such arguments do not always specify the benefits that self-reliance is meant to bring, nor are they much inclined to offer specific evidence of any damage done by Social Security and other pieces of protective legislation in the past. Since self-reliance is repeatedly invoked, however, and since it is a recurrent theme of the conservatives' case against additional social welfare benefits, it is important to identify the arguments and examine them individually.[55]

One reason for asking individuals to cope with risks on their own is to give them pride and self-respect and thereby make them more satisfied with their lives. Supportive evidence can be found in the aftermath of the welfare-to-work legislation of the mid-1990s. In reports on the effects of this law, one can read many accounts of poor women who were forced to get off welfare and enter the workforce only to find that they were happier having a job than living on checks from the government.

It is one thing, however, to have to rely on handouts from the government and quite another to collect benefits from a program to which one has contributed money over the years. There are few signs of discomfort on the part of recipients of Social Security and Medicare. Senior citizens seem very pleased by these programs and quite unwilling to give them up.[56] Surely, it strains belief to suppose

---

always increase well-being. On closer scrutiny, however, Veenhoven's study has several limitations. First, he measures only government outlays and thus does not rule out the possibility that countries with low public expenditures achieve good results through an artful combination of public and private expenditures. Second, he lumps together all of each government's social programs so that one cannot infer from his findings that every type of social legislation will fail to boost happiness. Third, he aggregates large groups of nations according to the total size of their welfare programs, and thus does not show that all generous welfare states are bound to fail. In fact, several countries with ambitious social programs, such as Denmark and Sweden, have unusually high levels of well-being.

Since Veenhoven's article appeared, several other scholars have tried to evaluate the effects on well-being of larger or smaller state social spending. The results have been mixed and the final verdict, therefore, seems still in doubt. Compare Angel Alvarez-Diaz, Lucas Gonzalez, and Benjamin Radcliff, "The Politics of Happiness: On the Political Determinants of Quality of Life in the American States" (draft paper, 2007); and Alexander Pacek and Benjamin Freeman, "The Welfare State and Quality of Life: A Cross-National Analysis" (draft paper prepared for Notre Dame Conference on New Directions in the Study of Happiness, October 22–24, 2006), with Christian Bjornskov, Axel Dreher, and Justine A.V. Fisher, "The Bigger the Better? Evidence of the Effect of Government Size on Life Satisfaction around the World," 130 *Public Choice* (2007), p. 267.

that the many millions who worry about being laid off, or falling ill without health insurance, or outliving their retirement savings are any happier at the prospect of having to face these challenges on their own.

A more common claim, however, is that protective legislation will weaken America by undermining people's resilience and self-reliance. According to this argument, even if such laws seem to be effective and large majorities accept them, shielding individuals from risk by removing their responsibility to protect themselves will ultimately sap the vitality of the nation and make it vulnerable to future challenges.

Those who worry about self-reliance often point to some golden age, usually in the eighteenth or nineteenth century, when social insurance was unknown and families allegedly grew strong by dealing with adversity with no help other than what their neighbors and churches could give them. Such claims, however, are historically questionable and impossible to prove. No index exists by which to measure the self-reliance and inner strength of our current population, let alone compare it with the character of the American people a century or more ago. Nor is it possible to determine whether any likely improvement in these human qualities is worth the hardship that results from leaving people to cope as best they can with financial hazards such as those described in this chapter.

A final reason for insisting on personal responsibility is that tax-payers should not be required to foot the bill for problems that prudent people should have been able to avoid. And yet, although it may be theoretically possible to save enough to prevent the misfortunes catalogued in this chapter, it is easy to overlook just how difficult it is for ordinary people to protect themselves against these risks. In trying to prepare for the possibility of unemployment, how are they to estimate the likelihood of being laid off, or the length of time it will take to find a new job, or the risk of having to settle for a much lower wage? In planning years ahead for retirement, how can they know how long they will live, whether they will need extended nursing home care, how many years they will be able to go on working, or how strong or weak the market will be when they retire and receive the cash value of their 401(k) account?

For some risks, of course, insurance policies are available to enable individuals to protect themselves. Still, it is impossible to know how large a pension or an insurance policy ought to be when the risks involved are so hard to gauge and the effects can vary so widely. Moreover, some forms of insurance, such as for nursing home care, are simply too expensive for many working families, while policies for other risks, such as unemployment or the effects of inflation in retirement, are either nonexistent or hard to find in the private market.

It is also unclear whether one can reasonably expect families with modest incomes to summon the willpower to save enough to guard appropriately against future contingencies. As David Hume once said, "there is no quality in human nature which causes more fatal errors in our conduct than that which leads us to prefer whatever is present to the distant and remote."[57] Even for those who are far-sighted, the cost of providing for all major risks—long-term health care, forced retirement, out-of-pocket medical costs, just to name a few—will seem prohibitive to many lower-income families.

There is likewise no country in which it is more difficult to save than the United States. Americans are on the receiving end of twice as much advertising as the citizens of virtually every other advanced democracy, subjecting them to a constant barrage of seductive pleas to consume more and more. Only in America would a cash-strapped public school display paid advertisements on the pages of its examination booklets.[58] National politicians who speak of self-reliance and personal responsibility practice massive deficit spending, while their counterparts in the states tempt constituents with state lotteries and legalized gambling. The very political leaders (and economists) who deplore the decline of personal saving worry publicly about lagging consumer confidence and urge the public to keep shopping. Business, for its part, displays great ingenuity in tempting people to assume additional debt by offering them more and more ways to enjoy the immediate pleasures of purchasing goods and services while postponing the burdens of paying the price. The marketplace teems with installment sales, no-down-payment deals on automobile purchases, and a plethora of variable rate and subprime mortgages. Meanwhile, modern technology makes it easy to buy on impulse by inviting people to purchase expensive goods with a single phone call or the touch of a computer key.

Nothing illustrates the problem better than credit cards.[59] The entire industry is based on exploiting human frailty. To banks and other issuers of cards, those who pay their bills on time, far from being praised for their punctuality and thrift, are referred to in the trade as "deadheads." No wonder. The profit to be made comes from delinquents who run up large credit balances and then have to assume huge interest costs and penalty payments for the money they owe. To obtain such customers, companies market cards aggressively to all sorts of vulnerable groups—students, unemployed families, even individuals emerging from bankruptcy. Armed with a battery of cards, people can then purchase goods without the immediate need to pay the price.

In such an environment, it is questionable whether lawmakers should approach issues of protective legislation by attempting to strengthen personal responsibility or improve the character of the people in other ways. Such judgments are always hazardous and tend to be highly partisan as well. The risk of error is especially great when members of Congress try to make moral judgments about how ordinary people should cope with financial hazards far greater than most lawmakers face in their own daily lives.

This does not mean that Congress should try to protect Americans from every common danger. Before forcing people to save to protect themselves against a particular contingency, legislators must ask whether the risks involved are sufficiently serious to justify requiring everyone to forgo income now to gain protection later. Before using general revenue to subsidize a new protective measure, lawmakers must decide that private insurance is either unavailable or too expensive for people of limited means and that the hazards involved are great enough to justify the cost to taxpayers. When social legislation does seem warranted, Congress must take great care not to create perverse incentives that will encourage unjustified claims or other forms of waste.

The judgments involved in these decisions are difficult enough without attempting to resolve them by defining a standard of personal responsibility to which all Americans should be held. Rather than embark on such a treacherous undertaking, legislators would be better advised to take experience as their guide and examine the way people actually behave. If large numbers of Americans are failing to protect themselves adequately against serious hardships, the odds are great that the risks involved are beyond the average person's ability to cope. In a country where fewer than half of all employees believe they are saving enough for their retirement, where 47 million people have not purchased health insurance, and where millions more have had the loss of a job propel them into bankruptcy, it is asking too much of human nature to expect families to protect themselves from all the financial risks they are facing today.

## Opportunities for Reform

How might the government act responsibly to give greater protection from the financial hazards that are causing such worry and distress among low- and middle-income American families? Social legislation is a notoriously complicated subject, and any attempt to describe a set of comprehensive reforms would require at least a volume by itself. For the purposes of this chapter, however, it is only necessary to indicate where feasible opportunities for reform exist, not to describe every detail of the remedy.

*Retirement*: Reforming pension laws is complicated by the current disagreement over whether working people are saving enough for their retirement. Whatever the answer turns out to be, however, particular groups of elderly persons will almost certainly experience hardships that could be mitigated or even avoided entirely by appropriate government action. For example, out-of-pocket health care costs currently eat up a quarter or more of the yearly income of 15 percent of retirees. It should be possible to cap such expenditures or devise some other way of keeping them within reasonable limits. In addition, since several other countries have enacted programs to defray the cost of long-term nursing home care, Congress should be able to do the same and thereby help families escape from having to pay crushing bills that force them into poverty.

Such protections would undoubtedly cost money, but that is not a sufficient reason for failing to protect individuals against serious hardships resulting from health problems that are seldom of their own making. Rather than allow such conditions to persist, it would be far better to use some of the tens of billions of dollars in tax deductions for pension contributions that are chiefly benefiting wealthier families who least need such subsidies.

It should also be possible to increase the minimum Social Security benefit in order to minimize the number of elderly Americans who currently live in poverty. Many of these retirees are not responsible for their condition; they are individuals who worked their entire life in low-paid jobs or widows who used up their retirement savings paying the medical bills of seriously ill husbands.[60] Even retirees who could have saved more earlier might be excused on compassionate grounds to spare them from having to live their declining years in genuine privation. The official poverty line in the United States is set sufficiently low that such relief will hardly deter younger workers from saving for their retirement.[61]

Still other steps could be taken to encourage more retirees to obtain annuities so that they do not run the risk of outliving their savings and having to subsist on Social Security alone. In principle, employees covered by a 401(k) plan can take their accumulated pension when they retire and buy an annuity. In practice, however, few of them do so, although researchers find that retirees with annuities are much happier than those without.[*] Companies could be required to offer their employees an option to convert their 401(k) savings into an annuity on their retirement. Such a conversion, in turn, could be made to occur automatically unless employees requested in writing to receive their account in cash. These steps would greatly increase the percentage of retirees receiving annuities while still preserving the right of retiring

---

[*]Constantijn W. Panis reports that retirees with incomes of $15,000–$30,000 who have annuities are much more likely to feel "very satisfied" with their situation than those with similar incomes who do not have an annuity. In fact, they are even slightly more satisfied than retirees without annuities who have incomes above $50,000. "Annuities and Retirement Well-Being," in Olivia S. Mitchell and Stephen P. Utkus (eds.), *Pension Design and Structure: New Lessons from Behavioral Finance* (2004), pp. 259, 265.

employees to receive their accumulated savings in cash if they so desired.[62]

In addition to the measures just described, lawmakers may decide after further study that current employees *are* saving too little, just as many analysts fear. If so, although a large increase in Social Security taxes may be unwise or impractical, Congress could consider requiring all employers to offer an optional 401(k) plan to their employees if they have not done so already. Under such a program, employers could contribute to the plan, but they would not have to do so. Unless employees were already covered, however, or requested specifically not to participate, a stipulated percentage of their earnings would be automatically withheld from their paycheck and placed in their retirement account.* In this way, having a pension to supplement Social Security would no longer depend on whether employees happened to work for a firm that offered such a benefit. By requiring reluctant workers to convey in writing their desire not to join, and by ensuring that a plan would be established in every workplace, Congress could greatly increase the number of employees with a private pension while still allowing individuals to refrain from participating if they did not wish to forgo the immediate use of the money.[63]

*Health care*: Whether or not President Obama succeeds in his efforts at sweeping health care reform, it should be possible to remedy the worst deficiencies of a health care system that currently leaves millions of Americans uninsured or underinsured. After all, America is the only advanced industrial country that has *not* managed to achieve universal coverage. While the details of a comprehensive plan are beyond the scope of this book, three elements are especially important. To begin with, the insurance plan should cover a full range of essential services, including appropriate long-term care, but

---

*Ideally, such a plan would be introduced in a time of rising wages so that workers would not have to choose between preserving their current income and saving adequately for their retirement. Additional steps could be taken to simplify choices and reduce the likelihood of improvident decisions. The number of alternative investment options could be reduced; the amount invested in the employer company's stock could be limited; a default option that offered protection against the risk of severe stock market declines at the time of retirement could be mandated, etc.

omitting items such as elective cosmetic surgery, over-the-counter medications, private hospital rooms, among others, that are not commonly included under existing insurance plans. In addition, all citizens and lawful resident aliens should be included, with coverage no longer dependent on employment. Finally, while copayments and other measures may be needed to prevent overuse, out-of-pocket charges should not be set so high that they discourage access to needed services, and the charges should be kept affordable by imposing a ceiling or some other device to ensure that such expenses do not consume an excessive percentage of family income.

Crafting a plan that meets these specifications will surely be expensive. Taxpayers may complain over the prospect of adding further costs to a system that with all its weaknesses is still the most expensive in the world. Even so, the financial burdens of past errors and excesses are scarcely a sufficient justification for perpetuating the hardships endured by millions of uninsured families whose members do not happen to work for an employer who provides health benefits. Since other nations have achieved universal coverage with much lower costs and often with better health results, it is surely possible to insure all Americans at a price the country can afford.

*Losing a job*: Although the loss of a job turns out to have surprisingly severe and lasting effects on well-being, it is the hardest to remedy of all the hazards in this chapter. Despite the fact that many layoffs in the United States appear to be unnecessary, it would be impossibly burdensome and difficult to require employers to seek government approval before downsizing their workforce. Forcing companies to give severance pay to all laid-off employees might prevent some needless layoffs, but it could also cause employers to avoid hiring full-time workers. Requiring companies to try other remedies, such as work-sharing, before resorting to layoffs could be hard to implement effectively and might seriously hamper employers needing to adjust to sudden market changes or downturns in the economy.

There is one simple step, however, that could address at least a small part of the problem. Every year, hundreds of thousands of employees are fired from their jobs for cause. In most cases, employers have good reason for their action. Quite often, however, they do not. Employees may be let go for acts they didn't commit or for personal reasons having nothing to do with their performance on the job, or they may be sacked without notice or warning or even any knowledge of the rules they have broken.

The United States is virtually alone among advanced industrial nations in failing to provide some simple form of redress for workers unjustly discharged. Those who work in unionized plants are routinely protected by contract clauses prohibiting firing employees without just cause. Statutes also prohibit firing workers on account of their age, gender, race, or religion. But nonunion employees who are discharged for other reasons, however unfair or insubstantial, have no recourse.

It would be relatively simple to provide relief in such cases. Although judicial remedies might be too costly and time-consuming, private arbitrators are readily available and widely used for just these purposes under collective bargaining agreements.[64] A number of nonunion employers have even instituted arbitration voluntarily. Ample precedent has developed over the meaning of just cause, and the procedures can be expeditious and quite inexpensive.

The value of extending such protection to nonunion firms would reach far beyond those cases in which employers were forced to reinstate workers or give them back pay. The principal benefit would be the prophylactic effect of inducing all employers to exercise greater care in discharging employees. Companies will doubtless resist this proposal, warning of burdensome red tape and diminished efficiency. Because the loss of a job takes such a toll on the well-being of employees, however, the remedy seems justified, especially now that so many unionized firms (along with employers in other countries) have long since grown used to such procedures.

Responding to layoffs is much more difficult. Of course, vast numbers of jobs could be saved if some way could be found to curb the irrational exuberances, excesses, and regulatory lapses that have periodically given rise to recessions in the past. It is hard to imagine any single improvement in policy that would do as much to avoid anxiety and distress. Unfortunately, however, one can scarcely count on public policy to achieve such miracles any time soon. When downturns do occur, deficit spending can limit the damage, and jobs programs can put people to work when unemployment rises. Still, there is little prospect of doing away with the large numbers of layoffs that occur every year, despite the distress they inflict on those who lose their jobs. At most, the government can try to ease the pain.

Enforcing the current 60-day notice period prior to layoff more rigorously and extending it to more employers would be one reasonable step, since timely advance notification has been found to avoid unemployment for some employees and to shorten the time out of work for others.[65] Uncoupling health insurance from employment and making coverage universal would also help. Above all, unemployment insurance coverage could be extended to reach many more workers than the roughly one-third to one-half who currently qualify under the stringent eligibility requirements now in effect.

These measures will not remove the loss of self-esteem that constitutes the heaviest blow to the unemployed. Still, there is no reason to add to the woes of laid-off employees by leaving them without the money to pay their medical bills and basic living expenses. As several experts have pointed out, the principal reason for the huge numbers of personal bankruptcies in this country is the lack of an adequate safety net to help individuals who have temporarily lost their job and their means of livelihood.[66]

Finally, more effective measures to assist the unemployed in finding new jobs would also make a difference. Existing programs have accomplished little in the past and hold scant promise for the future. The Federal Employment Service has been notably ineffective and attempts to revitalize it seem unlikely to succeed.[67] There is likewise little evidence that more short-term training will do much good, since dozens of such programs have been tried, and none has had much success.[68] To accomplish more, especially in an economy where skill demands have risen and managerial, technical, and professional employees are increasingly subject to layoffs, more extensive retraining is required.

Several possibilities are worth considering. One would be some sort of longer-term assistance for laid-off employees who wish to enroll in a community college or university to obtain the skills to start a new career and avoid having to accept another job at a much lower rate of pay. Another option would be a form of wage insurance that would pay employees up to half of any lost earnings if they were laid off but took a lower-paid, full-time job within six months of becoming unemployed.[69] The annual subsidy could be capped at some reasonable figure and the duration of the benefit limited to a fixed period such as two years. Such a benefit would give an incentive to laid-off workers to accept a lower-paying job that provided attractive opportunities either to obtain valuable on-the-job training and an eventual promotion or to take classes at night to qualify for a better position elsewhere.

Steps such as these, like the others briefly mentioned in this chapter, will hardly do away with all financial risk or remove all danger of economic ruin. Nor will they eliminate the need for families to exercise self-restraint to keep from living beyond their means. Through their combined effects, however, the government could limit the number of people who experience economic privation, ease the burden for those who do, and relieve the anxiety of countless others who live in the constant shadow of financial crisis.

The ultimate effects of these reforms on happiness are still not entirely clear in view of the doubts created by researchers studying the impact of social welfare spending on national levels of happiness. Further research on the effects of proposed remedies would doubtless help to address these uncertainties. Still, in view of the widespread worries and hardships resulting from the financial risks described in this chapter, it would be surprising indeed if well-designed measures to ease these burdens did not improve the well-being of millions of Americans.

# 7

## RELIEVING SUFFERING

Many of the multiple sorrows that befall human beings are beyond the power of government to remove. Many others inflict only transitory pain, since people recover surprisingly quickly from most of life's setbacks and disappointments. But a few afflictions stand out because they cause severe and prolonged distress, affect large numbers of people, and seem at least somewhat amenable to enlightened public policy. Three of the most prominent examples are chronic pain, sleep disorders, and depression. None of them is commonly numbered among the nation's high-priority illnesses. Yet all three offer exceptional opportunities to any government seeking to improve the well-being of the public.

### Chronic Pain

Chronic pain, by definition, is pure suffering and unhappiness. It is also surprisingly widespread and very costly to society. The American Pain Foundation has reported that 50 million Americans live with chronic pain.[1] Much of the suffering is borne by cancer patients, the terminally ill, and nursing home residents. But the many forms of pain experienced by those who work are estimated to cost the economy more than $60 billion in lost productivity alone.[2] If medical expenses, disability payments, and lost wages are added in, the total burden could approach $100 billion per year.

By all accounts, chronic pain can be effectively treated in the vast majority of cases. Cancer specialists estimate that at least 80 percent of patients with metastatic pain can have their suffering relieved.[3] Estimates for the successful management of other forms of serious pain range as high as 90 percent for those experiencing such distress during the course of severe illness.[4] Nevertheless, informed observers agree that many sufferers do not receive the care they need. Although pain is the principal reason why people consult a doctor, many who suffer do not seek help. Some are not aware of what can be done; others lack funds; still others resolve to soldier on stoically without assistance. Even more troubling is the fact that many who do ask for help do not receive adequate treatment from their doctor. In one study of hospitalized cancer victims, investigators found that 42 percent of these patients did not receive proper pain relief.[5]

Why do so many sufferers fail to get help from their doctor? The principal reason is that the most effective medications are typically morphine-based drugs called opioids. Because these drugs are also a source of addiction and abuse, they are classified as controlled substances under the Federal Controlled Substances Act. A well-known example is Oxycontin, which is a highly effective pain reliever but also an illegal drug whose improper use is said to have led to some 18,000 emergency room visits and up to 400 deaths from 2000 to 2003.[6] Few of those who abuse such medications are patients, and fewer still have become addicts as a result of being treated for chronic pain. Even so, the number of abuses seems to be increasing. Since pain is subjective, it is not always easy to distinguish patients who are truly suffering from those seeking pain relievers to satisfy a drug habit. In one way or another, Oxycontin and other opioids manage to find their way into the hands of drug dealers and addicts. In at least a small number of cases, irresponsible doctors are involved.

The law does not prohibit the use of opioids to relieve pain. Because of the risk of abuse, however, doctors and others who provide these medications are subject to strict regulation and oversight. All providers must register with the Drug Enforcement Agency and receive authorization to dispense such drugs. Agency personnel may investigate doctors on suspicion of violations and, where appropriate, call upon the Department of Justice for enforcement proceedings. If doctors are found to have violated the

Controlled Substances Act, they can lose their license to practice medicine or be forced to pay a civil fine of up to $25,000. In cases of deliberate violation, they may actually go to prison.

In addition to federal regulation, each state has its own drug laws enforced by police and other officials. Suspected physicians can be charged by the state attorney general or referred to medical licensing boards that have the power to hold hearings and suspend an offender's license to practice. In several states, criminal proceedings have been brought against doctors for allegedly prescribing excessive amounts of Oxycontin. Other states have imposed strict statutory limits on the amounts of pain-relieving drugs that physicians can prescribe.

Many state boards have been zealous in overseeing the use of opioids. Some critics have accused them of being too zealous. According to one author, "state medical licensing boards in the very decades in which an epidemic of undertreated pain was being reported, established a pattern and practice of taking draconian disciplinary actions against their licensees for alleged instances of 'overprescribing' opioid analgesics."[7]

Whether or not the authorities have gone too far, the current system of oversight seems very threatening to many physicians. Although the consequences of losing one's license to practice can be ruinous, licensing board decisions are not subject to careful review in the courts but can be overturned only when found to be "arbitrary or capricious." Even if a doctor is eventually vindicated in the courts, having one's practice disrupted for many months along with periodic bursts of negative publicity can ruin a career as well as causing intense and protracted worry. Faced with such possibilities, many doctors respond by refusing to dispense pain-killing drugs at all or prescribing very low doses in order to minimize the risk of legal difficulty.

The inhibiting effect of drug regulation is exacerbated by the vagueness and confusion that many doctors face in trying to interpret what the rules mean. Federal and state regulations are not always consistent. In 2004, for example, the Drug Enforcement Agency signaled a change in policy that departed significantly from the rules adopted by most state boards.[8] Even if there is no conflict, regulations are often hard to interpret—for example, when they prohibit the prescription of "excessive quantities" of a controlled substance or allow the use of opioids only after "all reasonable alternatives have been explored."[9] Further problems arise because many state boards and their employees are not trained in pain management and are poorly informed about the effects of pre-scribed drugs. Officials frequently exaggerate the risk that patients will become drug addicts—a result that has been shown in various studies to be extremely rare.

As it happens, few doctors have actually suffered penalties under state or federal law. Only 30 had their licenses suspended in 2003, although 950,000 providers are registered to dispense opioids. Nevertheless, the chilling effect of a few well-publicized proceed-ings has undoubtedly discouraged the appropriate use of opioids in many states. In separate surveys of primary care physicians in California and physician-members of the American Pain Society, 40 percent of the respondents indicated that fear of regulation led them either to avoid opioids altogether or to prescribe less than the optimum amounts.[10] In several states, the mere enactment of a law requiring doctors to file a copy of every opioid prescription with a state agency has had "an immediate and dramatic effect on prescribing practices of physicians."[11] Whether or not the doc-tors involved are overreacting, the result is likely to be unnecessary pain for their patients.

Added to the effects of regulation is the fact that many medi-cal schools have no required course in pain management, leaving the subject to be discussed, if at all, in isolated lectures scattered through other courses. This neglect has left many doctors with-out adequate knowledge of the basic facts about the use of pain-relieving drugs. For example, one survey of Texas doctors revealed that 25 percent believed erroneously that using opioids to treat pain carries a serious risk of turning patients into addicts.[12] This misconception arises from ignorance on the part of doctors of the difference between physiological dependence, which often occurs in treating patients but can be easily avoided by gradually reducing the dosage of the drug, and psychological dependence (the con-dition of drug addicts), which very rarely occurs if patients take the pain-relieving drug as prescribed. Physicians who do not understand this distinction will naturally hesitate before prescribing such drugs for their patients.

In recent years, the undertreatment of chronic pain has provoked growing anger on the part of patients and their relatives. As a result, a dozen or so states have passed laws declaring explicitly that drug regulations are not intended to interfere with the medical use of opioids by doctors. The Federal Drug Enforcement Agency has issued statements to the same effect. Even more importantly, the privately run agency that accredits hospitals has incorporated guidelines requiring the institutions they inspect to demonstrate compliance with a number of steps designed to ensure the proper use of effective methods to alleviate pain.

Another sign of the growing concern over unnecessary pain is the success of two civil actions brought by patients' families seeking damages resulting from the undertreatment of severe pain.[13] Prior to these lawsuits, doctors had nothing to fear if they did too little to relieve suffering but faced the frightening possibility of serious penalties and protracted legal proceedings if they were accused of prescribing opioids improperly. The predictable result was widespread undertreatment. Now, with the possibility of lawsuits and accreditation problems if they undertreat pain, doctors and other providers will presumably exercise greater care to alleviate such suffering properly.

While these developments may be steps in the right direction, the current situation leaves doctors in a very uncomfortable position. If a state board feels that they are overprescribing opioids, physicians face the threat of investigations and possible legal proceedings. Yet if they do not prescribe enough opioids, they may find themselves in a lawsuit brought by suffering patients or their families. Since rules are often vague or even in conflict with one another and since those responsible for enforcement are sometimes poorly informed about the medical facts, even the most conscientious doctors have reason to feel apprehensive.

Several steps are needed to resolve this dilemma and encourage the proper treatment of chronic pain without subjecting doctors to unnecessary risks. In order to overcome the pervasive ignorance and misunderstanding about the proper use of opioids and other controlled substances, medical schools should give pain management a more prominent place in the curriculum, not only for medical students but for residents as well. In addition, practicing physicians should be required to study the subject as part of their continuing education requirements, and drug enforcement officials should likewise receive appropriate training. Medical researchers should intensify efforts to find pain relievers that do not contain addictive drugs and develop better screening methods to help emergency room personnel identify patients who are likely to be seeking opioids for improper purposes. Government officials should take active steps to remove inconsistencies in state and federal laws affecting the use of drugs for medical purposes. State legislatures should review all laws that limit the amounts of pain-relieving drugs that physicians can prescribe to make sure that they are supported by sound medical evidence. Finally, lawmakers should work with representatives of the medical profession to develop "safe-harbor" legislation guaranteeing that doctors who follow clear guidelines for the use of opioids will not be subject to enforcement proceedings or other legal actions.

As matters now stand, serious chronic pain, like depression, offers an ideal opportunity to eliminate unnecessary suffering. Living with cancer is hard enough without forcing victims to endure acute distress that proper medication could readily alleviate. Coping with approaching death is likewise difficult enough without leaving up to "77 percent of patients suffering unrelieved, pronounced pain during the last year of life," to quote the words of Dr. Timothy Moynihan of the Mayo Clinic.[14] Since millions of Americans currently experience chronic pain, concerted efforts to minimize undertreatment deserve a prominent place in any comprehensive program to increase well-being in America.

## Sleep Disorders

One little-known fact about the state of health in America is the number of people who live with some form of persistent sleep

disorder that robs them of the restful nights they need to function effectively during the day. At least 30 million Americans suffer
from chronic insomnia. Another 6 million have obstructive sleep
apnea, which causes a temporary cessation of breathing due to
the obstruction of air passages or a malfunction of the brain's re-
spiratory center. Six million more have restless legs syndrome, an
uncomfortable itching, burning, or tingling sensation that compels
the sufferer to move constantly and thus interferes with sleep. Still
further millions are afflicted with narcolepsy, or disturbances of
the circadian rhythms, or one of a number of other conditions that
bring about drowsiness during the day or loss of sleep at night.[15]

The burden of these afflictions is substantial. Sleep disorders
are associated with a number of illnesses, including hypertension,
diabetes, heart attacks, and stroke. Almost 20 percent of all serious car accidents are brought about through lack of sleep (after
controlling for cases involving alcohol).[16] One 20-year Swedish
study found that sleep-disturbed employees had twice as many
job-related injuries as other workers.[17] Among the elderly, lack of
sleep is also a common cause of falling. The total cost associated
with problems of this kind is hard to estimate exactly but clearly
runs to tens of billions of dollars each year.

Apart from these tangible costs, sleep deprivation has remarkably bad effects on the well-being of sufferers. According to the experience sampling studies of Daniel Kahneman, using a five-point
scale to measure happiness, people who described their sleep as
"very good" had a mean level of enjoyment throughout the day
of 4.05 while those reporting "very bad" sleep reported a level of
only 2.80.[18] This difference turned out to be greater than that associated with any other factor, far greater, for example, than the
effect of income, or education, or a good job.

The testimony of sufferers gives an even more vivid sense of
how it feels to have a chronic sleep problem. Berkeley professor
Gayle Green, herself an insomniac, summarizes such reactions as
follows:

> Look on the web, read what insomniacs say on sleepnet.com and
> Talkaboutsleep.com, and you'll find stories of lives wrecked by this

affliction, marriages ruined, educations abandoned, jobs lost, careers destroyed. "I can't work, I can't date, I can't connect with anyone anymore. I had to drop out of school. I used to be a lawyer; now I'm the walking dead. I was a teacher once; there's no way I could face a classroom now. It's like being punished for something, only I don't know what I did."[19]

Paul Martin gives a more clinical description in his book, *Counting Sheep*: "sleep-deprived people perform badly on all aspects of creative thinking, including originality, flexibility, generating unusual ideas, being able to change strategy, word fluency. . . . All in all, they are worse at communicating their thoughts, feelings, decisions and actions."[20]

One would think that the prevalence of sleeping problems and the consequences to sufferers and to others would elicit a determined effort to cure these afflictions. But that is far from being the case. The title of a recent report by the Institute of Medicine describes the situation succinctly: *Sleep Disorders and Sleep Deprivation: An Unmet Public Health Problem*.[21] As the report points out: "millions of individuals suffering from sleep disorders remain undiagnosed and untreated." According to the *Harvard Medical School Guide to a Good Night's Sleep*, "despite some recent progress, fewer than 3 percent of Americans with persistent sleep problems get treatment because both patients and their primary care doctors often do not consider sleep an important health issue."[22]

There are various reasons for this neglect. No easy method is available to confirm a sleep disorder such as insomnia. It is, as Gayle Green says, "a subjective state. There is no blood test it shows up on, no biopsy or x-ray that picks it up, and it doesn't even show up on the EEG."[23] As a result, listeners often dismiss the complaints of sufferers as exaggerated. "Helpful" suggestions abound: "Drink less coffee." "Don't take naps after lunch." "Exercise more." Everyone seems to have a homespun solution. Before long, many an insomniac learns not to talk about the problem.

Efforts to obtain a doctor's help may also prove unavailing. Physicians in managed care plans often have too little time with a patient to diagnose the problem or devise a proper remedy. Worse yet, many doctors know too little to respond helpfully even if they had sufficient time. More than one-third of all medical schools do not include any coverage of sleep disorders in their curriculum, and the total average time allotted to the subject by the schools that do cover it is barely two hours.[24] Since sleep research emerged as a serious field of research only a half century ago, well-trained investigators are still in short supply. Proper diagnostic equipment is so scarce that sufferers often have to wait ten weeks or more for the standard polysomnogram procedure.

Finally, many who suffer from a chronic sleep disorder do not know that it is a genuine medical condition that can often be treated successfully. Instead, they take over-the-counter medications that can often cause withdrawal problems, or they find a doctor who will give them a prescription for Ambien, Lunesta, or some other drug to help them sleep. While the prescribed medications can be helpful, they can also have troubling side effects, such as sleepwalking, or going to the kitchen to eat, or even driving a car while asleep. Experts on sleep have differing opinions about the proper use of these medications. Some believe that they should not be used for extended periods, while others disagree.[25] Worse yet, many doctors don't prescribe the drugs at all, either because they are hypnotic and hence are subject to Federal Drug Enforcement Agency regulations or because doctors do not feel comfortable prescribing them for more than a limited period. As a result, by far the most commonly prescribed medications for sleep disorders are antidepressants, although they have not yet been proven to be effective for treating sleep disorders.[26]

This brief account should suffice to demonstrate the seriousness of the problem caused by the various forms of persistent sleep disturbance and by the way these conditions are currently treated. As an expert panel convened by the Institute of Medicine recently concluded: "Our findings confirmed the enormous public health burden of sleep disorders and sleep deprivation and the strikingly limited capacity of the health care enterprise to identify and treat the majority suffering sleep problems."[27]

Any serious attempt to remedy the situation would require action on several fronts. To begin with, the government would need to mount an educational effort to inform the public about the prevalence of persistent sleep disturbances and the possibilities that exist for effective treatment. Medical schools should spend more time on the subject in teaching medical students and residents as well as in continuing education courses for practicing physicians who need to know more about the causes, diagnosis, and treatment of sleeping disorders. More equipment is necessary to improve access and reduce waiting time for administering polysomnograms. Finally, the National Institutes of Health should increase the funds available for research, since current allocations for investigating sleep disorders are meager and have stagnated and even declined in recent years despite all that remains to be discovered in order to understand and treat these afflictions properly.

The sums required to do what is needed are not exorbitant in light of the prevalence of persistent sleep disorders and the toll they take on the well-being of millions of Americans. Such expenditures could even be a good investment. As the Institute of Medicine declared in its recent report: "The high estimated costs to society of leaving the most prevalent sleep disorders untreated are far more than the costs that would be incurred by delivering the proper treatment."[28]

## Depression

Depression is, almost by definition, a wretched condition. It is often characterized by deep melancholy, loss of energy and initiative, constant anxiety, and deterioration of judgment. Leonard Woolf gave this eloquent description of his wife, Virginia, during one of her recurring bouts of depression: "There was always a sense of some guilt, the origin and exact nature of which I could never discover. . . . In the early suicidal stage of the depression, she would sit for hours overwhelmed with hopeless melancholia, silent, making no response to anything said to her. When the time for a meal came, she would pay no attention whatsoever to the plate of food put before her. . . . If left to herself, she would have eaten nothing at all and would have gradually starved to death."[29]

Depression often weakens the immune system and creates a heightened risk of drug and alcohol abuse and even suicide.[30] It is also the principal cause of workplace disability. The total cost to American society is thought to exceed $80 billion per year, and the annual burden on employers from the loss of productive work alone accounts for more than $50 billion.[31]

Although estimates of the prevalence of mental illness vary widely, the rate of serious depression in the United States is generally thought to be higher than many people realize. According to one highly knowledgeable source, some 16 percent of Americans will suffer from at least one major depression during their lifetimes, and half or more of these will experience repeated episodes.[32] Every year, approximately 6.6 percent endure a major depressive episode lasting weeks, months, or even longer.[33]

If national rates of mental illness are inexact, comparative figures on the incidence of depression are even more unreliable. Those who study the subject, however, tend to believe that the United States and Canada have the highest or nearly the highest rates of any country in the world.[34] Experts differ over whether depression in America is increasing, but the most careful estimates suggest that the numbers are now rising very slowly.[35] Earlier claims of more substantial growth may well have been inflated because they were based on visits to doctors and failed to take adequate account of the fact that more people have become willing to seek professional help as the stigma of mental illness gradually diminishes.

Fortunately, advances in medicine make it possible to control the symptoms (and hence relieve the suffering and debility) of depression for 80 percent or more of those afflicted.[36] Patients can be treated either by psychotherapy or by drugs, but a combination of the two appears to be the most effective. Sustained, vigorous exercise may also be effective. For those who do not respond to any of these treatments, electric shock therapy is sometimes successful.

The policies and programs for treating the depressed in the United States have improved substantially since the days when sufferers were herded into public asylums and made to endure wretched conditions and inadequate care. Many of the discriminatory policies that used to limit the treatment of mental illness under health care plans and government programs have now been eliminated. The funds appropriated by the federal government have increased several times over, and the effectiveness of treatment has improved enormously.[37] No longer are the mentally ill regarded as outcasts and banished to isolated locations out of the sight of those fortunate enough to retain their sanity. Many fewer patients remain for extended periods in mental hospitals, and many more are integrated into normal communities with varying degrees of supervision and care.

Despite these encouraging signs, much more could still be done. The following rule of thumb describes the scope of the problem very starkly. Roughly speaking, of every six Americans who suffer from serious depression, only one is treated correctly, two are treated incorrectly, and three are not treated at all.[38] Poor people are especially likely to suffer without treatment, since they often lack the money to obtain needed services or the information to know where and how they can receive professional help.

There are several reasons for these disappointing results. One is a lack of adequate funding. Although mental health disorders account for a large part of the total burden of disease in the United States, they receive a far smaller share of federal health research funds and of all federal health care expenditures.

Another contributing cause is the inadequate training of medical personnel. In particular, primary care physicians, who represent the point of entry to America's health care system, are often insufficiently prepared to recognize mental illness or refer afflicted patients to doctors and facilities capable of giving them proper care.[39] With many physicians under managed care plans having only minutes to spend with each patient, symptoms of depression often go undetected and untreated, or, if diagnosed, are dealt with quickly by prescribing pills. These inadequacies help explain why two-thirds of those who see a doctor for their depression receive inappropriate treatment.

Still another reason for undertreatment is the failure of many depressed people to seek medical help. Part of the problem stems from the stigma that still attaches to mental illness and the consequent reluctance of many sufferers to disclose their condition. But a much more important cause is that those who do seek help are so often bewildered by the multiple agencies and offices that exist under our fragmented system of care. Being depressed and often poor with little education, they are the least able to cope with these complexities. Often, they simply give up trying.

Underlying these causes is a continuing skepticism toward mental illness that persists despite improving attitudes in recent decades. Seriously depressed people often believe that their case is hopeless or that they are somehow to blame for their condition and hence do not deserve help. A lurking suspicion abides with much of the larger public that mental illness is often imagined, that those afflicted should simply pull up their socks and get on with it, and that anyone who won't is probably weak-willed and unworthy.

The fear of being stigmatized in this way still keeps many depressed people from acknowledging their condition and asking for help. The lingering stigma itself helps explain the inadequacy of government funding and the political weakness of the mentally ill. It may have contributed at times to ill-advised policies, such as Congress's failure to appropriate enough money to pay for community housing and care following the wholesale release of patients from mental hospitals in the 1970s or Ronald Reagan's decision to cut large numbers of mentally ill people from federal disability rolls in the 1980s.

Traces of discrimination against the mentally ill have continued to appear throughout the health care system. According to a Robert Wood Johnson Foundation study, 72 percent of primary care physicians expressed frustration over their inability to obtain quality mental health care for their patients under insurance plans; only 18 percent made similar complaints about referrals to other types of specialists.[40]

Until recently, most private health insurance plans offered less comprehensive coverage for mental illness and required higher out-of-pocket payments than those provided for other forms of illness. For example, under one large group employer plan, individuals running up mental health bills of $35,000 had to pay $12,000 of their own money, while patients who incurred similar costs from other illnesses were only charged $1,500 out-of-pocket. The Federal Mental Health Parity Act of 1996 was supposed to end this type of discrimination, but restrictions in the law's coverage weakened its effectiveness.[41] In response, some 40 states passed parity laws of their own, but most of these laws cover only a restricted set of mental illnesses and do not protect government employees or persons covered by single employer plans, thus excluding a large fraction of the working-age population.

Even Medicare and Medicaid discriminated against the mentally ill until recently. For example, under Medicare, hospital coverage for mental illness was capped at 180 days over the beneficiary's lifetime until Congress prohibited the practice in 2007. No other type of illness is subject to such a limit. Moreover, the payments psychiatrists can receive under Medicare and Medicaid are still set at levels well below their normal fees. As a result, many psychiatrists will not accept mentally ill patients under the federal programs. Barely half of them will even take patients enrolled in managed care plans due to restrictions on fees and burdensome administrative requirements.

Fortunately, in the frantic negotiations for a federal "bailout" bill to stem the financial crisis during the fall of 2008, a provision was inserted prohibiting any discrimination between the treatment accorded to mental health problems and other forms of illness under private health insurance plans. It is still too soon to know exactly how this provision will be interpreted and enforced. Nevertheless, the new law appears to put an end to much of the lingering discrimination just described and hence represents a valuable advance in the long effort to place mental health on an equal footing with other types of sickness and disease.

Ignorance of the law creates additional barriers to proper mental health care. One survey of the elderly has shown that almost half of all those polled mistakenly said that they had no coverage for mental illness even though they were probably eligible for Medicare benefits.[42] Poor and uneducated sufferers also tend to be unaware of existing opportunities for care. Such findings suggest that the government should do more to inform individuals of their benefits. Under pressure to keep down costs, however, public officials rarely give a high priority to such efforts.

While no reforms of public policy can possibly guarantee proper care to all of the mentally ill who need it, further improvement seems well within the reach of government. It should be possible to raise the fraction of seriously depressed people who are properly treated to a point far above the current figure of one-sixth. Incentives could be provided to encourage better training for medical students, especially those seeking careers in primary care. Subsidies could be offered to induce more companies to refer their employees for psychiatric treatment and to encourage HMOs to refer patients to psychiatric care. It is not unreasonable to expect the government to do more to inform people of their benefits under Medicare and Medicaid and to provide some simple way to help the mentally ill cope with the confusing array of health care options and agencies and guide them to appropriate treatment. Nor is it impossible to create a health care system that covers all of the mentally ill and ensures the participation of enough psychiatrists to offer services to all who need them.

The steps just listed would undoubtedly cost money. Still, much of the expense would eventually be offset by restoring disabled employees to full-time productive work and by enabling more of the mentally ill on welfare to hold a steady job. More important, these reforms could give a substantial boost to the well-being of many millions of people who currently live large parts of their lives in a state of misery and despair.

There is nothing particularly original about the steps suggested for improving the treatment of depression—or for doing a better job of treating chronic pain and sleep disorders, for that matter. In all three cases, the actions recommended in this chapter are regularly mentioned in the writings of specialists on each subject. The chief contribution of happiness research, then, does not lie in developing novel remedies but in pointing to neglected needs and sufferings that offer unusual opportunities to improve the well-being of millions of Americans.

# 8

## MARRIAGES AND FAMILIES

Researchers agree that love, friendship, and positive relations with other human beings contribute much to happiness, a result that will hardly surprise anyone. Of these experiences, close ties within the home matter most both for parents and for children.[1] Helping to build such relationships, however, represents a far greater challenge to policy-makers than finding ways to protect people from economic hardship or from the suffering caused by depression and chronic pain. As the late Senator Daniel Patrick Moynihan once observed, "If you expect a government program to change families, you know more about government than I do."[2] Still, warm human ties are so important to happiness that it is worth considering whether policies exist that can do something to strengthen marriages and families in ways that will foster caring relationships and promote the healthy development of children.

### Helping Marriages

As pointed out in chapter 1, both marriage and divorce can affect happiness in substantial ways. According to one study averaging national surveys from 1970 to 1994, 42 percent of married couples described themselves as "very happy" compared with 17 percent of divorced men and women, 21 percent of couples that were separated, and 26 percent of individuals who had never married.[3] These results, of course, are partly due to the fact that happier people are more likely to get married and stay married. Yet researchers have concluded from longitudinal studies that marriage itself is partly responsible for the increased well-being, although the positive effects often fade after two or three years.[4]

Successful marriages appear to have more lasting effects on the well-being of children. In one study that divided adults into seven groups according to the quality of their parents' marriage, investigators found that the happiest group was made up of individuals who grew up in a home where parents were content and seldom in conflict with one another.[5] In another long-term study, investigators asked Harvard students in the 1950s to describe the nature of their relations with their parents. Examining the medical records of the same individuals 35 years later, researchers found that those who had previously described their relations with parents as warm and close experienced fewer than half as many serious illnesses over the intervening years as those who characterized their relations with their parents as cold and distant.[6]

Divorce and separation have the opposite effect. Studies have repeatedly shown that the breakup of a marriage can result in a substantial decline in well-being that lasts for many years.[7] In addition to losing her husband and experiencing failure in an important relationship, a wife who becomes divorced can suffer a loss of income that causes persistent worry over finances along with unsettling changes in lifestyle and environment. Husbands tend to suffer more psychologically than their wives from the breakup of a marriage. They are more likely to regret their divorce and to experience depression and other forms of distress.[8]

Divorce can cause equally serious problems for children. Although most sons and daughters weather such a rupture without lasting difficulty, a substantial minority experience significant distress or even severe psychological problems. Children may blame themselves for the divorce. A parent's remarriage may bring new tensions into the home. One careful study by Harvard economists even found that the rising divorce rate was the single factor most highly correlated with the threefold increase in teenage suicide after 1970.[9]

In explaining the problems encountered by children of divorced parents, researchers differ over the extent to which these hardships are attributable to divorce per se. Some have argued that the difficulties are likely to result from the marital conflicts that typically precede a divorce rather than the divorce itself and that ending a bad marriage can often leave children better off than before.[10] Although this controversy is not fully resolved, the weight of the evidence suggests that both intense parental conflict *and* divorce can cause subsequent problems for children but that marital conflict is not usually severe enough for divorce to be preferable from the standpoint of the children's well-being.[11]

Many children of divorced parents grow up in a household with only one adult. The same is true for most children of parents who never marry. Although young people can flourish under these conditions, the odds of encountering serious problems increase. Reviewing numerous studies of single-parent families, one analyst has concluded: "For children, growing up in a household with two married parents is associated with better school performance, fewer emotional and behavioral problems, less substance abuse, less abuse or neglect, less criminal activity, and fewer out-of-wedlock births. These results persist even after controlling for income, education, and other observed factors."[12] According to James Q. Wilson, children born into single-parent homes are twice as likely to drop out of school, have children out of wedlock, or be incarcerated.[13]

The findings just summarized are particularly worrisome for the United States in view of the deteriorating condition of traditional families over the past several decades. The percentage of married adults describing their marriage as "very happy" has dropped substantially since 1970. The divorce rate, which had gradually increased over the twentieth century, began to rise more rapidly in the 1970s and climbed to 50 percent before finally leveling off after 1990. From 1970 to 1998, the proportion of adults currently married fell from 69 percent to 58 percent.[14] As marriage rates declined, births out of wedlock, which made up only 5 percent of all children in 1960, steadily rose to account for almost 33 percent by the end of the century. As a result of these trends, the percentage of children living with a single parent increased from 8 percent in 1960 to 28 percent in 2005.[15]

Today, the divorce rate in the United States is the highest of all advanced countries. The percentage of children who are born out of wedlock is also high, though not the highest. The United States continues to outstrip all other advanced nations in the prevalence of teenage pregnancies, even though the level declined sharply after 1990. As a result of these trends, America now stands alone in the percentage of children under 18 who grow up in a home without both biological parents.

Many young people with single parents reside in low-income, inner-city neighborhoods. A series of problems has made conditions in these communities especially dire.[16] Unemployment has soared as manufacturing firms have relocated, moved jobs overseas, or gone out of business. An influx of drugs has offered an easy source of income for many black youths who find regular work hard to get. Mandatory prison sentences for dealing drugs have sent many of these young men to jail for years, surrounding them with the worst kind of role models. Once out of prison, they find that employers are reluctant to hire them, thus intensifying the pressure to return to a life of drugs and crime.

The effects of these trends on black communities have been devastating.[17] Twenty percent of all black men born between 1975 and 1979 were incarcerated by their early 30s, including 36 percent of those who did not go to college and an astonishing 69 percent of high school dropouts. More than 70 percent of black men in prison have fathered children by the time they went to jail. For them, there can be no chance of acting as a parent. Moreover, with so many men behind bars, young black females in many inner-city neighborhoods far outnumber young black males, making marriage highly unlikely for large numbers of these women.

Even where conditions are not so bleak, the challenge of developing effective measures to strengthen marriages and families has proved daunting. Efforts to solve one problem often worsen others. Tougher child support enforcement may discourage out-of-wedlock births, but it may also keep fathers from acknowledging their children and helping to raise them. Changes in the law that make it harder to divorce may also keep children locked in families marked by persistent conflict or even abusive behavior.

Another difficulty for policy-makers is the frequent conflict between effective family programs and strongly held cultural and religious values. For example, teaching about birth control, distributing contraceptives, and easing inhibitions on abortion have been shown to do much more to reduce teenage out-of-wedlock births than programs urging sexual abstinence. Even so, proposals of the former kind often provoke intense public and political opposition.

With these problems in mind, policy-makers can use three different strategies to strengthen marriages and families. The first is through education—by telling teenagers how and why to avoid becoming pregnant, or teaching better skills of communication and conflict avoidance to young couples before and during marriage, or imparting parenting skills to couples expecting their first child. Programs of this kind have proved especially successful in reducing teenage pregnancy, with declines as high as 50 percent or more among the young people enrolled.[18] Teenagers are an especially attractive target, not only because they are often unprepared to be parents but also because at least two-thirds of their pregnancies (and almost all the pregnancies of unmarried teenagers) are unintended.

Successful interventions of this kind can do a lot to increase opportunities and improve the well-being of young women. Teenage single mothers are especially likely to regret their pregnancy, remain unmarried, and drop out of school before graduating. Their children also have a higher risk of being born prematurely with low birthweights and are much more likely than children of older parents to repeat a grade or drop out of school. Education is an inexpensive strategy for avoiding this litany of misfortunes. The cost of such programs has been estimated at only $1,000 per participant.[19] In view of the burdens to society that often result from out-of-wedlock births, it is likely that much, if not all, of the cost would be recouped in eventual savings, quite apart from the beneficial effects for all those spared from unintended and unwanted pregnancies.

For older couples, marital and premarital education can be effective in reducing conflict and improving communication. Although the evidence is mixed (presumably because program quality varies greatly), several researchers have found that these classes substantially lower the incidence of divorce.[20] For example, a study of one government program found that only 4 percent of couples receiving instruction had split up after five years compared with 25 percent of families that did not have such classes.[21] Since divorce often causes lasting distress, there is much to be said for any program that can improve the odds of keeping marriages intact. This conclusion seems all the more compelling since marital difficulties are often short-lived; in fact, a recent large-scale study found that two out of three unhappily married adults who decided not to seek divorce or separation reported being happily married five years later.[22]

At present, only an estimated 40 percent of recently married couples receive any counseling or education to help them build a successful relationship, and many of these programs are poorly designed. Quite possibly, expanding and improving such efforts would help more marriages to succeed, although further research is needed to determine how long-lasting the results will be. Fortunately, a number of pilot projects are already underway, funded by a program to strengthen marriage established under George W. Bush. Before long, officials should know much more about which forms of counseling work best and how long the effects will last. Since marriage classes cost only a few hundred dollars per couple, compared with an estimated cost to society of $30,000 for each divorce, interventions of this kind could turn out to be a very inexpensive way of contributing to happiness.[23]

The second approach to strengthening marriage is to alter incentives in ways that will discourage out-of-wedlock pregnancy and persuade low-income couples to marry. For example, the combination of tougher child-support enforcement and stricter requirements for women on welfare to go to work has raised the cost of pregnancy for both parties. That may be one reason why teenage births out of wedlock began to decline after 1990.

In principle, at least, it should be possible to make marriage more attractive for low-income couples when the woman does become pregnant. Contrary to popular opinion, most of these couples are still romantically involved when their baby is born. According to one study, 90 percent feel that the chances they will wed each other are at least 50-50, and 75 percent believe that marriage is "almost certain."[24] (As it happens, however, only 15 percent are married by their child's third birthday.) Far from feeling trapped by becoming a parent, the vast majority of the men are pleased at the prospect of being fathers. Most of them continue to see their child regularly during the first year and eventually lose contact only because the mother denies access or becomes involved with another man or because one member of the couple moves to another city.[25]

A common explanation for the failure to marry is that low-income couples are often irresponsible. The truth is more complicated. Recent research indicates that although poor couples cohabit rather casually, they take marriage much more seriously and think carefully before making this commitment.[26] Large majorities of poor women would like to have a husband and agree that a lasting marriage would be best for them and for their children. Their reasons for not marrying are much more likely to be financial rather than resulting from a frivolous attitude toward family and parenthood. Either they cannot afford to lose the child care subsidies, earned income tax credits, or welfare benefits they would forfeit by marrying a wage-earning man, or they cannot find a mate who has steady work and an income large enough to support a family.[27]

These economic obstacles could be alleviated by such measures as a higher minimum wage and an expanded earned income tax credit coupled with better job training and greater efforts to persuade boys to stay in high school and graduate. Innovations such as career academies, which provide extensive vocational education and work-internships during high school, deserve encouragement. Congress could also examine ways to reduce the financial disincentives to marriage that poor women face by having to give up various means-tested benefits if they marry a steady wage earner.

Several other steps are worth studying to lessen the adverse effects of incarceration on marriage and parenthood in inner-city neighborhoods.[28] Congress could review the use of mandatory jail sentences for drug offenses and other nonviolent crimes to determine whether the deterrent effects are sufficient to justify the devastating consequences for families in inner-city communities. Congress should also consider creating public works programs in high unemployment areas to provide an alternative to drug dealing as a source of income. Efforts could likewise be made to expand prison rehabilitation and job assistance programs that have proven effective in lowering recidivism.

The third approach to strengthening families is to take steps that will encourage better care of children. Some of the reasons why having children often fails to increase the well-being of parents (and part of the explanation for the decline of women's happiness in recent decades) may have to do with conditions that public policy can address. If parents could take paid parental leave for adequate lengths of time, they might feel less torn between the necessity to work and their desire to care properly for their infant children. If they could readily find decent child care at prices they could afford, they might not have to struggle so hard to deal with their children's needs while still showing up on time for work. If they had guaranteed health insurance, they wouldn't have to worry constantly over how to manage if a child falls ill.

America has been especially backward in encouraging the kinds of interaction between parents and newborns that research has shown to be critically important to a child's later development.[29] Most working parents would like to take time off when a child is born, but the United States is the only advanced, industrialized country that does not require employers to offer paid parental leave. Even the current federal law requiring unpaid leave applies to only half the workforce. Moreover, it allows only a three-month absence from work despite findings by behavioral scientists that full-time employment during the first six months of a baby's life "appears to lead to lower cognitive ability in early childhood and into middle childhood."[30] In sharp contrast to America, other highly advanced industrial democracies require an average of ten months of paid parental leave, and Scandinavian countries actually provide for periods ranging from eighteen months to three years.[31]

There is no convincing reason why the United States should not follow these examples and insist on paid parental leave for at least six months for all families.* Such a requirement would put the

---

*Because health care insurance is linked to employment and hence must be paid for by employers, paid leave can be more expensive in America than in other countries. As a result,

well-being of parents and infants ahead of questionable claims of burdening businesses and hampering economic growth that have not been persuasive in other advanced nations. Greater efforts might also be made to increase part-time jobs in the public sector for mothers of small children so that they can work but still have ample time for parenting. Sweden has had such success with this approach that Swedish mothers spend more time with their small children than American mothers even though a higher percentage are employed.

In addition to the specific interventions just discussed, lawmakers could consider more comprehensive efforts to strengthen families. Over the years, the federal government has funded and evaluated a number of pilot programs of this kind. Several of them have enjoyed at least modest success. One of the most promising was the Minnesota Family Investment Program, which substantially increased child care support, wage subsidies, and other benefits to married couples. Evaluators found that the program cut the divorce rate substantially, improved the school performance of children, reduced domestic violence, and slightly increased the chances that unmarried mothers on welfare would marry.[32] A subsequent pilot program for poor women in Milwaukee offering wage supplements, job-search assistance, subsidized health insurance, support for child care, and community service jobs for those who couldn't find work boosted marriage rates significantly in addition to increasing employment and reducing depression among participants.[33]

Much more research and experimentation are needed to test these results and try to bring the programs to scale before their success is assured. Still, the results are promising enough to hold out hope that opportunities exist for encouraging marriage and improving the prospects for parents and children within populations where marriage and family seem most endangered. A comprehensive program to promote healthy marriages might include expanded programs of premarital education, steps to reduce the economic barriers that

---

compulsory paid leave might lead some employers to end their health care plans or to avoid hiring women of childbearing age. This is one more reason in favor of a fundamental reform of our health care system.

deter poor couples from marrying, and increased efforts to reduce school dropouts, create jobs in low-income communities, and improve the economic prospects of low-income families through measures such as an expanded earned income tax credit. While these initiatives would be expensive if they were implemented nationwide, the investment could eventually pay large dividends in well-being by increasing the odds of successful marriage and enhancing opportunities for a better life among parents and children in many of the most economically disadvantaged American families.

Reflecting on the various initiatives to promote successful marriages, one can understand Senator Moynihan's skepticism about the capacity of governments to improve family life. Human relationships may be the most important source of happiness, as many psychologists claim, but changing the way people feel about one another remains a formidable challenge at best. Still, some barriers to marriage are economic and can be lessened through government assistance (although much care is needed to avoid perverse incentives and other unintended consequences). Other problems can be avoided through education and counseling to avoid unwanted teenage pregnancies and improve the ways families communicate and resolve their differences. With further research and experimentation, such methods could become even more successful.

Will happiness increase as a result? Researchers have yet to explore this question thoroughly. But if one examines the adverse effects that divorce can have on couples, or the troubles experienced by children of unwed teenage mothers, or the problems encountered by many young people growing up with single parents, the odds are good that successful interventions will improve well-being, and at surprisingly little long-term cost to the society.

## Helping Children

In addition to measures to promote stronger, happier marriages, other possibilities exist to enhance the well-being of children. The opportunities begin even before a child is born. It is well established that prenatal care commencing early in pregnancy will substantially reduce infant mortality and premature births. Nurse-visit programs to expectant mothers can improve the odds of giving birth to healthy babies by discouraging alcohol consumption and smoking and improving nutrition during pregnancy.[34] The effects of such efforts on well-being are obvious. The death of an infant destroys any opportunity for a happy life. Premature and low-birthweight babies can at least survive, but they have a much higher than normal incidence of blindness, deafness, and cognitive deficiencies along with a greater likelihood of dropping out of school and suffering other misfortunes.

The percentage of pregnant women in the United States who receive timely and continuous prenatal care has improved in recent years due to expanded eligibility under Medicaid. Even so, participation rates are lower than in several other advanced democracies, such as France, Denmark, and Sweden. Moreover, while the federal government has long made an effort to supply proper nutrition to low-income mothers and infants, the program has never been funded sufficiently to accommodate more than 60 percent of the eligible mothers, even though it is widely thought to yield savings in Medicaid and other costs that could more than repay the added cost. It is not surprising, then, that America lags behind most other leading democracies in the incidence of infant mortality and premature births. Although infant mortality rates in America have dropped substantially in the past 40 years, they have fallen even faster in many other countries. As a result, the United States fell from twelfth to twenty-ninth among the nations of the world from 1960 to 2004.[35] The percentage of low-weight, premature births in America is also said to exceed that of most prosperous countries.[36]

Once a child is born, the nature of the home environment, and in particular, the amount of stimulation the infant receives, have marked and lasting effects. The affection and attention given to children can influence their health and resilience decades later. The volume of talk that babies hear before age three affects their IQ and the size of their vocabulary even at age nine.[37] Since parents differ greatly in the degree of stimulation they provide, cognitive differences inherited at birth can be magnified significantly by the time young children begin school. Those from affluent families tend to have home environments rich in reading, games, and other challenging activities. In contrast, by the age of four, children in low-income households have heard an average of 32 million fewer words than their counterparts in well-to-do families.[38] It is no wonder, then, that so many poor children enter kindergarten less prepared than their peers.

Since two-thirds of all mothers with children under six work outside the home, a majority of women with preschool children leave their offspring in the care of others—a relative, a neighboring family, or a child care center. The quality of these arrangements varies enormously. The care provided by relatives or a neighboring family is unregulated and largely depends on the adults involved. Much of it is poor. One national study concluded that fully one-third of all these informal venues were of such low quality that they threatened children's cognitive and emotional development.[39]

Over the past several decades, child care centers have steadily grown in popularity and now claim the largest share of small children. They, too, differ widely. As one leading investigator declared, "few experienced observers would doubt that center quality in the United States varies from excellent to dreadful and is, on average, mediocre."[40] Much of the difference reflects the wide disparities among the states in applicable regulations. Some states demand low staff-infant ratios and require that caregivers be certified and even have a college degree. Their centers are much more likely to be of good quality but will often charge rates that are out of reach for many families. Most states have far looser requirements. Many of their centers pay their caregivers only slightly more than the minimum wage and turnover is very high. As a result, their rates are more affordable for families of modest means, but some are of such low quality that they threaten the healthy development of children and ought to be closed.

The evidence is mixed on whether the timing and amount of infant child care has positive, negative, or negligible effects on children's intellectual and language development. Informal care in another household does not necessarily inhibit cognitive development or do lasting emotional or behavioral damage, but poor-quality care is generally thought to have negative effects.[41] As for center-based care, studies suggest that many programs are of insufficient quality to help children much either cognitively or emotionally.[42] There is dispute, however, over whether high-quality child care does a great deal to aid the development of children. Although most investigators have concluded that the cognitive effects of high-quality care are "consistent, positive, and strong," some researchers have found that excellent care has only small positive effects.[43]

In the wake of the welfare reforms of 1996, governments have substantially increased the subsidies available to low-income families for child care. Still, only a modest fraction of eligible families are receiving subsidies. Expanding access to child care, therefore, continues to deserve a high priority. Much greater sums would be required to give all low-income mothers access to affordable centers of high quality with properly trained and compensated staff. Until there is more agreement on the lasting effects of excellent child care, mounting such an expensive program would probably be premature. There are other interventions that promise to have greater positive effects on the later lives of small children from low- and middle-income families.

The Perry Pre-School Project is the most carefully studied and most celebrated prototype of such programs. Begun in 1962, it enrolled 123 poor African American children aged three and four with very low IQs in the range of 70–85. The program offered daily two-and-one-half-hour classes with low student-teacher ratios and included weekly visits with parents and children in their homes. Researchers monitored the results carefully by comparing outcomes with those of a control group of similar children who were not enrolled in such a program. These evaluations continued into adulthood and turned out to be invaluable in calculating the full effects of the preschool experience.

As the organizers hoped, children in the project made significantly larger cognitive gains than members of the control group, but the gains tended to diminish over the next few years. Surprisingly, however, other benefits became evident as time went on. In comparison with the control group, fewer graduates of the experimental program dropped out of school or had to repeat a grade or enroll in a special education class. By early adulthood, more had attended college and more were employed. Fewer committed crimes or were on welfare, or used drugs.[44] As a result, although the initial costs of the program were substantial, the eventual benefits were great enough to yield almost nine dollars for every dollar invested.[45]

The Perry program must surely rank as one of the most influential social experiments of all time. It had a major role in persuading Congress to launch the national Head Start program, which currently reaches over 900,000 children and costs $6 billion per year. In addition, by the year 2000, 40 states had created their own prekindergarten programs and were contributing $3 billion per year and enrolling almost one million additional children.

Welcome as these developments are, the subsequent history parallels the experience of many other social programs in America. Although access to Head Start is restricted to low-income families, appropriations have only been sufficient to accommodate 60 percent of the eligible children. Most programs are only a half day in length, and spending per student rarely comes close to that of the Perry program. The training of teachers is often limited (only half of the states with preschool programs require teachers to have a BA), the pay they receive is generally well below that of school teachers, and class sizes tend to be larger than those of the Perry project. These deficiencies naturally take a toll on the effectiveness of the programs. Although the Education for America Act of 1994 declared as its first objective that all children should arrive at kindergarten ready to learn, the best estimates are that 30–40 percent of all children in the United States are still entering kindergarten unprepared.[46]

The government has done little to encourage systematic evaluation over time to measure the long-term benefits of the Head Start program rigorously or to determine which aspects of the program have the greatest effect on gains in cognitive ability, school performance, and subsequent behavior. As a result, no one can be completely sure what Head Start has accomplished. Existing studies have reached differing conclusions.[47] Some investigators have even failed to find clear evidence of positive, lasting results. All in all, however, the weight of the evidence seems to indicate that although early IQ gains disappear fairly quickly, graduates of Head

Start often achieve significantly higher levels of high school graduation, college attendance, and employment. Fewer graduates have to repeat grades or enter special education classes. Fewer seem to be arrested or enter the welfare rolls.

According to one well-known expert, W. Steven Barnett of Rutgers University, the positive effects of Head Start programs "are large enough to make a meaningful difference in the lives of children from low-income families: for many children, pre-school programs can mean the difference between failing and passing, regular or special education, staying out of trouble or becoming involved in crime or delinquency, dropping out or graduating from high school."[48] Professor Barnett would agree, however, that the gains from Head Start are substantially smaller than those of the more expensive Perry program.[49] According to one estimate, it would require a boost of approximately 50 percent in current preschool funding to bring the proficiency of children from poor families up to approximately the national average at the time they enter kindergarten.[50]

No investigator has inquired into the effects of successful early childhood programs on the happiness of participants. Nevertheless, one must assume that children who grow up to earn more money, commit fewer crimes, take fewer drugs, and experience less unemployment will tend to be happier than those with worse records. Certainly, those other citizens who escape being beaten, robbed, or shot because of reduced levels of crime will also be spared much distress as a result.

In addition to the well-being it would bring, a truly effective, comprehensive program of preschool education promises to be a remarkably good investment in the long run. Although America currently spends many times less per capita on its preschool programs than it spends on K–12 education, Nobel economist James Heckman has concluded that "the best evidence supports the policy prescription: invest in the very young and improve [their] basic learning and socialization skills."[51] Following this prescription could eventually return the costs several times over.

According to one projection, the initial cost of a properly constructed, comprehensive nationwide program (similar to the Perry project) would be substantial, amounting to $19 billion per year, assuming that classes had begun in 2004.[52] (The incremental cost, of course, would be considerably smaller, since federal and state officials are already spending billions on preschool education.) Because many of the benefits, such as lower rates of unemployment and criminal behavior, emerge much later in the lives of participants, seventeen years would have to pass before the benefits began to equal the costs. By 2050, however, the estimated surplus of benefits over costs would grow to $167 billion per year.[53] Since much of the surplus would enrich the public treasury (because of higher tax payments and lower education, welfare, and prison costs), the investment would not only benefit society but more than repay the government as well.

Of course, it would be naïve simply to assume that a vast nationwide preschool effort could achieve the same beneficial results as a small pilot project. There are obvious problems in taking a successful pilot program to scale without losing much of its value in the process. Other experimental preschool initiatives, however, strongly suggest that the Perry project was not a fluke.[54] Although the most carefully evaluated pilot programs have differed in their design and operation, each has produced benefits several times greater than the money invested. One of these initiatives, the Chicago Child-Parent Centers, is far larger than the other pilot projects, enrolling 5,000 children per year, yet still has realized benefits greater than seven times the cost.[55] Moreover, a statewide program, initiated by Oklahoma, that is open to all four-year-olds, mandates small class sizes, and requires teachers to have a college degree and a certificate in early childhood education has achieved gains in prereading and spelling that are not far below those of the Perry project.[56]

While programs of this kind offer hope for overcoming much of the initial disadvantage of growing up in low-income homes, more experimentation and research are required before lawmakers can be confident that a large-scale effort will produce the anticipated results. The pity is that this preliminary work was not completed years ago. For reasons that are hard to fathom, the government was prepared to invest billions of dollars in a stripped-down program of suboptimal quality but unwilling to spend modest amounts to evaluate its long-term effects or to experiment with other models in order to find the one most likely to offer the best results. Had such studies been done, America might already have a program in place capable of providing more equal opportunities for millions of low- and middle-income children along with reduced crime, smaller high school dropout rates, and fewer people on welfare. Fortunately, the chance to secure these gains still remains. By pressing forward with all possible vigor, the government could hasten the day for achieving major benefits to society and, even more important, creating more equal opportunities and a happier, more fulfilling life for millions of American children.

# 9

## EDUCATION

People often misjudge what will bring them enduring happiness or pain.[1] It stands to reason, then, that any serious attempt to increase well-being should give a prominent place to education. Schools and universities are the obvious institutions to assume this responsibility by trying to cultivate interests and supply the knowledge that will help young people make more enlightened choices about how to live their lives.[*]

Researchers exploring happiness have done much to identify the activities and behaviors that tend to contribute most to an enjoyable and satisfying life. Among these pursuits, work and career are undoubtedly important. Employment is essential for most people if only to earn the money they need to survive and enjoy much else in life. The lack of a job can cause acute distress, a point brought home most vividly when workers are laid off. For many people, work is not merely a means to other ends but an absorbing and deeply satisfying activity as well. For many more, it is a source of friends and companionship. It also brings self-respect, helps people grow and mature, and gives meaning and purpose to many lives.

That said, work is far from the only source of happiness. For a majority of people, it is probably not the most important. Daniel Kahneman has discovered through experience sampling that almost all of the enjoyable activities of the day tend to occur outside one's job—in leisure and active recreation, meals with family and

[*]Some readers may not instinctively associate the work of educational institutions with the activities of government. Yet almost 90 percent of all high school students attend public institutions, and the same is true of almost three-quarters of the students who enroll in colleges and universities.

friends, playing with children.[2] Other surveys exploring people's satisfaction with life have revealed that work may have less to do with happiness than aspects of life such as close friendships, perceived health, or civic and community activities.[3] Researchers have also found that most elderly people are more satisfied in retirement than they were when they were employed.[4] These findings suggest that an education that is truly designed to promote well-being should not just train students for jobs but try to cultivate a wide range of interests and prepare students for a variety of pursuits that tend to increase satisfaction with life.

## Schools

In annual surveys to learn what parents want from the public schools, respondents regularly agree that teachers should prepare their students broadly, not just for productive work but also for successful relationships with other people, for civic responsibilities, and for fruitful and rewarding leisure activities.[5] Yet this is not the mission that America's political leaders have been stressing in the last few decades. Washington officials have repeatedly made clear that the national interest in the public schools lies chiefly in seeing to it that all young people are properly trained for jobs in the twenty-first-century economy so that they can help the United States grow and compete successfully with other countries.

Sustained federal interest in the quality of public education began in the late 1950s after the launch of Sputnik awakened a fear that the Soviet Union might be pulling ahead of the United States in science and engineering. Twenty-five years later, the Soviet threat had receded only to give way to fears that America was falling behind Japan and Europe in the emerging global economy. This worry clearly underlay the highly influential report on public education, *A Nation at Risk*, issued by the Department of Education in 1983.[6] The report began not with a fulsome declaration of education's importance but with a somber warning: "Our once unchallenged preeminence in commerce, industry, science, and technological innovation is being overtaken by competitors throughout the world." As Douglas Harris, Michael Handel, and Lawrence Mishel later observed: "There are more economic terms than educational ones throughout the report. The title could very well have been *An Economy at Risk*."[7]

Since 1983, while public education has continued to occupy a prominent place on the national agenda, the emphasis has consistently been on training young people for productive jobs. In policy circles, students become "human capital" that schools must develop to enhance economic growth and competitiveness. As Bill Clinton put it in his State of the Union address in 1994: "We measure every school by one high standard: Are our children learning what they need to know to compete and win in the global economy?"[8] George W. Bush was no less explicit in his statement in 2007 reauthorizing the No Child Left Behind program: "We need to make sure that our country is more competitive and that our children can take advantage of the best jobs this country has to offer by expanding access to advanced placement courses and strengthening math and science education."[9] President Obama too has made job skills, competitiveness, and economic growth the chief reasons for investing more heavily in our schools and colleges.[10]

The views expressed by these political leaders have plainly influenced the government's education policies. Vocational objectives dominate. The No Child Left Behind legislation stresses accountability by requiring all school districts to test their students regularly. The mandated tests, however, are focused on reading and mathematics, skills that officials consider essential to a productive workforce. In contrast, tests of civic education are emphasized far less; the sole examination on this subject is not administered every year but only once every ten years, and the results rarely get much attention in the press. There has likewise been no official effort to measure progress in other aspects of a broad education—such as music appreciation, art, or moral reasoning—that could help students live fuller, more satisfying lives.

The government's emphasis on basic skills has shifted the attention of principals and teachers from the full range of school activities toward an effort to raise student scores on the high-stakes tests that have assumed such importance in public policy. This tendency has been especially marked in elementary schools. Sixty-two percent of all school districts report that they have increased the time students spend in the early grades on English language studies and mathematics.[11] To compensate, 36 percent of the districts decreased the time spent in social studies, 28 percent reduced the time devoted to science, 10 percent cut the time given to arts and music, and 9 percent took time away from physical education.[12] The reductions were substantial, averaging roughly one-third of the time previously available for each of the subjects that gave up minutes to English and math.

The effects of the law on high schools appear to be less pronounced. Students are taking more courses than they did 20 years ago in math, science, and reading, but they are also earning more credits in social studies and the arts.[13] More than 75 percent of high school seniors complete at least one course in civics or government, and almost all have taken courses in American history. The rewards and penalties of federal legislation have undoubtedly caused school officials to devote more attention to the vocationally related subjects that are regularly tested and for which schools are held accountable. In fairness, however, the courses in reading and mathematics that educators stress do not merely impart vocational skills but prepare the mind for many activities that can contribute to a full and flourishing life.

If there are shortcomings in the high schools, then, they do not lie primarily in the curriculum. A greater cause for concern is whether teachers actually succeed in nurturing a breadth of interests that will persist in later life. On this score, surprisingly little is known. In keeping with the government's priorities, many researchers have studied the impact of education on subsequent earnings, but very few have tried to determine whether high schools foster continuing intellectual, civic, and artistic interests or contribute to a lasting involvement in active sports and exercise.

What little is known is not encouraging. One survey of 81 high school valedictorians found that only a half dozen retained significant intellectual interests a decade later.[14] A leading study of political involvement concluded that most high school civics courses had only a slight impact on voting rates or involvement in political and community activities after graduation.[15] More generally, since researchers find that education, as such, has virtually no direct effect on well-being, it is quite possible that schools accomplish little (beyond equipping people for jobs) that contributes to happiness in later life. One should not be surprised, therefore, to learn that inquiries into the use of time reveal that Americans have responded to the gradual increase in leisure hours not by pursuing interests they learned to enjoy in school, such as reading, recreational sports, or civic activities, but by watching more television.[16] These findings underscore the need to try to foster lasting interests in activities that have been shown to be more closely associated than television with higher levels of well-being.

One step toward this goal might be to impart the knowledge, interest, and commitment required for active and informed civic involvement. Civic education has always been considered a basic aim of the nation's teaching institutions. Today, more than 80 percent of Americans believe it to be a "very important" function of the public schools.[17] Active participation in political and civic affairs has also been shown to be a source of satisfaction to participants as well as contributing to strong communities and effective democracy. It is all the more critical in a country like the United States where civic involvement has been declining, voting turnouts are relatively low, and the society is comparatively weak in labor unions and other political grassroots institutions capable of mobilizing and informing communities of low and moderate incomes about matters of politics and government.

By all accounts, our schools are not now doing enough to acquaint students with even the basic facts about their government and their responsibilities as citizens. A survey in 1998 by the Department of Education found that roughly three-quarters of American high school seniors were "not proficient in civics; one-third lacked even a basic comprehension of how the government operates, and fewer than one-tenth could give two reasons why citizens should participate in the democratic process."[18] Although earlier tests of civic knowledge are not strictly comparable, the results strongly suggest that the civic literacy of high school seniors has been declining steadily since the late 1960s.[19] According to one study, the knowledge of government among high school graduates today is in most respects equal only to that of high school dropouts in the late 1940s.[20]

Classroom time is likewise poorly used in many schools to convey an appreciation of why politics matter and why students should take an interest in the political process. In one survey of high school students, almost 90 percent reported that the most frequent activity in civics classes involved reading and filling out work sheets and that the teaching tended to consist of dry institutional descriptions.[21] Another report by political scientists found that texts on American government are filled with facts but are often short on vivid descriptions of how government functions, how citizens can get involved, and why politics are relevant to much that students care about.[*]

To the credit of the schools, much progress has occurred in encouraging, or even requiring, students to engage in some form of active community service. Between 40 and 50 percent of high school students currently participate.[22] Such experiences can help instill habits of civic involvement that frequently endure after graduation, bringing personal satisfaction to students and benefit to their communities. Service activities can also foster an empathy for the problems of people in need that no amount of classroom work can duplicate. Still lacking in most high schools, however, is an effort to capture the full benefit of such experience by integrating it into the curriculum in ways that allow students to reflect on their efforts and see connections between the problems they have witnessed and their responsibilities as citizens.

A second component of a broad education is a greater understanding and appreciation of the arts. Although almost every school system includes the arts in its curriculum, such courses are widely undervalued and often provided only as an elective. Their

---

[*]According to the most careful review of high school government and civics texts, the former are the most deficient. By and large, they "fail to challenge the student to think critically or creatively," and do not relate the work of government to issues that concern students. Civics texts were considered significantly better in these respects. James D. Carroll, Walter D. Broadnax, Gloria Contreras, Thomas E. Mann, Norman J. Ornstein, and Judith Stiehm, *We the People: A Review of U.S. Government and Civics Textbooks* (1987), p. v.

goals are typically poorly defined.* They are frequently taught by untrained and underqualified teachers and are among the first subjects to be cut back or abandoned when time and money are in short supply.[23]

Methods of instruction are often poorly designed to arouse lasting interest or deeper understanding. Many teachers of the visual arts do not make special efforts to help their students to improve their powers of observation, or to evaluate what they see more critically, or to develop their imagination to envisage what they cannot observe directly. Music classes often consist of participation in student orchestras and bands but do little to help students understand more about music so that they can listen more perceptively. Rarely is research done to discover which methods of instruction are most successful in helping students acquire enduring interests either as amateur practitioners or as consumers of art. In short, schools seldom make the most of the opportunity to give students new ways of apprehending works of art that could excite their interest and enhance their capacity to appreciate much else around them.[24]

Exercise and sport afford still further examples of unrealized opportunities to help students acquire interests that could contribute to a full and satisfying life. Since active forms of recreation are among the pursuits that bring great satisfaction to many people (and since only one-quarter of American adults devote the amount of time to physical exercise that doctors recommend), schools should presumably give a high priority to developing a desire to participate in active recreational sports. This is seldom the case at present, however. Recent studies find that the amount of physical activity drops precipitously from three hours per day for the average nine-year-old to only 49 minutes on weekdays and half an hour on weekends by the time students reach 15.[25] This result is all the

---

*There is much controversy in learned journals about the purposes of arts education. As is often true of other marginalized subjects, such as introductory writing courses in college, academic articles on the subject are typically pitched at a high level of theoretical abstraction that seems curiously detached from what is actually going on in classrooms across the country. See, e.g., Ronald E. Neperud, *Context, Content, and Community in Art Education* (1995).

more disappointing, since research has shown that vigorous exercise can make remarkable contributions to students' well-being by enhancing mental alertness and school performance; counteracting stress, anxiety, and depression; avoiding obesity; and improving health and longevity.[26] To achieve this promise, educators need to do much more than prescribe a desultory hour in the gym each week while concentrating their effort and resources on the best athletes in a few high-profile team sports that are rarely practiced after graduation. Rather, schools would do better by exposing all their students to a variety of strenuous lifetime sports, from tennis and running to swimming and rowing, in an effort to foster habits of physical activity that will endure through later life.

Should high schools take a more direct approach and begin to teach their students what psychologists have learned about happiness? Already one can find a few examples of such courses, although they are rare. In an effort to prevent depression, psychologist Martin Seligman and his colleagues from the University of Pennsylvania offer a program based on happiness research to groups of students ranging in age from 8 to 15.[27] The course not only features class presentations for parents as well as children; it even includes a series of practical exercises to increase well-being. In one week, members of the class may practice being grateful for individuals and experiences that have improved their lives. In another, students may commit to performing a specified number of acts of kindness and generosity to others. In still another, students will write about a particular setback they have encountered recently and discuss why the experience distressed them and how they may have misinterpreted the event or overreacted to it.

It is easy to parody exercises of this kind and write them off as quirky digressions from the serious intellectual work that schools ought to provide. In defense of Professor Seligman, however, each of the practical assignments, and others like them, rests on a body of experimental work indicating that the exercises do increase the happiness of a large fraction of participants.[28] Some of the studies have even found that students in experimental classes that included exercises of this kind continued to experience greater well-being than control groups many months after their instruction ended.

Professor Seligman's course appears to have succeeded handsomely. In a series of separate evaluations comparing his students with control groups, the program was found to cut the incidence of depression in half over a two- or three-year period.[29] Since up to 20 percent of young people are thought to experience mental health problems in the course of a year, one can only applaud efforts of this kind, especially when the teaching is done by instructors as competent as those on Professor Seligman's team.

Other groups have experimented with short high school programs designed to address a wide range of problems and risks.[30] Some try to alleviate stress or help students have successful marriages; others seek to prevent HIV-AIDS, pregnancy, drug and alcohol abuse, or suicide. Successful interventions of this kind can reduce distress and increase well-being in important ways. So long as they have been rigorously evaluated to ensure effectiveness and are staffed by well-trained instructors, they deserve every encouragement.

As the research on happiness becomes better known, more and more high school teachers and principals are likely to consider offering courses on the subject in the regular curriculum. The arguments for doing so seem reasonable, even laudable. Teenagers are interested in knowing how they can lead happier, more fulfilling lives. Rising levels of suicide, depression, and drug and alcohol abuse all point to a troubled, unhappy existence for many adolescents. Why not respond to these signs of need by giving courses that speak directly to the quest for a satisfying life?

Tempting as it is to answer in the affirmative, it is far from clear that schools should try to offer such courses, especially ones that include practical exercises to increase well-being. The reason is that most high school teachers are not adequately prepared to teach such material. Few of them will have ever taken a rigorous course on happiness or been sufficiently trained in psychology to evaluate the writings on the subject with a practiced eye.

There are many ways by which untrained instructors can distort what is known about the subject.[31] Pop psychology books on happiness abound, and their pages are often filled with half-truths, unproven theories, misstatements of what psychologists have found, and unsubstantiated opinions on "the good life." Even more serious problems can occur when untrained instructors offer practical exercises in how to achieve greater happiness. It takes considerable knowledge and experience to keep from emphasizing such exercises at the expense of other attitudes essential to a mature, successful life. Urging students to practice gratitude and emphasize the good in their lives can lead them to accept events and conditions that deserve their disapproval. Well-meaning efforts to build confidence and self-esteem can cause young people to overestimate their capacities and ignore weaknesses they need to overcome. Teaching students to emphasize the positive can engender an unwarranted optimism that avoids serious problems. In short, moderation and balance are as important in the pursuit of happiness as in most other human endeavors. Enthusiastic and untrained teachers may overlook this point or simply not know how to deal with it properly in their classes.

The problems just described expose a troubling dilemma. Learning more about the sources of sustained happiness and dissatisfaction can clearly be of great value to students. Since 40 percent of young people do not go to college, many of them will never discover what is known about the subject if they cannot study it in high school. At the same time, naïve or distorted teaching about happiness can do more harm than good and expose schools to unwelcome controversy from angry parents and other concerned groups. Ideally, it would be helpful to develop thoughtful course materials and train qualified instructors to teach them. As a practical matter, however, schools are unlikely to take these steps for a long time, if ever. For the present, then, given the dearth of qualified instructors, most high schools will probably be wise to forgo such courses and concentrate on teaching more familiar subjects that can nurture the breadth of skills and interests that will contribute to a rich and rewarding life.

## The Effects of Higher Education on Happiness

High school seniors graduate and come to universities with a remarkably materialistic view of what a college education can provide. It was not always thus. In the 1960s, entering freshmen were chiefly interested in developing values and a meaningful philosophy of life. Only 40 percent felt that making "a lot of money" was a "very important" goal.[32] Toward the end of that decade, however, student ambitions began to change. By the mid-1970s, their priorities were completely reversed. Making "a lot of money" was now "very important" for 75 percent of entering students, while acquiring a meaningful philosophy of life remained a major goal for only 40 percent.[33] Since then, aspirations have stayed at about these levels, with making money continuing to be the preeminent reason for attending college. This is hardly cause for rejoicing. Much research has shown that people who set great store on becoming rich tend to be *less* happy than those who have other goals.[34] If that is the case, a majority of freshmen arriving at college are already on the wrong path to a full and satisfying life.

Fortunately, colleges have long insisted that all their students acquire at least some minimal breadth of learning. Even those who choose a vocational major must normally complete at least one year of general education courses that are designed to encourage a variety of interests by exposing students to the sciences, social sciences, and humanities.

Outside the classroom, colleges maintain a large number of extracurricular programs to serve a variety of interests—orchestras, glee clubs, athletic teams and intramural sports, newspapers, drama groups, and a host of other activities. Organizations of Young Democrats and Young Republicans are a fixture on most campuses, while student government gives added opportunities to develop political interests and skills. Community service programs have recently expanded to the point that half or more of the senior class in many colleges will have worked in homeless shelters, tutored children from poor families, visited prisons and old-age homes, or assisted people in need in some other way. This feast of extracurricular pursuits can help students explore new interests, acquire lifelong avocations, and learn to live and work more easily and harmoniously with other people.

Despite this impressive breadth of activity, the widespread preoccupation with making money has definitely left its mark on the undergraduate curriculum. In order to compete for applicants, colleges have felt impelled to offer more and more vocational majors, and students have responded by gravitating increasingly to programs that prepare them for higher-paid professions and occupations. From 1970 to 1990, the number of business majors rose threefold to become by far the most popular undergraduate concentration. Close to three-fifths of all undergraduates in four-year colleges now choose vocational majors. Even liberal arts concentrators pursue majors that often look suspiciously like preprofessional programs designed for undergraduates seeking a PhD and an eventual academic career.

Whether vocational or not, college majors consume up to half of all the courses students take in college. Since roughly a quarter of the undergraduate curriculum is typically made up of electives to allow students to pursue special interests, little time is left to accomplish all the other ambitious aims of a liberal arts education—exploring a wide range of interests, preparing for citizenship, learning to write acceptable prose, studying foreign languages, and more. As a result, many of these ambitious goals are achieved only partially at best for a majority of students.

For all the breadth of extracurricular activity, moreover, many colleges develop these programs in response to student desires instead of making them part of a conscious plan to help undergraduates acquire skills and interests to enrich their later lives. Most of the funds colleges spend on such activities go to support a half dozen high-profile sports that few students will play after they graduate. Little money and administrative effort are devoted to trying to give as many undergraduates as possible opportunities to gain a competence in the arts that will enable them to continue either as amateur painters, musicians, and photographers or at least as knowledgeable consumers and patrons of the arts. Moreover, while extracurricular activities are a vital part of undergraduate life for 18- to 21-year-olds attending residential four-year colleges, a majority of students on campuses today are older, study part-time, and commute rather than live in dorms. Outside activities are likely to play a much less important part in their college careers. In short, though extracurricular programs can kindle lifelong interests, they tend to do so fortuitously rather than through conscious effort and are likely to have such effects less frequently among the growing numbers of older undergraduates than they have with younger students who live on campus.

Much work has gone into measuring the changes in student attitudes, interests, and values as they progress through college. Despite the limitations just described, the results, on the whole, are encouraging. The percentage of seniors who believe that there is intrinsic value in a broad liberal arts education grows by an average of 25–30 percentage points, while the proportion who value their education chiefly as a way to increase their earning power declines by a net 17 points.[35] The percentage of seniors who claim to have serious intellectual and aesthetic interests rises significantly.[36] Student interest in politics and civic activity also tends to increase moderately, although there is some evidence of decline in civic engagement among students enrolled in such popular majors as business, education, and engineering.[37] Moral reasoning improves, especially for the minority of students taking courses in the subject, and researchers consistently find that the improvement has at least a modest effect on actual behavior.[38]

Less is known about the persistence of these interests and attitudes over the years following graduation. As with high schools, much of the work on the long-term effects of college involves its impact on subsequent earnings. But researchers have also discovered that community service seems to inspire students to devote more time to civic affairs during subsequent years even after controlling for initial differences in civic and social concern.[39] Political scientists have also found that voting rates and civic activity of all kinds are much higher among college graduates than among those with only a high school education, although it is still not entirely clear how much these effects are due to the education students receive and how much to initial differences between the attitudes and interests of those who choose to go to college and those who don't.[40] As for other aims of college, such as fostering intellectual and aesthetic interests, there are bits and scraps of evidence suggesting persistent effects among a minority of graduates, but the findings are too sparse to draw firm conclusions.

Happiness scholars have also examined the impact of college on well-being in later life. Overall, the verdict seems to be that added years of education have very little direct effect on happiness, accounting at best for only a tiny share of the variance among adults. True, college does have positive indirect effects.[41] Those with more years of education tend to be happier. Still, this result seems to be largely due to the fact that people who go to college get better-paid jobs and have enough self-discipline to develop healthy habits, not because universities have given them the breadth of interests and capabilities to live richer, more fulfilling lives.

Much still needs to be explored about these long-term effects to discover what kinds of colleges, courses, or other undergraduate experiences tend to be associated with greater happiness in later life and which cause more participation in the kinds of activities associated with a satisfying life. The dearth of such inquiries is striking. It is surely odd that faculties that have devoted so much time and effort to giving a broad education and nurturing humane values pay so little attention to discovering the effect of their efforts on the lives of their alumni. Achieving the goals of a liberal education is a formidable challenge for which there are few obvious answers. Only by investigating the results can educators hope to learn how they can do more to enrich the lives and enhance the well-being of their students in the decades following graduation.

## Improving the Contributions of Higher Education

Critics within the academy have periodically questioned whether colleges do enough to prepare students to think deeply about what it means to lead what Alexander Meiklejohn described as "a life worth living." Allan Bloom dealt forcefully with this problem in his best-selling polemic in 1987, *The Closing of the American Mind*.[42] More recently, Yale law professor and former dean Anthony Kronman has sounded the alarm again.

[T]he question of how to spend one's life, of what to care about and why, the question of which commitments, relations, projects, and pleasures are capable of giving a life purpose and value . . . , this question was taken more seriously by most of our colleges and universities in the middle years of the twentieth century than it is today. Increasingly few teachers of the humanities believe that they have either the competence or duty to offer their students an education in the meaning of life.[43]

Professor Kronman's point is undoubtedly accurate for most colleges. While any student determined to explore the meaning of life can usually find courses with readings fit for the task, few colleges do much to encourage such study, let alone offer classes specially designed for the purpose. Most programs of general education do little more than require students to take one or two courses—any one or two—in each of the major bodies of knowledge—the humanities, the sciences, and the social sciences. It is only by the merest chance that the courses chosen will help undergraduates think deeply about the purposes of their lives, since few of these offerings were ever intended for this purpose. Surely educators can do better than that. It would be fruitless to require undergraduates to study the history of philosophy or the Great Books if they are not inclined to do so. But the search for a meaningful life seems plainly important enough to warrant a serious effort by the faculty to devise and encourage an optional course of study designed to expose students to the best that has been written on the subject.

At the same time, although such courses can help students think about how to live a fulfilling life, it is much less clear how much they do to help students achieve this goal. The Great Books are better at raising questions than supplying answers. They contain a wealth of views from powerful minds, but the opinions vary too widely to offer much guidance. Their chief contribution lies in helping students to see through superficial answers and to appreciate the complexity of the quest for meaning and fulfillment. For many students, as for Professor Kronman, that is precisely what makes them so valuable. Without disputing this view, one wonders whether there is more that colleges can do to help their students decide how they can lead a fuller, more satisfying life.

An obvious step in this direction would be to offer courses based on what researchers have discovered about well-being. A number of colleges are doing just that. Indeed, if interest in Great Books courses has declined, the opposite is true of offerings by behavioral scientists on happiness. Although such courses vary in content and approach, most of them follow one of two models.

One approach is simply to study what is known about happiness—the methods by which it can be measured, the accuracy of the results, and the wealth of experimental findings about the sources of well-being and distress and the duration and intensity of their effects. The makeup of such courses is similar to that of most college classes in the behavioral sciences, but the relevance of the material to the lives of students often makes them very popular. At Harvard, for example, a recent course on happiness attracted over 800 undergraduates, making it capable of reaching half the entire student body over a four-year period.[44]

The second way of teaching the material is similar to the first but also includes practical exercises of the sort employed by Professor Seligman—expressing gratitude, analyzing unpleasant events to cast them in a better light, or performing acts of kindness, among others. Some of the instructors who teach such classes describe their effects in terms normally found in advertisements for a New Age spa. According to one syllabus, the course in question will "develop a zest for living a virtuous, satisfying, and meaningful life."[45] Another makes an even bolder claim that "as a result of attending this class, you will also experience a personal transformation in which you become a more positive person."[46] Still another professor is more reserved, declaring only that "it is my hope that you will be able to apply some of the research findings on happiness to your own life."[47] Most instructors, it should be added, make no claims of this kind at all.

Courses on happiness, like Great Books courses, cannot tell any given student how to lead a satisfying life. The research yields results that, at best, simply express probabilities that certain activities and conditions will bring satisfaction, lead to unhappiness, or have no lasting effect one way or the other. The findings will not hold for everyone and may have little or nothing to say about many questions individual students are facing. Nevertheless, the conclusions—like many of the findings one reads concerning exercise or diet—are at least worth knowing in deciding how to live one's life.

Some will question whether colleges should take the added step of offering practical exercises to help students increase their well-being. Syllabi for such courses that claim to "transform lives" or to bring about "a personal transformation" not only seem pretentious but may strike some people as uncomfortably close to indoctrination. Still, so long as the courses are optional, clearly described, and taught by a professor properly trained for the task, it is hard to see why they should be discouraged. After all, many college courses are offered with a view toward influencing students in one way or the other. Indeed, colleges often declare in their brochures that the principal aim of their entire liberal arts education is to help students grow and change in ways that will enrich their lives. Since such statements usually rest on little more than intuition and hope, one can hardly complain about a set of practical exercises whose claims have at least some basis in empirical research.

Apart from teaching courses on happiness, universities have a growing opportunity to reach out to members of older age groups to encourage new intellectual interests that can provide fresh sources of pleasure and enlightenment. Awakening lasting interests among 18-year-olds has always been a formidable challenge, well worth trying but with highly uncertain results. Now, universities can pursue this goal with greater confidence in the results by taking advantage of a quiet revolution that has occurred on campuses throughout America over the last 40 years. Without much notice or fanfare, older Americans have increasingly come to realize that formal education need not end in one's 20s but can usefully extend throughout one's life. Often, the number of adults who come back to campus for further study exceeds the number of traditional students enrolled in degree programs at the undergraduate and professional school levels. Most of these newer students enroll for professional reasons to catch up on recent developments in their field or to prepare for a change in the nature of their work. But many come simply to widen their horizons and pursue some new intellectual interest. Their numbers are bound to grow as more and more adults look forward to lengthy retirements with abundant free time at their disposal.

Too often, universities have tended to view this growing interest in education simply as a means of making money. As a result, high-priced executive courses for corporations abound as do luxury cruises for well-to-do alumni. While there is nothing wrong with such programs, universities would also do well to reach out, either through conventional courses or via the Internet, to all those harboring a serious desire to explore a new field of learning. By so doing, they could further the goals of liberal learning while enhancing the lives of many people beyond the normal college age.

In addition to courses, colleges have other ways to help their students live more satisfying lives. One of the decisions undergraduates make that is likely to have long-lasting effects is the choice of what occupation to enter. By now, researchers have compiled an impressive quantity of pertinent facts about the common satisfactions and frustrations of careers in the more prominent professions. It would be more than a little odd for a college to provide its students with detailed information about the various professional schools to which they might apply without giving them the best available evidence about the kind of life they may lead once they finish their training.* As Arthur Levine and Jeanette Cureton point out in their "portrait" of undergraduates, most students want to do well financially *and* do good in the world but have very little idea about how to combine the two.[48] Colleges should draw upon the extensive literature on vocations in an effort to help students answer such questions.

---

*Such assistance seems all the more useful since the satisfaction derived from different occupations is far from obvious. While jobs with higher prestige and income tend to yield higher than average levels of satisfaction, as one would expect, the ten occupations that rank the highest are often surprising. In order of their level of satisfaction, they are: clergy, physical therapists, firefighters, education administrators, painters-sculptors, teachers, authors, psychologists, special education teachers, and operating engineers. The occupations associated with the highest levels of satisfaction with life follow a similar pattern, with the clergy again topping the list. Tom W. Smith, "Job Satisfaction in the United States," National Opinion Research Center/University of Chicago (press release, April 17, 2007).

In law, to take but one profession, much information is available on the lives of practitioners. Essays have been written based on numerous interviews with attorneys that identify the key ingredients in a satisfying legal career and the aspects of legal practice that often cause anxiety and dissatisfaction. Materials are available describing different kinds of legal work including courtroom advocacy, corporate counseling, and public interest law, among others. Elaborate statistics have been compiled on lawyers' earnings, rates at which young attorneys leave law firms or quit the profession altogether, even levels of stress, alcohol and drug abuse, divorce, and suicide. Clearly, such information can be relevant to students contemplating a legal career, whether they receive it in a course on the legal profession or in some convenient form outside of class.

There is also no reason why colleges should be the only unit of the university to disseminate such information. Once students enter a professional school or elect a vocational major, they will still need to make important decisions about the specialized field and the kind of setting or organization in which to practice. Again, abundant information is available for several professions on the common satisfactions and discontents that these choices entail.

Such information is all the more useful, since several professions have undergone major changes in recent decades that have significantly affected the quality of life for many of their members. Interesting new settings have emerged in which to work: charter schools, start-up businesses in exciting fields, specialized publishing houses, health maintenance organizations, online magazines, and nonprofit groups of all kinds. At the same time, many professions have gradually become less of a calling and more like a business. Public school teachers seem to have lost some of their autonomy in the classroom as districts struggle to raise standardized test scores and meet stricter standards of accountability. Corporate owners of newspapers and television networks have tended to become more bottom-line oriented, cutting news staff and pressuring journalists to feature more human interest and sensational stories that will appeal to wider audiences. Health maintenance organizations have pressed their doctors to see more patients, do more paperwork, and accept closer supervision to control costs. Publishing houses have been taken over by large companies that sometimes seem more concerned with the bottom line than with high literary standards. In every profession one hears stories of increased stress, longer hours, and greater difficulty maintaining a healthy balance between work and family.

Law practice offers a good example of the kind of sweeping changes that have altered the nature of professions and the satisfactions they afford.[49] New opportunities to practice have emerged with the establishment of legal staffs in universities and other large nonprofits, bigger in-house law offices in major corporations that assign their members a wide variety of problems, and public interest firms that fight for any one of a number of causes. Meanwhile, the more traditional law firms are hiring larger numbers of young lawyers, intensifying the competition for partner status. Every attorney in these firms is now held accountable by having to record the hours each day for which clients can be charged. Associates are judged in part by the number of hours they bill, creating incentives to work longer. Instead of enjoying virtual tenure, as they once did, partners are now evaluated increasingly on the amount of new business they bring in and may be asked to leave the firm if they are not "adding sufficient value." In return for greater stress and longer hours, these changes have led to starting salaries that often reach six figures for especially outstanding recent graduates along with annual incomes in the millions of dollars for senior partners in leading firms.

These new conditions may seem attractive to some students and dismaying to others. In either case, it is important to know the facts before one chooses where to practice. At present, at least half of the beginning lawyers in large firms leave voluntarily within three years.[50] Such a heavy turnover is wasteful for the firms involved as well as for the individuals who depart. Some of the exodus, at least, might be prevented if every law school exposed its students to what is now known about the benefits and disadvantages of large-firm practice and the pros and cons of working in other legal settings.

Whatever form of practice they choose, students in professional schools should have an ample opportunity not merely to acquire technical proficiency but to reflect on how they can find meaning and fulfillment in their careers beyond financial success. Such opportunities can come through a variety of courses. Most students ought to learn about their profession—its history, current problems, and future possibilities. Discussion courses on common ethical dilemmas confronting practitioners are also useful in helping students understand how they can work in a manner compatible with their values. Some students may benefit from studying biographies of well-known practitioners. Others may need a more imaginative approach. For example, the psychiatrist and author Robert Coles used to teach courses in any one of several different professional schools using novels and short stories that raised moral issues and other dilemmas common to the calling in question. Students who might be reluctant to disclose their inner doubts and fears about trying to live a fulfilling professional life would enter into intense debates about the questions facing fictional characters. Many participants were passionately engaged by these discussions and continued to correspond with Professor Coles for years afterward.

Courses of the kind described in the preceding paragraph can often be found in professional schools. What is much less common is a conscious effort to consider how best to provide each student with opportunities for serious thought about what it might mean to "live greatly" in their profession. Schools of law, business, and medicine have all been criticized repeatedly for failing to convey the values and ideals that should animate their profession and its practitioners.[51] However difficult the task, any faculty concerned about the well-being of its graduates ought to provide students with some vision of this kind so that they can ponder it and think how it could help to guide their own careers.

## The Ultimate Importance of Education

Both John Stuart Mill and John Maynard Keynes predicted that continued growth and progress would eventually lead to sufficient prosperity to free people from their preoccupation with getting and spending and allow them to cultivate the humane interests that would bring them a deeper satisfaction.[52] Today, the predicted prosperity has arrived in the United States, but there is little sign that concerns over money and possessions have diminished or that people have turned in large numbers to the creative and reflective pursuits that thinkers like Keynes had in mind. However prosperous the nation becomes, most people continue to believe that a bit more money is the key to lasting happiness.

Schools and universities are the institutions best equipped to help young people in their search for a truly satisfying life. Granted, teachers cannot tell students what will make them happy. But schools and universities can do their best to supply them with the knowledge, skills, and interests that will aid them in their search. If educators can provide such help, they will do more than benefit their students. They will also affect what government officials can accomplish in proposing policies to increase well-being. In a democracy, after all, citizens must perceive what sort of life will be truly satisfying before the government can do a great deal to assist them.

At present, few government officials and educators pay enough attention to preparing young people for a full and rewarding life. In keeping with the primacy of economic growth, federal policy toward public schools is preoccupied with developing a competitive workforce. Invariably, government leaders justify each new policy initiative as an investment in future economic progress and prosperity. School officials have mainly gone along; they often have little choice in the matter. As a result, their attention has now come to focus primarily on improving basic skills as measured by standardized test scores.

Government officials have much less influence over college curricula. University officials are still committed to the broader purposes of the liberal arts and continue to maintain an impressive variety of courses and activities. Yet higher education is not immune from the economic forces and priorities of the larger society. In order to attract students, whose chief reason for attending college is to prepare themselves for well-paid careers, most colleges have concentrated their effort and attention during the past 30 years on expanding and improving vocationally oriented majors. Moreover, in an age filled with references to the "knowledge-driven economy" where innovation and scientific discoveries are increasingly seen as the key to economic progress, university funding increasingly mirrors the needs of the marketplace. Federal research support has moved toward fields with "economic potential," and professors with valuable expertise are richly rewarded for consulting with industry. Meanwhile, faculty salaries in literature, art, and, more generally, the humanities have gradually lost ground along with student interest in these subjects.[53]

The time has surely come to reconsider these priorities. Educators and policy-makers alike need to place more weight on purposes other than acquiring vocational skills. There is much more to education than becoming a productive member of the workforce and more to schools and universities than producing "human capital." In the last analysis, what Thomas Jefferson wrote almost 200 years ago still rings true today: "I look to the diffusion of light and education as the resource most to be relied on for ameliorating the condition, promoting the virtue, and advancing the happiness of man."[54]

# 10

## THE QUALITY OF GOVERNMENT

Earlier chapters have discussed a sample of the ways by which the federal government could try to increase well-being and relieve distress: a more vigorous campaign to alleviate mental illness and chronic pain, a comprehensive effort to strengthen marriage and family, a series of measures to enhance people's peace of mind by giving them greater protection from the financial risks arising from retirement, illness, and the loss of a job. The focus of this chapter, however, is not on new programs to improve lives but on people's feelings about the government itself. One of the interesting findings from the recent research on happiness is the discovery that how government functions and how citizens think it functions have significant effects on their well-being. Hence, it is worth asking whether opportunities exist to give people greater satisfaction with the way their government is performing.

If popular impressions of government have a bearing on happiness, there is ample reason to worry about the situation in the United States. For most of the past 30 years, a majority of Americans have believed that the country "is moving in the wrong direction," and they blame the government for much that has gone wrong.[1] According to opinion polls in 2007, fewer than one-third of Americans trusted the federal government to do the right thing all or most of the time.[2] A survey of people's confidence in 25 different sectors of society ranked the federal government next to last.[3] For a number of years, more people have felt that the federal government, rather than big business or organized labor, is the greatest threat to the nation.[4] Large majorities have believed that Washington creates more problems than it solves and that its actions usually make problems worse rather than better.[5]

## How Well Has the Government Performed?

Are these harsh judgments justified? Has the government truly performed this badly? It is hard to give a convincing answer, since there is no authoritative way to assess the government's record. Public officials are involved in too many activities serving too many different purposes to measure their performance objectively. Lacking definite standards, therefore, evaluations of government are unusually vulnerable to ideological bias or personal prejudice of one sort or another.

With these difficulties in mind, one promising approach is to examine the government's record in trying to achieve the aims that are widely accepted as important by the public.[6] While people differ sharply over the best *means* to achieve society's goals, there is broad agreement among Americans on the important *ends* for the nation to pursue. Some 75 goals can be identified that command almost universal support, such as robust economic growth with low inflation and unemployment, quality health care for all at affordable cost, universal education with high levels of academic proficiency, and safe levels of air and water pollution. In each case, the government has much to do with the amount of progress made, and for many goals, Washington's policies are decisive. As a result, charting the nation's progress in pursuing these objectives offers a useful starting point for evaluating the government's performance.

Overall, the record seems impressive. From 1960 to 2000, the United States made substantial progress toward at least two-thirds of the 75 goals. In only one-quarter of the cases did the country lose ground, and most of these involved objectives such as lower crime rates, less cheating in school, and more charitable giving (as a percentage of personal income), where the government's influence over the results is relatively tenuous.

At the same time, the record just summarized, while encouraging, does not reveal how well a truly effective government could have performed. Conceivably, such a government might have made progress toward virtually all of the consensus goals and the amount of progress might have been greater.

The best way to explore this possibility is to compare the record of the United States with that of other leading democracies. If our government is performing at a high level, it ought to stand up very well in relation to these countries. Fortunately, data are available to compare our progress toward the same widely accepted goals with the record of six other leading nations—Britain, Canada, France, (West) Germany, Japan, and Sweden.

Evaluated in this way, the performance of the United States seems much less impressive.[7] In two-thirds of the 75 cases, our progress is below average for the group of seven nations. In fully half the cases, America stands at the bottom of the list or close to it. While the federal government may not be primarily responsible for every case in which America lagged behind, the record overall suggests a 40-year performance that is mediocre at best compared with that of other leading democracies.

A useful way of testing this conclusion is to compare it with the findings from a World Bank study of the record of 212 national governments using very different methods of evaluation.[8] The Bank has examined six separate aspects of performance on the basis of independent assessments made by a variety of commercial and nonprofit organizations. One of the advantages of its report from the standpoint of this study is that all of the six aspects (described below) have been found to be significantly related to the well-being of citizens.[9]

1. *Voice and accountability*: The degree to which citizens participate in choosing their government and the degree of freedom accorded to speech, association, and media expression.
2. *Political stability*: The unlikelihood of destabilizing the government by violent or unconstitutional means, including the incidence of terrorism and similar types of violent protest against the government.
3. *Effectiveness of government*: The quality of policy formation and implementation and the quality of the civil service.
4. *Quality of regulation*: The ability of the government to formulate and implement policies and regulations that promote economic development and protect the public against common risks.
5. *Rule of law*: The likelihood of crime and violence, the effectiveness of the police and courts, and the extent to which officials abide by the rules of the society.

6. *Control of corruption*: The extent to which officials use power for private gain and the degree to which the government is influenced by special interests.

The World Bank ratings have only been compiled since 1996. Over that period, the United States has consistently ranked among the highest on the list of 212 nations studied. Nevertheless, as table 5 makes clear, America's ratings have declined since the rankings began in all but one of the categories evaluated.

Moreover, although the United States compares very well with the great majority of countries in the World Bank study, many of these nations are desperately poor, others have only recently become democracies, and still others are notably corrupt and undemocratic. It is more instructive, therefore, to contrast America's ratings with those of the six leading democracies referred to earlier in assessing the comparative progress of the United States from 1960 to 2000. (See table 6.) This exercise shows that America lags well behind most of the other countries in the comparison group.

TABLE 5
Evaluation of U.S. Government

(The following ratings are on a scale of +2.5 to −2.5 for the first two columns and +3 to −3 for the other four.)

| Year | Voice and accountability | Political stability | Effectiveness of programs | Quality of regulation | Rule of law | Control of corruption |
|------|--------------------------|---------------------|----------------------------|------------------------|-------------|------------------------|
| 1996 | 1.31 | 0.94 | 2.12 | 1.28 | 1.74 | 1.75 |
| 2002 | 1.35 | 0.30 | 1.78 | 1.47 | 1.57 | 1.90 |
| 2006 | 1.08 | 0.31 | 1.64 | 1.47 | 1.57 | 1.30 |

The figures above are taken from Daniel Kaufman, Aart Kraay, and Massimo Mastruzzi, "Governance Matters VI: Aggregate and Individual Governance Indicators 1996–2006," World Bank Policy Research Working Paper 4280 (July 2007), pp. 76–93.

The figures for the United States regarding political stability are comparatively low, despite the stability of our democracy, because they include the incidence of terrorist acts against the government. Since terrorist acts by foreign agents do not necessarily have much relevance to the effectiveness or quality of government, one might reasonably argue that the results have little or no bearing on the discussion in this chapter. Nevertheless, it should be noted that omitting political stability entirely from table 6 does not change the overall ranking of the United States compared with the six other governments listed.

TABLE 6
Comparative Evaluation of National Governments

| | United States | Canada | France | Germany | Japan | Sweden | United Kingdom |
|---|---|---|---|---|---|---|---|
| Voice and accountability | 1.08 | 1.46 | 1.40 | 1.48 | 0.91 | 1.55 | 1.42 |
| Political stability | 0.31 | 0.94 | 0.46 | 0.83 | 1.11 | 1.13 | 0.46 |
| Effectiveness of programs | 1.64 | 2.03 | 1.20 | 1.52 | 1.29 | 2.00 | 1.83 |
| Quality of regulation | 1.47 | 1.53 | 1.06 | 1.39 | 1.27 | 1.44 | 1.76 |
| Rule of law | 1.57 | 1.85 | 1.31 | 1.77 | 1.40 | 1.86 | 1.73 |
| Control of corruption | 1.30 | 1.90 | 1.44 | 1.78 | 1.31 | 2.24 | 1.86 |

The figures above are taken from Daniel Kaufman, Aart Kraay, and Massimo Mastruzzi, "Governance Matters VI: Aggregate and Individual Governance Indicators 1996–2006," World Bank Policy Research Working Paper 4280 (July 2007), pp. 76–93.

The figures for the United States regarding political stability are comparatively low, despite the stability of our democracy, because they include the incidence of terrorist acts against the government. Since terrorist acts by foreign agents do not necessarily have much to do with the effectiveness or quality of government, one might reasonably argue that the results have little or no bearing on the discussion in this chapter. Nevertheless, it should be noted that omitting political stability entirely from table 6 does not change the overall ranking of the United States compared with the six other governments listed.

An even simpler way of expressing America's comparative position is to add the scores of each country for the six relevant aspects of government to form a single set of aggregate figures.

| Sweden | 10.22 |
| Canada | 9.71 |
| United Kingdom | 9.06 |
| Germany | 8.77 |
| United States | 7.37 |
| Japan | 7.29 |
| France | 6.87 |

Taken together, the World Bank ratings and the progress made toward common goals from 1960 to 2000 give a fairly clear picture. On the one hand, our government's performance is certainly not as disastrous as large majorities of the public seem to think. Compared with all the countries of the world or judged by our record of progress over several decades, the government has done relatively well. On the other hand, measured against the record of a sample of leading democratic nations with which we normally compare ourselves, our performance according to both methods of evaluation has been well below average.

## Improving Performance

Why hasn't our government performed better? Conservatives often blame excessive government intervention. Liberals frequently take the opposite view and complain that official programs are too modest, pointing out that most other leading democracies have governments that collect far more in taxes than ours does and spend far more generously on public programs. Neither of these explanations is entirely persuasive. Since several countries with better records tend to have higher taxes and more extensive government programs than the United States, the conservative case seems unconvincing. The liberal argument is somewhat stronger, since a number of government programs in the United States are scantily funded compared with similar programs in other advanced democracies. Nevertheless, our record is none too impressive even in fields such as public education and health care where America's spending from all sources is as high, or in the case of health care, considerably higher than that of other leading democracies.

Looking further at America's record in achieving a variety of goals, one begins to see a pattern.[10] Most of our successes, as in science and technology, occur in fields in which individual creativity and talent are especially important and the government can stimulate progress simply by distributing funds on the basis of merit. However, in addressing more complicated social problems, such as poverty or health care or public education, which require more intricate planning and execution, our record is much less impressive. One can easily find stunning successes achieved by individual schools or hospitals or nonprofit groups, even in highly depressed neighborhoods. But when it comes to taking the successes and transforming them into a statewide or nationwide system, the results are usually disappointing.

One important reason for the difficulty in addressing complex problems is the remarkable fragmentation of government authority in the United States.[11] Federalism divides the powers of government among national, state, and local bodies. The desire for checks and balances has led to a further division of authority at every level among three separate branches, each designed more to check the excesses of the others than to work harmoniously together. Finally, in most legislatures, a lack of strong party discipline gives unusual autonomy to each member, thus dividing power even further. The result is to make it more difficult to craft coherent legislative programs or to avoid a clutter of special exceptions and concessions to accommodate individual lawmakers. The difficulty of enacting and implementing laws in such a fragmented system does much to account for the complexity, the inconsistencies, and the lack of coordination characteristic of our tax laws, our health care legislation, our antipoverty programs, and much more.

Another distinctive feature of American government is a proliferation of detailed regulations administered through a highly contentious, adversarial system of enforcement marked by much litigation and long, frustrating proceedings.[12] This feature too owes much to fragmentation not only in the government but in the economy as well. The multiple divisions of government lead to duplicative, overlapping regulatory agencies, disputes over which level of authority has jurisdiction, and frequent intervention by courts and other independent oversight bodies. Unlike most other advanced democracies, there are no powerful employer and labor organizations to work with the government in devising and implementing rules. As a result, regulations are seldom arrived at by negotiating uniform and mutually acceptable industry-wide agreements but must be imposed from above on unions (where they exist) and individual employers. The resulting rules rarely fit the varied circumstances of all of the different firms and industries to which they apply and thus tend to cause resentment. Moreover,

without strong labor or management groups with which to negoti-
ate and administer agreed-on rules, regulations must be enforced
by the government on a case-by-case basis with layers of review to
avoid errors and overreaching on the part of public officials. In a
nation with many hundreds of thousands of separate, competing
enterprises, enforcement is necessarily slow, contentious, and expensive, often irritating everyone involved.

Finally, many examples of weak performance occur when the
government is attending to the needs of poor and working-class
Americans.[13] Basic forms of social protection, such as health care,
unemployment insurance, paid parental leave, and others, are not
guaranteed by the government, as they are in most other advanced
democracies, or they exist at reduced levels of support and often
reach only a fraction of those in need. As a result, among the leading democratic nations of the world, the United States has the
highest levels of poverty (including among children), the fewest
people lifted out of poverty by government programs, and the largest segment of the public without health or unemployment insurance of any kind.

In part, lower levels of protection for people of modest means
reflect the conflicted attitudes of the public toward social and protective legislation. Large majorities have consistently affirmed that
the government should be doing more to help the poor and needy.[14]
Beneath the surface, however, many people are ambivalent, partly
because of the racial and ethnic divisions in the society, partly because of a fear that many of the so-called needy are malingerers or
otherwise undeserving of help, and partly because of a reluctance
to pay the taxes required to finance more extensive programs of
assistance.[15] Reinforcing these hesitations and doubts is the lack of
any strong labor party or union movement to champion the cause
of poor and working-class citizens. Large segments of the population are consequently much weaker politically than their counterparts abroad. The results are starkly evident if one compares the
situation of the elderly, who are represented by a powerful interest
group, with that of children, who are not. Over the past 40 years,
poverty rates among senior citizens have been cut by two-thirds,
and all Americans over 65 are covered by Medicare or some other

health insurance program. For children, the situation is reversed. Close to 20 percent of all children live below the poverty line and many of them lack any health insurance whatsoever.

This political environment does not rule out major legislative initiatives, such as Social Security, Medicare, or the Civil Rights Act. But such advances tend to come only occasionally either in time of crisis or through a fortuitous combination of skillful leadership and an issue commanding unusually strong support among the American people. These exceptional conditions cannot be maintained. They typically give way before long to the normal difficulties of governing such a vast, fragmented, complicated nation.

Under these conditions, is it possible to achieve a sustained improvement in the quality of government? In theory, at least, one way to obtain better performance would be to change the basic structure of government. But there is no consensus among political scientists on a different set of institutions or procedures that could produce better results, nor is there even agreement that *any* fundamental change in the basic structure would improve performance substantially. It is also hard to conceive of a change of this kind that could command the support of the American people, who overwhelmingly approve of our political system even as they complain bitterly about the results. If any strong consensus exists in America, it is that the shortcomings of Washington are due to the behavior of politicians rather than the system in which they work.[16]

It is also theoretically possible to achieve better results through a sustained improvement in the quality of government officials. But this way forward seems equally likely to end in disappointment. One can certainly point to high officials who have seemed inept in carrying out their responsibilities. But Congress and the upper levels of political appointees are already packed with Rhodes scholars, Phi Beta Kappas, and graduates of America's leading colleges and professional schools. Admittedly, there is greater room for improvement in the quality of the permanent civil service, but attempts to reform the bureaucracy have been repeatedly tried without much success. Besides, what bothers people most about their government has much less to do with civil servants than with the behavior of elected officials.

Inspired leadership remains the last, best hope of those who yearn for better government, and inspired leadership can undoubtedly make a difference. Unfortunately, however, no system of government yet devised has succeeded in consistently producing outstanding leaders. Such a feat would be particularly difficult in the United States, where the problems of governing are challenging enough to require leadership of a very high order indeed.

## Improving Procedures

If it is so difficult to restore confidence by improving the government's performance, what strategies are there that could lessen the cynicism and distrust that currently blight public attitudes toward the work of public officials? One possibility to explore is to enact procedural reform rather than attempt to improve the quality of leadership or tamper with the Constitutional structure. Opinion surveys suggest that Americans are less upset about the *policies* in Washington than they are about the *processes* by which decisions are made.[17] Specifically, large majorities believe that legislation is influenced far too much by lobbyists armed with campaign contributions and other favors they render to members of Congress. Similar majorities feel that politicians are not as dedicated to the public welfare as they are to their own reelection. To preserve their place in Congress, elected officials are said to squander taxpayers' money on "pork barrel" projects while gerrymandering the shape of their legislative districts to include more voters of their own party and fewer people who might vote against them.

These criticisms have more than a grain of truth. Special interests almost certainly have significant influence. The millions they donate to political candidates and parties must buy something of value. Lobbyists claim that they only contribute to gain access to plead their case, but the facts suggest otherwise. Although special interests may have less effect on major policy decisions than most people believe, the many dubious exceptions, subsidies, and regulatory exemptions that crop up repeatedly in Congressional legislation all speak eloquently to the power of campaign contributions.

The public is also correct in suspecting that politicians are preoccupied with holding on to power. No wonder. Few people would choose to endure the grind and stress of a prolonged election campaign if they did not have an exceptional desire to gain political office and a fierce determination to keep it. These tendencies become all too evident when the time comes to draw new district lines for future elections or to vote on campaign finance laws that might limit the advantage incumbents enjoy in raising money for elections.

Finally, although Americans may exaggerate the amount of waste in government, they are surely correct in concluding that some waste occurs. The cumulative costs of questionable tax breaks for particular industries and earmarked funds for favored constituents are substantial enough to lend some substance to the public's concern. From inflated food prices to unregulated practices by banks and credit card companies to repeated cost overruns in military procurement, citizens pay a stiff penalty for powerful lobbyists in Washington and the influence they are able to exert.

It should be possible to boost the public's confidence somewhat by taking steps to discourage the objectionable practices just described. There are clearly added measures the government could adopt to counteract the impression that politicians are in the grip of special interests. Public funding of election campaigns could help, especially if it included reasonable limits on independent expenditures. So could efforts to close the remaining loopholes that allow lobbyists to bestow special favors on legislators.

Greater use of impartial bodies to make and enforce the rules of politics could also build confidence in the fairness of the system. An independent ethics commission might diminish the suspicions aroused by a Congress that insists on policing itself, a practice that naturally creates suspicion that the rules are not being strictly enforced. An amply staffed Federal Election Commission that is not composed of political loyalists chosen by the president and Congress could also help bolster confidence that campaign finance rules are being administered properly. Independent redistricting commissions could eventually overcome the impression that politicians gerrymander electoral districts to ensure their own reelection and give an unfair advantage to the party in power.

Finally, measures to curb earmarks and the pork barrel spending they engender might do something to persuade citizens that lawmakers are more concerned with the public welfare than with their own reelection. Every year, hundreds of special projects are approved at the request of individual legislators. These expenditures, although they make up only a small fraction of the total federal budget, give rise to a never-ending series of media reports reinforcing the popular impression that huge amounts of taxpayers' money are being wasted on bridges to nowhere and other useless projects to improve the image of individual lawmakers.

Apart from helping restore confidence in politicians, these reforms might contribute modestly to the government's performance. Cutting down on earmarks and special interest subsidies would save money that could be used for worthier purposes. Even greater improvements could come about by passing effective campaign finance laws. Such legislation might not only curtail the influence of lobbyists. It could also help bring about greater political equality and counter the weakness of lower-income Americans that contributes to the government's failure to give adequate protection against excessive financial risks, encourage greater equality of opportunity, and extend our social legislation to all those in need.

To the credit of Congress, lawmakers have already acted on numerous occasions to tighten the rules governing campaign contributions, ethical practices, and pork barrel spending. Nevertheless, in virtually every case, the measures taken are only partial steps. Invariably, the media ferret out the loopholes that remain and publicize the ways by which lawmakers get around the reforms and restore the preexisting practices. As a result, although the new rules may do *some* good, the impression left with the public is one of phony remedies and continued efforts by incumbent politicians to curry favor with large contributors and ensure their own competitive advantage in future elections. Without more sweeping and uncompromising efforts to achieve higher standards, continued piecemeal reform will not do much to change the prevailing image of Washington as a place where well-paid lobbyists thrive at public expense and politicians use their power to protect themselves from electoral defeat.

It will not be easy to enact truly effective procedural reforms along the lines just described. Doing so will require lawmakers to check their instinctive desire to maintain their political advantage through their ability to raise campaign money from interest groups, gerrymander their election districts, and spend taxpayers' money on showy projects in their home districts. Even if reformers can muster the necessary support, it is very difficult to construct procedural rules that can withstand the determined efforts of interest groups to find new ways of influencing the officials who wield such power to influence their success and prosperity. More important still, it is doubtful that procedural reforms alone, helpful as they would be, can overcome the deep suspicion and cynicism that so many citizens harbor toward their government and the politicians who control it. Further steps are needed if Americans are to gain the full satisfaction of living under a government that, for all its faults, still ranks among the most successful democracies in the world.

## Encouraging More Accurate Perceptions of Government

A closer look at popular sentiment suggests that the public has too jaundiced a view of its government. Granted, one can easily point to ineffective policies, major errors of judgment, periodic cases of corruption and mismanagement. Still, the recurring popular impressions that "the country is heading in the wrong direction" and that "when the federal government tries to solve a problem, it generally only makes things worse" are flatly contradicted by the evidence of substantial progress over the past 50 years toward a large majority of the goals widely supported by the public.[18] In a survey taken in 1997, Americans were asked whether they felt that the country was making progress, standing still, or losing ground in 17 areas of general concern, such as crime, health care, the quality of education, poverty, and the federal deficit.[19] In 11 of the 17 areas, a majority believed that the country was losing ground, and a plurality agreed in 3 other cases. In none of the areas did as many as one-quarter of the respondents feel that any progress had occurred. In fact, however, the record clearly showed that significant progress had been made in most of the cases.

Several other familiar charges against Washington are equally extreme. While many public programs may not be models of efficiency, Americans tend to exaggerate the extent to which the government wastes money. Most people believe that over half of every dollar collected for Social Security is spent on overhead and administration, although the actual figure is only slightly more than 1 percent.[20] Similarly, the average American has believed for years that the federal government wastes approximately half of every dollar it receives in revenue, even though a long series of blue-ribbon commissions created to study inefficiency in the federal government have invariably failed to identify waste on a scale anywhere close to matching this figure.[21]

There are likewise indications that the popular view of politicians is too harsh. Barely one-quarter of the public have a positive impression of Congress as a whole, and opinion polls consistently rank members of Congress among the least trustworthy on a list of familiar occupations.[22] In 2006, only 8 percent of Americans were prepared to agree, even "somewhat," that "most politicians are honest."[23] Curiously, however, large majorities continue to feel that *their own representative* in Congress is doing a good job.[24] It is hard to imagine how so many individual lawmakers in Congress can earn the praise of most of their constituents if the institution and its members are failing so miserably.

Most Americans also believe that elected politicians lose touch "pretty quickly" with the people who elected them and do not really care what the voters think.[25] Yet there has probably never been a time when politicians spent as much time examining opinion polls and focus group results to find out what the voters think about a wide variety of issues. Moreover, most close observers who have watched the work of Congress over many years do not feel that the quality of the members has declined, as opinion polls would suggest.[26] Those with longer memories recall the days when big city machines regularly sent political hacks to Washington to carry out the bidding of their local boss and bags of money were delivered to lawmakers by lobbyists on the floor of Congress.

So long as Americans harbor such negative impressions, they are bound to feel frustrated and upset with the way their government is performing. If the public were well enough informed to have a more balanced, accurate view of Washington, the prevailing mood might improve, at least to some degree.

The media—newspapers, radio, and television—have an obvious responsibility for correcting distorted impressions of the kind just described, since they are the principal institutions in our society for informing the public about the government. Of course, ferreting out stories of ineptitude, corruption, and mismanagement is one of the media's most important responsibilities. Honest and responsive government depends on it. Still, tales of wrongdoing and failure must be balanced with accounts of success and accomplishment in order to give an accurate picture of the government's performance.

It is far from clear that the media are succeeding in this task. Rather than trying to convey a fair and balanced view of government, newspapers and television feed the public's appetite for stories of scandal and ineptitude. Positive accounts of the government's performance appear much less often and less prominently than stories recounting failures, wrongdoings, and disappointments of various kinds.* Studies of media content suggest that the ratio of unfavorable to favorable news stories has increased substantially over past decades, especially in the coverage of Congress. In 1972, for example, two out of every three media stories about Congress were unfavorable. In 1982, the ratio increased to three of every four stories. By 1992, nine of every ten stories about Congress had come to be predominantly negative.[27] Since then, media coverage has continued to be predominantly hostile through the early years of the twenty-first century.[28]

Since the United States made progress in this period toward most of its widely accepted goals, such negativity cannot be convincingly

---

*As Mark J. Rozell points out in a study of newspaper coverage, "editors rarely devoted much space to agencies' success. Agencies that adopted regulations to protect the public received little if any credit. Offices that successfully accomplished their goals did so without notice. Editors provided no counterweight to the heavy emphasis on bureaucratic ineptitude and mistakes." *Media Power, Media Politics* (2003), p. 112.

explained by the actual performance of legislators and candidates. Rather, it seems to reflect a growing inclination on the part of the media to emphasize what has gone wrong, perhaps in an effort to attract attention and stem the gradual erosion of readers and viewers.

Experts on the media tend to confirm this assessment. Doris Graber, a long-time student of political reporting, has concluded that "excessive negativism is another serious and entirely deserved accusation. . . . Whatever is done (by politicians) is attributed to self-serving reasons—namely political advantage and power and, above all, the desire to win elections."[29] According to Professor Mark Rozell, who examined the press coverage of Congress from 1946 to 1992, reporting "focuses on scandal, partisan rivalry, and interbranch conflict rather than the more complex subjects such as policy, process, and institutional concerns."[30] Coverage over the same period, according to Rozell, "has moved from healthy skepticism to outright cynicism."*

Independent analysts make similar criticisms of the media's treatment of elections. Much of the coverage emphasizes the strategic ploys of candidates or evaluates the odds of who will emerge victorious. Small mistakes and slips of the tongue get more attention than serious policy proposals. Speculation over the candidates' "real motives" trumps substantive discussions of major issues. As Stephen J. Farnsworth and S. Robert Lichter conclude:

> [T]he "game" frame dominates, leaving viewers with a sense of politicians as scoundrels. Candidates get little opportunity to speak for themselves, as the average length of a sound bite has fallen to less than eight seconds. . . . In addition, reporters and producers are far more negative than positive in their assessments about most candidates, and reporters and anchors have a very unsatisfying record on that cardinal journalist matter of just plain getting the facts right and being fair to the candidates.[31]

---

*Even motion pictures have gotten into the act. According to David Paletz, who has studied the subject, "movies misrepresent and overdramatize (Congress's) process, omit its positive and workaday side, and portray members as egocentric and expedient." *The Media in American Politics: Contents and Consequences* (1998), p. 234.

These tendencies, evident even in the most widely watched news programs, are exacerbated by political pundits and talk show hosts, many of whom make it their specialty to denigrate public officials and amplify their mistakes and misadventures.

The way in which the media describe politics has an effect on the audience. Political scientists John Hibbing and Elizabeth Theiss-Morse have found that television reporting does not change viewers' cognitive impressions but does generate significantly more negative emotions toward Congress and its members.[32] Joseph Capella and Kathleen Hall Jamieson have also studied the effect of television reporting on viewers. They conclude that most of the coverage is framed in strategic and oppositional terms, suggesting "motives that are self-interested and which in turn are interpreted to mean that political actors are both self-interested and not focused on the best interests of the public."[33] When Capella and Jamieson tested such coverage on live audiences, they found that cynicism increased, whereas material that focused on issues had the opposite effect.[34]

Improving the media's performance could be difficult. Despite the public's professed dislike of negative reporting, it may well be that tales of scandal and failure attract the interest of readers and viewers more readily than sober accounts of hard work and modest legislative achievements. Trapped in a fierce competition for gradually declining audiences, media executives may feel compelled to emphasize corruption and ineptitude. If so, the media are not likely to present a more balanced view of government unless owners come to recognize that negativism can actually dampen the interest of readers and viewers in the longer run. For their part, reporters will need to exercise considerable imagination to find interesting ways of recognizing the positive accomplishments of politicians and government programs. Such an effort seems possible only if the profession comes to regard the challenge as a matter of responsible journalism and begins to attack it with the same seriousness that many reporters display in pursuing other journalistic values, such as avoiding partisan bias or obtaining adequate confirmation of serious charges against a public figure.

## Curbing Unrealistic Expectations

Voters can also judge their government unfairly if they harbor exaggerated expectations of how public officials ought to perform. Many Americans seem to react in just this way. Large majorities of the public believe that "with all its faults, the American system of government is the best in the world," and that "there is no problem that America cannot solve with proper leadership."[35] When asked in the 1990s whether the lack of progress in the United States resulted from failings of leadership or from the difficulty of the problems, only 17 percent of respondents replied that the problems were too difficult.[36] With attitudes like these, the public is bound to blame political leaders when they fail to produce effective solutions to even the most contentious and intractable problems.

There are similar indications that the public gravely underestimates the difficulty of enacting effective legislation in a Congress made up of legislators representing many varied interests and priorities and possessing sharply different ideological views about the government's proper role. Because most Americans agree on the *goals* of society, people seem to feel that lawmakers should be able to sit down together, use their common sense, and agree on appropriate *means* to achieve these ends. They greatly overestimate the amount of agreement among the voters on important policy issues and fail to recognize how much people differ about what methods to use or which goals deserve priority. As a result, while often expressing a preference for a divided government in which one party controls the legislature and the other the White House, Americans are impatient with all the arguing, the delays, and the compromises that occur before legislation can be passed.

In one revealing survey, an overwhelming 86 percent of Americans agreed that "elected officials should stop talking and take action," while 52 percent "agreed" and another 8 percent "strongly agreed" that "compromise is selling out one's principles."[37] Apparently, the prevailing ideal of good government is of a Congress composed of decent, sensible people who reluctantly stand for election and then roll up their sleeves and quickly decide what needs to be done to move the country forward. Disappointed by what they see instead, many people assume that most of the arguments and compromises that constantly occur take place because politicians are venal beings under the baneful influence of special interests.

The attitudes just described have been aptly summarized by Professors Hibbing and Theiss-Morse following an extensive analysis of surveys and focus groups probing popular opinions about Congress.[38] After documenting the public's impatience with the process of enacting legislation, the authors declared:

> People do not wish to see uncertainty, conflicting options, long debate, competing interests, confusion, bargaining, and compromised, imperfect solutions. They want government to do its job quietly and efficiently, sans conflict and sans fuss. In short, we submit, they often seek a patently unrealistic form of democracy.[39]

Americans also find it difficult to recognize, let alone understand, the kinds of compromises politicians have to make in order to win elections, reach agreement on a controversial bill, or simply fulfill their responsibility to represent the wishes of their constituents. Even experienced political commentators will blame politicians for behavior that is inevitable, or even appropriate, in a healthy democracy. A statesmanlike accommodation that allows an important bill to pass becomes a craven retreat to those who oppose the measure. Editorial writers assail legislators for supporting measures the authors dislike despite the fact that a majority of the constituents the lawmakers are supposed to represent clearly favor the bill. Candidates are criticized for becoming artificial figures whose every word is scripted by professional political advisers even though politicians can hardly do otherwise when their speeches are scrutinized meticulously by reporters and opponents and even minor slips become front-page news. Members of Congress are widely condemned for being preoccupied with their own reelection when the burdens and sacrifices our system requires of political candidates virtually ensure that those who seek and win election will have a preternatural desire to gain and hold on to political power.

The media bear some of the responsibility for failing to educate the public about the constraints under which elected politicians operate or to explain the necessity of protracted argument and repeated compromise in a legislature representing diverse interests. Journalists may also help perpetuate an unrealistic view of Congress's role under a Constitution designed more to check the transgressions of an overreaching government than to facilitate legislation. Following a review of media coverage, Professor Rozell concludes that reporters seem to conceive of the legislature as a "reform-oriented, progressive, policy-activist Congress that works effectively with a strong, ambitious, president. . . . This image of what Congress should be is clearly incompatible with the traditional role of the legislative branch (as envisaged by the authors of the Constitution)."[40]

Now that the media no longer concentrate simply on reporting the facts but spend much time interpreting the news and describing what lies behind activities in Washington, there should be ample opportunity to convey a better understanding of why progress and consensus are often hard to achieve. Commentators should be able to explain the difficulties of legislating in a large and diverse nation with a Constitution designed more to prevent mistakes and avoid concentrated power than to promote efficient government. However, if "interpretation" simply means speculation about the "true motives" of political leaders and if references to interest groups consistently emphasize selfish aims without acknowledging the plausible arguments they often make or the legitimate role they play in a democracy, the public is bound to believe that the legislative process is largely a struggle among self-absorbed actors who have little concern for the public interest.

The media, of course, are not solely responsible for educating the public about the inevitability of conflict and compromise in a large, diverse, and complicated society. The job of creating realistic expectations about the government begins with our schools and colleges. This is not to say that educators should teach unthinking patriotism or convey a sugar-coated view of government that ignores legitimate problems. Politicians and officials can be held accountable only if the public (and the media) can perceive their weaknesses and shortcomings. At the same time, no government will be judged fairly if its citizens do not have a reasonable and realistic appreciation of the way our democracy functions and the inherent difficulties that beset its work. At a minimum, the public must understand the legislative process; the system of checks and balances; the role of public opinion, interest groups, and other forces that influence policy-making; and the necessity of argument, disagreement, and compromise in governing a vast nation filled with differing interests and values.

The way in which civics is taught in most high schools too often fails to convey such understanding. A group of political scientists who conducted a study of civics textbooks in 1987 concluded that the content frequently consisted mainly of dry, factual descriptions of government institutions and procedures that conveyed little appreciation of how the political process works and why it works as it does. According to the authors, "eighty percent of the civics books and half of the government books minimize conflict and compromise."[41] Moreover, "most of the texts do not deal extensively with the changing forms of political action, e.g., the influence of the media, interest and lobbying groups and political action committees."[42] With readings such as these, students can hardly emerge with a reasonable understanding of why lawmakers and interest groups behave as they do or how to distinguish between failures of government that result from incompetence or irresponsible behavior on the part of politicians and those that are chiefly due to the nature of the system in which officials function. These deficiencies are particularly unfortunate in light of recent research suggesting that properly taught courses in civics can have significant effects in reducing cynicism toward government.[43]

Colleges hardly do a better job. Although their brochures regularly proclaim a commitment to prepare students for citizenship, very few college faculties have developed courses specifically for this purpose, let alone imposed requirements to ensure that all undergraduates receive some minimum of civic education. Few faculties have even devoted serious thought to how one might go about preparing students for citizenship.[44] Instead, the prevailing attitude seems to be that a well-rounded liberal education will automatically serve the purpose adequately.

A careful look at what actually occurs in college gives ample cause to question this assumption. Surprisingly few students acquire sufficient knowledge to understand how the legislative process works, let alone comprehend the basic issues being discussed. Barely one-third of all undergraduates take so much as a single course on American government and politics. Fewer than half complete a basic economics course. Only a small fraction enroll in courses on subjects such as international affairs or political philosophy.[45]

College curricula today are dominated by the major, often vocational in nature, which typically takes up almost half of all undergraduate courses. As a result, little time remains for achieving all the other purposes of a college education including civic education. What's more, one recent study found that several of the most popular college majors, such as business, engineering, and education, actually tended to undermine active citizenship.[46] The more courses students took in these subjects the less likely they were to be civically engaged once they graduated.

Apparently, then, like so much else on campus, preparation for citizenship is typically treated as an option along with volleyball, choral singing, or courses on film studies. A few colleges have recently begun to develop promising programs for preparing citizens, but these examples are still very rare. As Carol Schneider, president of the Association of American Colleges and Universities, reports: After "five years of active discussions on dozens of campuses, . . . I have been persuaded that there is not just a neglect of but a resistance to college-level study of United States democratic principles."[47]

To be fair, colleges do improve basic skills, especially critical thinking, that contribute to constructive citizenship. Moreover, college graduates vote at much higher rates and know considerably more about politics and government than those whose education ended with high school. While much of this improvement reflects the greater interests and knowledge of those who choose to go to college, some of the progress is presumably attributable to undergraduate courses and extracurricular experiences.

At the same time, colleges could undoubtedly accomplish more if they paid closer attention to the task. They could certainly do a better job of conveying realistic expectations of government. As matters now stand, the extensive surveys and focus groups conducted by Professors Hibbing and Theiss-Morse have shown that college graduates are just as intolerant of legislative conflict and compromise as citizens with only a high school diploma.[48] Such findings are hardly surprising, since so few undergraduates take even a single course on American government.

All in all, it is hard to generate much enthusiasm for the way schools and colleges are fulfilling their civic responsibilities. Preparing students for active citizenship is simply not a high priority either for national education policy or for the nation's schools and colleges. It should be. In describing the attitudes of young Americans, a recent report by a group of political scientists concludes by observing that "their impression of 'politics' is dominated by negative images of partisan bickering, corruption, lying, and a sense that politics is boring, confusing, and a realm that is for people (such as the rich and powerful) other than themselves."[49] This description hardly augurs well for democracy or the satisfaction Americans take from it. Welcome as it is, the enthusiasm young people displayed during the presidential election of 2008 will not provide a permanent cure for the underlying problem. Schools and universities will need to place a much higher priority on preparing citizens and devote much more thought and imagination to the task if they are to improve on the current record and help their students gain the understanding of the political process that a healthy democracy requires.

## The Importance of Diminishing Pessimism and Distrust

Perhaps it is only human nature to be wary of politicians and to complain about their work. In the United States, however, unrealistic expectations and inaccurate perceptions have combined with the familiar shortcomings of politicians and bureaucracies to produce a disillusionment that is out of proportion to the government's actual performance. As a result, Americans have much less trust in political leaders and much less confidence in the agencies of government than citizens in countries with especially high levels of well-being, such as Denmark, Holland, or Switzerland.[50] These negative feelings could well be one of the reasons why the world's most prosperous country is not the world's happiest.

Strengthening trust in government and avoiding excessive cynicism toward politicians have an importance that goes beyond increasing happiness. The attitudes of the public have serious consequences for the quality of our democracy quite apart from their effect on levels of well-being. The negative attitudes toward public officials that so many citizens share limit the attractiveness of government as a career and make it harder to recruit and retain capable people. The lack of confidence in the political process among lower-income Americans aggravates political inequality by weakening their desire to go to the polls. An even more serious effect of the low regard for government is the dangerous gap it has helped create between the functions people expect the state to perform and the taxes they are prepared to pay to support these services. If most Americans believe that the government wastes half of every dollar it receives, it is only natural for them to resist giving more to Washington and to conclude that political leaders should fund desired programs and services by cutting waste instead of raising revenues. If the government truly makes every problem it touches worse, why should anyone contribute more to help it do its work?

The mismatch between expectations and resources creates a toxic situation with dire consequences for the country. Pressed by constituents for new services and benefits, yet constrained from raising taxes, Congress often responds by creating more programs than it can pay for. It then makes up the difference by incurring deficits that burden future generations, or by shifting expenses to hard-pressed states through unfunded mandates of one sort or another, or by underfunding programs so that they cannot possibly deliver their promised benefits. In these ways, negative attitudes have a self-fulfilling tendency to make the government less effective than it might be, a result that adds to the public's cynicism toward politicians, diminishes well-being, and hampers efforts to deal with problems that urgently need to be addressed.

It is important to recognize how serious this problem has become. Unless the situation improves, the government is not likely to stop the escalating federal deficits, or keep the nation's crumbling infrastructure in good repair, or ensure adequate health care for all its citizens. Still less will it be able to afford new measures that could improve the well-being of the people and bring America closer to its most cherished ideals by helping all its citizens succeed according to their aspirations and abilities.

# 11

## THE SIGNIFICANCE OF HAPPINESS RESEARCH

After 35 years of intensive research, what have investigators discovered that adds significantly to the teachings of that champion of happiness, Jeremy Bentham? Essentially, researchers have succeeded in doing what Bentham could not accomplish: to devise a way of measuring how happy people are and how much pleasure or pain they derive from the ordinary events and conditions of their lives. As a result, investigators are often able to reach conclusions that can help lawmakers decide which legislative programs are most likely to improve the well-being of the citizenry. It is true that many of these findings merely echo what some philosopher or theologian said centuries ago. Nevertheless, since prominent thinkers have so often disagreed with one another in discussing happiness, the new research does a valuable service by providing empirical evidence to suggest which insights are correct and which seem to be invalid.

Investigators have achieved this result by the simple technique of asking individuals either to describe their feelings at particular times during the day or to estimate how happy or satisfied they feel about the lives they are leading. The answers may not always be accurate. When collected from large numbers of people, however, they give a fairly reliable picture of what conditions and experiences of life tend to be associated with happiness or distress, how intensely people feel such emotions, and how long the sentiments last. The findings correlate significantly with independent evidence of happiness ranging from activity in the brain to the estimates of friends and relatives. All in all, they seem at least as accurate as many of the statistics commonly used by policy-makers in Washington and other centers of government.

The results of this research are reassuring in several critical respects. The vast majority of Americans appear to be happy most of the time. Even in the lowest income quartile of the population, more than 80 percent profess to be more happy than not. Moreover, the happiness they feel does not seem to come primarily from mere pleasure-seeking or from selfishly looking out for number one. Rather, apart from such basic conditions as how well people feel, how much freedom they enjoy, and whether they possess the necessities and comforts of life, the most important sources of happiness seem to include having close relationships with family and friends, helping others, and being active in community, charitable, and political activities. Thus, the successful pursuit of happiness promises not merely to be self-serving but to contribute to a better, stronger, more caring society. At the same time, happy people tend to live longer, enjoy better health, work more effectively at their jobs, and contribute more to strong, effective democratic government and flourishing communities. All in all, therefore, happiness seems to represent a most appropriate goal for a government to pursue, just as Bentham maintained more than two centuries ago.

Would it really make much practical difference, however, if governments began to pay serious attention to the findings of happiness scholars? Very little, public officials might reply. After all, in a democracy, lawmakers know they are accountable to the voters and must pay close attention to what their constituents want. Almost everything the government does is meant in one way or another to increase the well-being of the citizenry. Legislators do not have to read academic studies to figure out what people need. The people themselves are the best judge of that, and common sense and opinion polls will suffice to keep their representatives informed of what they want.

At first glance, this response seems plausible. Surely, lawmakers know a lot about the needs of the people they represent. They hardly need researchers to tell them that married couples tend to be happier than people who are divorced or separated, or that people who lose their jobs are unhappy, or that individuals who are depressed or in chronic pain feel miserable.

True enough. Yet research on happiness contradicts this commonsense view on one crucial point. People do *not* always know what will give them lasting satisfaction. They tend to focus too much on their initial response to changes in their daily lives and overlook how soon the pleasure of a new car or a pay raise or a move to warmer climes will disappear and leave them no happier than before. Conversely, they often fail to realize how quickly they will adapt to most of the misfortunes that befall them once the initial shock has passed away.

The prevailing culture accentuates these misimpressions. A vast barrage of commercial advertising reinforces the continuing desire for more goods and services by emphasizing the immediate enjoyment they will bring. In a materialistic society that places great emphasis on the things money can buy, success is frequently measured in financial terms, while wealth and the possessions it provides become an important source of status and respect from neighbors and peers. Earning the wherewithal to satisfy these desires often leads to worry and stress while requiring constant attention and long hours of work that diminish family life and limit the time for more satisfying pursuits.

Since business executives and corporations are well supplied with money and organizational skills, commercial interests and priorities have a potent influence in government circles. Backed by this political clout and by the public's constant desire for more goods and services, economic growth becomes the highest priority on the domestic agenda. Environmental policy, labor policy, tax policy, and much else must be shaped to satisfy the imperatives of an expanding economy. Education reform is dominated by the need to prepare a more effective workforce. Other aspects of life that contribute to well-being, such as marriage, child-rearing, and leisure receive less attention and must usually give way when they conflict with economic goals.

How might these priorities be affected if policy-makers began paying serious attention to the research on happiness? Clearly, the most profound question raised by this new body of work is whether growth should retain such a dominant place on the domestic agenda. What several investigators have done is to challenge prevailing policies at their core by marshaling evidence to show that the constant preoccupation with growth has *not* helped Americans become any happier over the past 60 years despite the doubling and redoubling of the Gross Domestic Product.

Happiness scholars are not the first to raise this issue. Philosophers have questioned the value of accumulating wealth and possessions for at least 2,500 years, while scientists began to express concern several decades ago about the effects of continued economic growth on natural resources and the environment. But the claims of philosophers were assertions unaccompanied by evidence. As for the scientists' forebodings, the more alarming predictions of impending doom were usually refuted by subsequent events, while more restrained, carefully documented warnings could be satisfied by measures that did not seriously interfere with growth itself. In contrast, a number of happiness researchers have marshaled empirical evidence that calls in question not just the side effects of economic activity but the value of growth itself.

Not all happiness investigators share these doubts, and analysts have made persuasive arguments on both sides of the question. If it should turn out, however, that growth no longer adds significantly to the happiness of Americans, both policy-makers and the general public may eventually have to consider whether it is sensible to invest so much time and effort and put the environment to so much risk in a ceaseless struggle to expand the output of goods and services.

For now and in the foreseeable future, however, there is little chance that researchers will bring about drastic changes in economic policy. Even if it should turn out that growth does not bring added happiness, there is no way at present to stop the economy from growing without creating problems that would outweigh any hoped-for benefits. The necessary changes in behavior and outlook would be so profound and the practical and political problems so numerous and difficult that such a transformation would probably take generations.

For the time being, then, the doubts researchers have raised about the value of growth are likely to have more modest effects. At most, they may persuade policy-makers to be more skeptical of those who assume that maximum growth should be the overriding goal to which all other domestic policies must accommodate and to become more attentive to other aspects of life that can contribute importantly to well-being.

With such a change of emphasis in mind, government officials could draw upon the new research to rethink their priorities and make a more balanced effort to promote well-being. For example, happiness research reinforces the importance of programs to strengthen marriage and family; encourage active forms of leisure; cushion the shock of unemployment; guarantee universal health care and a more secure retirement; improve child care and pre-school education; treat mental illness, sleep disorders, and chronic pain more effectively; and focus education policy on a broader set of goals. Progress on these fronts could well do more for well-being than such familiar proposals as redistributing income, putting more people in prison, subsidizing even further the retirement savings of the well-to-do, or promoting the kind of suburbanization that brings longer commutes and added traffic.

One can easily think of other policies to consider beyond the ones described in this volume. Environmental policy is a prime example, not only because of the long-term risk of catastrophic damage from global warming but also because at least one longitudinal study has found that reductions in air pollutants such as lead and nitrogen dioxide lead to perceptible gains in happiness.[1] In law enforcement, happiness research would suggest paying more attention to groups affected by crime, such as residents in inner-city neighborhoods who live in fear of being beaten, robbed, or shot, or victims of crime who would benefit from enforceable rights to be informed of progress in apprehending their wrongdoer and to appear in court to submit their views on plea bargains and sentences.[2] Even more could be done to improve well-being by requiring a more thoughtful and more rigorous review with greater Congressional participation before entering into major wars, such as those in Iraq and Vietnam, that have caused so much death, injury, and psychological harm, not to mention such vast destruction and expense.[3]

In contemplating this altered agenda, lawmakers should be pleased to discover how little it would cost the nation. Some important measures, notably universal health care, would require substantial sums to implement properly. But other useful steps, such as more extensive premarital counseling, more effective relief of chronic pain, more attention to crime victims, and a broader set of educational goals, would be far less expensive. Better yet, such valuable measures as universal preschool, or public financing of elections, or proper attention to sleep disorders and depression, though they would require initial investments, could more than pay for themselves eventually. Still other initiatives, such as efforts to discourage earmarks or revise sentencing policies for victimless crimes, would reduce government outlays almost immediately. Any success in avoiding unnecessary wars, of course, would yield far greater savings. Overall, then, a comprehensive effort to promote well-being is one of the few important government initiatives that could ultimately cost the public little or nothing. If obstacles to such reforms exist, they are more likely to involve a lack of political will than a shortage of money.

Still another important item in a revised political agenda would be a fresh look at government itself. One of the more interesting findings from the research on happiness is how much the quality of government and the trust and confidence people have in their public officials contribute to well-being. With this insight in mind, efforts to improve the government's performance and increase respect for its work take on added significance, especially at a time like the present when public confidence and trust have sunk to such low levels. Sustained improvement in the quality of public policy will be very hard to achieve. But lawmakers could take some practical steps to build greater confidence in the political process through measures to reduce the influence of money and special interests and to curb redistricting abuses, unethical practices, pork barrel earmarks, and other efforts by politicians to place their own reelection above the general welfare.

Helpful as these reforms would be, they are unlikely by themselves to bring about a substantial increase in trust and confidence. For that to happen, the media, along with schools and colleges, will need to educate the public to counteract the widespread tendency to expect too much of government, exaggerate its faults, and overlook its accomplishments. In recent decades, these attitudes, reinforced by an insufficient understanding of our Constitutional system and its effects on policy-making, have contributed to a widespread cynicism toward politics that hampers the work of government and ultimately diminishes the public's well-being. The remedy is surely not to promote some sort of mindless patriotism or to ignore the errors and misadventures of our public officials. Rather, schools, colleges, and the media all need to take the responsibility for civic education more seriously and give the public a more balanced, realistic appreciation of how the political and policy-making processes work and why they often involve such prolonged arguments and awkward compromises.

Beyond these specific changes, almost any successful effort to increase happiness will require greater understanding by the people of the actual sources of well-being. Despite the many possibilities for useful government initiatives, no democratically elected government can stray too far from the wishes of the voters, no matter how enlightened its officials may be and how committed they are to furthering the well-being of their constituents. If Americans have a faulty perception of what will bring them lasting satisfaction, policy-makers will find it hard to do a great deal for them.

One modest but important step that the government could take to increase understanding would be to publish annual reports on the well-being of the American people using the best survey methods and the most comprehensive data available. Such information would regularly call attention to the subject and stimulate debate about the findings. Over time, public awareness would increase and people's conception of national progress might come to include much more than the familiar measures of economic growth, stock market trends, unemployment, and standardized test scores that currently attract so much attention from policy-makers and the media.

More information and increased public awareness, though helpful, will not suffice to realize the full potential for increasing happiness. People must also have a better appreciation of the causes of their own happiness and dissatisfaction. Government cannot assume this responsibility for them. In a democracy, public officials have only a limited power to increase well-being. They can do a lot to relieve suffering by mounting more effective efforts to deal with chronic pain and depression, avoid needless wars, or limit financial risk. It is much more difficult for governments to change behavior in positive ways that will bring about stronger marriages, greater civic engagement, more active uses of leisure, or closer social ties. Policymakers can offer incentives and create opportunities, but education will ultimately accomplish more than legislation in helping people to pay more informed attention to these aspects of their lives.

At present, both our schools and our colleges are doing less than they should to help young people acquire the variety of interests or recognize the kinds of experience that are most likely to contribute to a full and satisfying life. In crafting an education policy, officials have focused too heavily on the need to train a productive workforce at the expense of other reforms that could do as much or more to increase well-being. Most educators try to take a broader view, but multiple pressures lead them to concentrate primarily on vocationally oriented knowledge and skills. To serve their students well, schools and colleges need encouragement to adjust their priorities and do more to cultivate a breadth of interests and convey the kinds of knowledge that students need to make wiser choices about their lives.

For education, then, as for many other areas of public policy, the study of happiness could have important implications. Its potential value can only grow. Serious empirical research on happiness is only a few decades old and hence is still in its infancy compared with most other fields in the social sciences. Over time, its methods will improve and its findings will become more reliable and detailed. New research will throw fresh light on more and more facets of human experience and trace the effects of more and more conditions of life on the well-being of different groups of people. Thus, the policy implications described in this book offer only a preliminary glimpse at what may eventually come to light.

At this point, it is still too early to tell how much attention policymakers will eventually give to such research. Yet even if they never pay much heed, the study of happiness promises to contribute in another important way. Until now, the results of the new research have barely entered the consciousness of the general public. As the work matures and a clearer consensus emerges around its central findings, a wider debate is likely to occur not only over the role of growth but over larger questions about how to use our abundance "to live wisely, and agreeably, and well."[4] Whatever Congress does or does not do, such discussion, nourished by a growing body of research, is bound to contribute to the evolution of society and the refinement of its values. That alone will be an accomplishment of enduring importance to humankind. And in the fullness of time, who knows? Public policy may even begin to change as well.

# NOTES

## Introduction

1. Quoted in Vijay K. Shrotryia, "Happiness and Development: Public Policy Initiatives in the Kingdom of Bhutan," in Yew-Kwang Ng and Lok Sang Ho (eds.), *Happiness and Public Policy: Theory, Case Studies, and Implications* (2006), pp. 193, 201.

2. See, e.g., Jigme Y. Thinley, "Gross National Happiness: A Paradigm for Intelligent Urbanism" (paper submitted at 3d International Conference on Gross National Happiness, Bangkok, Thailand, January 3–5, 2007); Brook Lerner, "Bhutan's Novel Experiment," *National Geographic* (March 2008), p. 124.

3. Daniel Kaufman, Aart Kraay, and Massimo Mastruzzi, "Governance Matters VI: Aggregate and Individual Governance Indicators 1996–2006," World Bank Policy Research Working Paper 4280 (July 2007), pp. 76–93.

4. The treatment of Nepalis in Bhutan is described by Tessa Piper, "The Exodus of Ethnic Nepalis from Southern Bhutan," 14 *Refugee Survey Quarterly* (1995), p. 52.

5. See, e.g., Vijay K. Shrotryia, note 1; Brook Lerner, note 2; Bob Frame, "Bhutan: A Review of Its Approach to Sustainable Development," 15 *Development in Practice* (2005), p. 216.

6. See Raksha Arora, "A Well-Being Report Card for President Sarkozy," http://www.gallup.com/poll/103795/WellBeing-Report-Card-President-Sarkozy.aspx (January 17, 2008).

7. Nick Donovan and David Halpern, *Life Satisfaction: The State of Knowledge and Implications for Government* (2002). David Cameron is quoted in Rana Foroohar, "Money v. Happiness: Nations Rethink Priorities," *Newsweek* (April 5, 2007), p. 3.

8. Darrin M. McMahon, *Happiness: A History* (2006), pp. 200–221.

9. Ibid., p. 261.

10. Jeremy Bentham, *Introduction to the Principles of Morals and Legislation* (J. H. Burns and H.L.A. Hart, eds., 1996), pp. 39–40.

11. Ibid., pp. 38–41.

12. See chapter 1 for further discussion.

13. Richard A. Easterlin, "Does Economic Growth Improve the Human Lot? Some Empirical Evidence," in Paul A. David and Melvin W. Reder (eds.), *Nations and Households in Economic Growth: Essays in Honor of Moses Abramowitz* (1974), p. 89; and Easterlin, "Feeding the Illusion of Happiness: A Reply to Hagerty and Veenhoven," 74 *Social Indicators Research* (2005), p. 74.

14. E.g., Daniel Kahneman and Richard H. Thaler, "Anomalies, Utility Maximization, and Experienced Utility," 20 *Journal of Economic Perspectives* (2006), p. 221. See also Daniel Gilbert, *Stumbling on Happiness* (2006).

15. Juliet B. Schor, *The Overspent American: Why We Want What We Don't Need* (1998), p. 15.

16. Alberto Alesina, Rafael Di Tella, and Robert MacCulloch, "Inequality and Happiness: Are Europeans and Americans Different?" 88 *Journal of Public Economics* (2004), p. 2009.

17. Ruut Veenhoven, "Return of Inequality in Modern Society? Test by Dispersion of Life-Satisfaction across Time and Nations," 6 *Journal of Happiness Studies* (2005), p. 457.

18. Ruut Veenhoven, "Well-Being in the Welfare State: Level Not Higher; Distribution Not More Equitable," 2 *Journal of Comparative Policy Analysis: Research and Practice* (2000), p. 91.

## Chapter 1: What Investigators Have Discovered

1. E.g., Carol Graham, Soumya Chattopadhyay, and Mario Picon, "The Easterlin and Other Paradoxes: Why Both Sides of the Debate May Be Correct" (draft paper for Princeton Conference on International Differences in Well-Being, October 2008), p. 4; Rafael Di Tella and Robert MacCulloch, "Happiness Adaptation to Income Beyond Basic Needs" (draft paper for Princeton Conference on International Differences in Well-Being, October 2008), p. 7. See generally Ed Diener, "Subjective Well-Being," 95 *Psychological Bulletin* (1984), pp. 542, 543; Mihaly Csikszentmihalyi and Maria Mei-Ha Wong, "A Cross-National Comparison," in Fritz Strack, Michael Argyle, and Norbert Schwarz (eds.), *Subjective Well-Being: An Interdisciplinary Perspective* (1991), pp. 193, 194.

2. Ed Diener, Eunkook M. Suh, and Shigehiro Oishi, "Recent Findings on Subjective Well-Being," 24 *Indian Journal of Clinical Psychology* (1997), p. 25.

3. Angus Deaton, "Income, Aging, Health, and Well-Being around the World: Evidence from the Gallup World Poll," National Bureau of Economic Research, Working Paper No. 13317 (August 2007).

4. Ed Diener, Eunkook M. Suh, Richard E. Lucas, and Heidi L. Smith, "Subjective Well-Being: Three Decades of Progress," 125 *Psychological Bulletin* (1999), pp. 276, 292, figure 3.

5. E.g., Ronald Inglehart, Roberto Foa, Christopher Peterson, and Christian Welzel, "Development, Freedom, and Rising Happiness: A Global Perspective (1981–2007)," 3 *Perspectives on Psychological Science* (2008), p. 264. The authors found that happiness remained the same from 1981 to 2007 in the United States, Switzerland, and Norway and declined in Britain, Austria, Belgium, and West Germany; p. 276.

6. Ed Diener and Robert Biswas-Diener, *Happiness: Unlocking the Mysteries of Psychological Wealth* (2008), p. 73.

7. Rafael Di Tella and Robert MacCulloch, "Gross National Happiness as an Answer to the Easterlin Paradox?" 16 *Journal of Development Economics* (2007), p. 22. Three Italian economists, however, have argued that Di Tella and MacCulloch did not include the decline in social capital and that the paradox could have been explained by taking account of this factor. Stefano Bartolini, Ennio Bilancini, and Maurizio Pugno, "Did the Decline in Social Capital Depress Americans' Happiness?" (unpublished paper, 2008).

8. Betsey Stevenson and Justin Wolfers, "Economic Growth and Subjective Well-Being: Reassessing the Easterlin Paradox," Brookings Papers on Economic Activity (Spring 2008), p. 1.

9. Ruut Veenhoven, "Return of Inequality in Modern Society? Test by Dispersion of Life-Satisfaction across Time and Nations," 6 *Journal of Happiness Studies* (2005), p. 475.

10. See, e.g., Richard A. Easterlin, "Does Economic Growth Improve the Human Lot? Some Empirical Evidence," in Paul A. David and Melvin W. Reder (eds.), *Nations and Households in Economic Growth: Essays in Honor of Moses Abramowitz* (1974); Ronald Inglehart, Roberto Foa, Christopher Peterson, and Christian Welzel, note 5, p. 276.

11. Rafael Di Tella and Robert MacCulloch, note 1.

12. Erzo F. P. Luttmer, "Neighbors as Negatives: Relative Earnings and Well-Being," 121 *Quarterly Journal of Economics* (2005), p. 963.

13. Alois Stutzer, "The Role of Income Aspirations in Individual Happiness," 54 *Journal of Economic Behavior and Organization* (2004), p. 89. See also Lee Rainwater, "Family Equivalence as a Social Construction," in Olivia Ekert-Jaffe (ed.), *Standards of Living and Families: Observation and Analysis* (1994), pp. 23–40.

14. Robert D. Putnam, *Bowling Alone: The Collapse and Revival of American Community* (2000), p. 192.

15. Juliet B. Schor, *The Overspent American: Why We Want What We Don't Need* (1998), pp. 14–15. Schor's figures are derived from polls from the Roper Center for Public Opinion Research, University of Connecticut.

16. Angus Deaton, note 3; John F. Helliwell, Haifang Huang, and Anthony Harris, "International Differences in the Determinants of Life Satisfaction," in Tridip Ray, E. Somanathan, and Bhaskar Dutta (eds.), *New and Enduring Themes in Development Economics* (2009). Another group of scholars has found that Deaton's result may be partly explained by the wording of the Gallup survey. Apparently, asking people to evaluate their life on an 11-point scale from "best possible" to "worst possible" tends to result in a greater emphasis on income than when they are simply asked how happy or satisfied they are with their lives. Ed Diener, Daniel Kahneman, William Tov, and Raksha Arora, "Income's Differential Impact on Judgments of Life versus Affective Well-Being" (draft paper, September 30, 2008). This difference may result from the fact that the Gallup survey tends to elicit comparisons between one's own life and that of people in other nations of the world.

17. Betsey Stevenson and Justin Wolfers, note 8.

18. Ruut Veenhoven and Michael Hagerty, "Rising Happiness in Nations 1946–2004: A Reply to Easterlin," 79 *Social Indicators Research* (2006), pp. 421, 429.

19. Rafael Di Tella and Robert MacCulloch, note 1; Carol Graham, Soumya Chattopadhyay, and Mario Picon, note 1.

20. See, e.g., Linda J. Sax, Alexander W. Astin, William S. Korn, and Kathryn Mahoney, *The American Freshman: National Norms for Fall 2003* (2003).

21. Tim Kasser and Allen D. Kanner, *Psychology and Consumer Culture: The Struggle for a Good Life in a Materialistic World* (2004). See also Martin E. P. Seligman, *Authentic Happiness: Using the New Positive Psychology to Realize Your Potential for Lasting Fulfillment* (2002), p. 55. Other researchers, however, have found that those who care a lot about money and do in fact make a lot of money are not especially unhappy. Carol Nickerson, Norbert Schwarz, Ed Diener, and Daniel Kahneman, "Zeroing In on the Dark Side of the American Dream," 14 *Psychological Science* (2003), p. 531.

22. Carol Nickerson, Norbert Schwarz, Ed Diener, and Daniel Kahneman, note 21, p. 535.

23. Ibid., p. 531.

24. Ed Diener and Mark E. Suh, "Subjective Well-Being and Age: An International Analysis," in *Annual Review of Gerontology and Geriatrics* (1997), p. 304.

25. See, e.g., Yang Yang, "Social Inequalities in Happiness in the United States, 1972 to 2004: An Age-Period-Cohort Analysis," 73 *American Sociological Review* (2008), pp. 204, 220.

26. Betsey Stevenson and Justin Wolfers, "The Paradox of Declining Female Happiness," *American Economic Journal: Economic Policy* (forthcoming).

27. Yang Yang, note 25, pp. 218–20.

28. E.g., Michael Argyle, *The Psychology of Happiness* (2d ed., 2001), pp. 105, 125; Bruno S. Frey, *Happiness: A Revolution in Economics* (2008), pp. 97, 105; on TV and movies compared with more active forms of recreation, see Nick Donovan and David Halpern, *Life Satisfaction: The State of Knowledge and Implications for Government* (2002), pp. 5, 25. For earlier studies showing that "television rates as average to below average in enjoyment, especially in relation to more active uses of free time," see John P. Robinson and Geoffrey Godbey, *Time for Life: The Surprising Ways Americans Use Their Time* (1997), p. 242.

29. E.g., Marissa L. Diener and Mary B. McGovern, "What Makes People Happy?" in Michael Eid and Randy J. Larsen (eds.), *The Science of Subjective Well-Being* (2008), p. 347; David G. Myers, "Close Relationships and the Quality of Life," in Daniel Kahneman, Ed Diener, and Norbert Schwarz (eds.), *Well-Being: The Foundations of Hedonic Psychology* (1999), p. 374.

30. Jonathan Gardner and Andrew J. Oswald, "How Is Mortality Affected by Money, Marriage, and Stress?" 23 *Journal of Health Economics* (2004), p. 118 (being married has a much greater effect on longevity than income; it is comparable to not smoking for men and has roughly half the effect of not smoking for

women). See also Andrew J. Oswald, "Happiness and Economic Performance," 107 *Economic Journal* (1997), pp. 1815, 1825; Raymond Cochrane, "Marriage and Madness," 3 *Psychology Review* (1996), p. 2; Susan Kennedy, Janice K. Kiecolt-Glaser, and Ronald Glaser, "Immunological Consequences of Acute Chronic Stressors," 61 *Journal of Medical Psychology* (1988), p. 77.

31. Alois Stutzer and Bruno S. Frey, "Does Marriage Make People Happy or Do Happy People Get Married?" 35 *Journal of Socio-Economics* (2006), p. 326. David G. Myers reports that the prevailing opinion of researchers is that the association between marriage and well-being is mainly due to the beneficial effects of marriage; "Close Relationships and the Quality of Life," in Daniel Kahneman, Ed Diener, and Norbert Schwarz (eds.), note 29, pp. 374, 380.

32. Compare Bruno S. Frey, *Happiness: A Revolution in Economics* (2008) (although happiness declines quite rapidly after its peak around the time of marriage, it remains above the levels experienced several years *before* marriage for five to six years), with Richard E. Lucas and Andrew E. Clark, "Do People Really Adapt to Marriage?" 7 *Journal of Happiness Studies* (2006), p. 405 (marriage gives only a short-term boost to happiness, based on a longitudinal study of German couples).

33. Richard E. Lucas, "Time Does Not Heal All Wounds: A Longitudinal Study of Reaction and Adaptation to Divorce," 16 *Psychological Science* (2005), p. 945.

34. Ibid. It is not entirely clear why separations cause more unhappiness than divorces. Perhaps it is because separations tend to be more recent so that respondents will have had less time to adapt. Perhaps it is that those who divorce are likely to have been unhappier in their marriage, on average, than those who have merely chosen to separate.

35. Daniel Gilbert, *Stumbling on Happiness* (2006).

36. Marsha D. Somers, "A Comparison of Voluntarily Child-Free Adults and Parents," 55 *Journal of Marriage and the Family* (1993), p. 643.

37. See Robin Simon, "The Joys of Parenthood Reconsidered," 7 *Contexts* (2008), p. 40. According to a Danish study, after the birth of the first child, parents gain no further satisfaction by having additional children. Hans-Peter Kohler, Jere R. Behrman, and Axel Skytthe, "Partner + Children = Happiness? The Effects of Partnership and Fertility on Well-Being," 31 *Population and Development Review* (2005), p. 407.

38. Daniel Gilbert, note 35, p. 22.

39. Norval D. Glenn and Sara McLanahan, "The Effects of Offspring on the Psychological Well-Being of Older Adults," 43 *Journal of Marriage and the Family* (1981), p. 409.

40. Kei Nomaguchi and Melissa A. Milkie, "Costs and Rewards of Children: The Effects of Becoming a Parent on Adults' Lives," 65 *Journal of Marriage and the Family* (2003), p. 356.

41. National Opinion Research Center survey reproduced by Elizabeth Warren, "Unsafe at Any Rate," *Democracy Journal* (Summer 2007), p. 11; Darrin R.

Lehman, Camille B. Wortman, and Allan F. Williams, "Long Term Effects of Losing a Spouse or Child in a Motor-Vehicle Crash," 52 *Journal of Personality and Social Psychology* (1987), p. 218.

42. Ed Diener and Robert Biswas-Diener, *Happiness: Unlocking the Mysteries of Psychological Wealth* (2008), p. 52 and, more generally, pp. 47–67.

43. Meliksah Demir and Lesley A. Weitekamp, "I Am So Happy 'Cause Today I Found My Friend: Friendship and Personality as Predictors of Happiness," 8 *Journal of Happiness Studies* (2007), p. 181. On the relative effect of friends and spouses, see Toni C. Antonucci, Jennifer E. Lansford, and Hiroko Akiyama, "Impact of Positive and Negative Aspects of Marital Relationships and Friendships on Well-Being of Older Adults," 5 *Applied Developmental Science* (2001), p. 68.

44. John F. Helliwell and Robert D. Putnam, "The Social Context of Well-Being," in Felicia A. Huppert, Nick Baylis, and Barry Keverne (eds.), *The Science of Well-Being* (2007 ed.), p. 435.

45. Compare Marianne Tait, Margaret Y. Padgett, and Timothy T. Baldwin, "Job and Life Satisfaction: A Reevaluation of the Strength of the Relationship and Gender Effects as a Function of the Date of the Study," 74 *Journal of Applied Psychology* (1989), p. 502, with Jeffrey S. Rain, Irving M. Lane, and Dirk D. Steiner, "A Current Look at the Job Satisfaction/Life Satisfaction Relationship: Review and Future Considerations," 44 *Human Relations* (1991), p. 287, and John F. Helliwell and Haifang Huang, "How's the Job? Well-Being and Social Capital in the Workplace," National Bureau of Economic Research, Working Paper No. 11759 (November 2005). Another recent study, however, concludes that satisfaction with work has little effect on satisfaction with life. Joseph C. Rude and Janet P. Near, "Spillover between Work Attitudes and Overall Life Attitudes: Myth or Reality?" 70 *Social Indicators Research* (2005), p. 79.

46. Timothy A. Judge and Shinichiro Watanabe, "Another Look at the Job Satisfaction–Life Satisfaction Relationship," 78 *Journal of Applied Psychology* (1993), p. 939.

47. John F. Helliwell, Haifang Huang, and Robert D. Putnam, "Are Trust and Social Capital Neglected Workplace Investments?" (unpublished paper, 2008).

48. Andrew E. Clark and Andrew J. Oswald, "Unhappiness and Unemployment," 104 *Economic Journal* (1994), p. 648; Liliana Winkelmann and Rainer Winkelmann, "Why Are the Unemployed So Unhappy? Evidence from Panel Data," 65 *Economica* (1998), p. 1.

49. Daniel Nettles, *Happiness: The Science Behind Your Smile* (2005), p. 111; Richard Layard, *Happiness: Lessons from a New Science* (2005), p. 64.

50. Bruno S. Frey and Alois Stutzer, "What Can Economists Learn from Happiness Research?" 40 *Journal of Economic Literature* (2002), pp. 402–3.

51. Daniel Nettles, note 49, p. 111; Richard Layard, note 49, p. 64.

52. Morris A. Okun and Linda K. George, "Physician and Self-Ratings of Health, Neuroticism, and Subjective Well-Being among Men and Women," 5 *Personality and Individual Differences* (1984), p. 533.

53. The classic study is Philip Brickman, Dan Coates, and Ronnie Janoff-Buhlman, "Lottery Winners and Accident Victims: Is Happiness Relative?" 2 *Journal of Personality and Social Psychology* (1978), p. 917.

54. See, e.g., Abbot L. Ferris, "Religion and the Quality of Life," 3 *Journal of Happiness Studies* (2002), p. 199.

55. Richard Layard, note 49, p. 64. David G. Myers reports that 41 percent of Americans with "strong" religious beliefs were "very happy" compared with 31 percent of those who indicated that they were only "somewhat" or "not very" religious. *The Pursuit of Happiness: Discovering the Pathway to Fulfillment, Well-Being, and Enduring Personal Joy* (1992), p. 183.

56. Jeffrey C. Jacob and Merlin B. Brinkerhoff, "Mindfulness and Subjective Well-Being in the Sustainability Movement: A Further Elaboration of Multiple Discrepancy Theory," 46 *Social Indicators Research* (1999), p. 341; Kirk W. Brown and Tim Kasser, "Are Psychological Well-Being and Ecological Well-Being Compatible? The Role of Values, Mindfulness, and Lifestyle," 74 *Social Indicators Research* (2005), p. 349.

57. Bruno S. Frey and Alois Stutzer, "Happiness Research: State and Prospects," 62 *Review of Social Economy* (2005), pp. 207, 213.

58. Elizabeth W. Dunn, Lara B. Aknin, and Michael I. Norton, "Spending Money on Others," 319 *Science* (2008), p. 1687.

59. Peggy A. Thoits and Lyndi N. Hewitt, "Volunteer Work and Well-Being," 42 *Journal of Health and Social Behavior* (2001), p. 115. Research involving East Germans who were abruptly denied the opportunity to continue volunteering suggests that volunteering is more a cause than a result of greater happiness. Bruno S. Frey and Alois Stutzer, note 57, pp. 207, 213.

60. Ronald Inglehart, Roberto Foa, Christopher Peterson, and Christian Welzel, note 5, pp. 264, 272.

61. See table 2, p. 24.

62. In fact, one investigation of the results from the most recent World Values Survey found that freedom was the most potent factor contributing to a rise in happiness levels in 45 of 52 countries surveyed from 1981 to 2007. Ronald Inglehart, Roberto Foa, Christopher Peterson, and Christian Welzel, note 5, p. 264.

63. Ibid., p. 271.

64. See Grant Duncan, "After Happiness," 12 *Journal of Political Ideologies* (2007), pp. 86, 91–96.

65. Robert Biswas-Diener and Ed Diener, "Making the Best of a Bad Situation: Satisfaction in the Slums of Calcutta," 55 *Social Indicators Research* (2001), p. 329.

66. Margaret W. Maitlin and David J. Stang, *The Pollyanna Principle: Selectivity in Language, Memory, and Thought* (1978).

67. For a careful analysis of trends in well-being in Eastern Europe, see Richard A. Easterlin, "Lost in Transition: Life Satisfaction on the Road to Capitalism," *Journal of Economic Behavior and Organization* (forthcoming).

68. See table in Kaare Christensen, Anne M. Herskind, and James W. Vaupel, "Why Danes Are Smug: Comparative Study of Life Satisfaction in the European Union," 333 *BMJ* (2006), p. 1289, downloaded from www.bmj.com.

69. Ibid.

70. See table 2 in Rafael Di Tella, Robert J. MacCulloch, and Andrew J. Oswald, "The Macroeconomics of Happiness," 85 *Review of Economics and Statistics* (2003), pp. 809, 811.

71. Daniel Kahneman and Jason Riis, "Living, and Thinking About It: Two Perspectives on Life," in Felicia A. Huppert, Nick Baylis, and Barry Keverne (eds.), *The Science of Well-Being* (2007 ed.), pp. 285, 295.

72. Ibid., pp. 297–98.

73. Daniel Kahneman, Alan B. Krueger, David A. Schkade, Norbert Schwarz, and Arthur A. Stone, "A Survey Method for Characterizing Daily Life Experience: The Day Reconstruction Method," 306 *Science* (2004), pp. 1776, 1778.

74. Daniel Kahneman and Jason Riis, note 71, p. 295.

75. Alberto Alesina, Edward Glaeser, and Bruce Sacerdote, "Work and Leisure in the U.S. and Europe: Why So Different?" National Bureau of Economic Research, Working Paper No. 11278 (April 2005), p. 30.

76. The Conference Board, "In Pursuit of Satisfaction: U.S. Job Satisfaction Declines" (news release, February 23, 2007). See also Lynn Franco, "Job Satisfaction Continues to Wither," The Conference Board, Executive Action No. 69 (September 2003); David G. Blanchflower and Andrew J. Oswald, "Well-Being, Insecurity, and the Decline of American Job Satisfaction" (unpublished paper, July 22, 1999).

77. The Conference Board, note 76.

### Chapter 2: The Reliability of Research on Happiness

1. Jeremy Bentham, "Article on Utilitarianism," in Amnon Goldworth (ed.), *Jeremy Bentham: Deontology, Together with a Table of the Springs of Action and the Article on Utilitarianism* (1983), p. 297.

2. Quoted in Darrin M. McMahon, *Happiness: A History* (2006), p. 219.

3. See, e.g., Daniel Kahneman and Jason Riis, "Living, and Thinking About It: Two Perspectives on Life," in Felicia A. Huppert, Nick Baylis, and Barry Keverne (eds.), *The Science of Well-Being* (2007 ed.), p. 285.

4. See Anna Alexandrova, "Subjective Well-Being and Kahneman's 'Objective Happiness,'" 6 *Journal of Happiness Studies* (2005), p. 301.

5. Ed Diener and Martin E. P. Seligman, "Beyond Money: Toward an Economy of Well-Being," 5 *Psychological Science in the Public Interest* (2004), pp. 1, 21.

6. Victoria H. Medvec, Scott F. Madey, and Thomas Gilovich, "When Less Is More: Counterfactual Thinking and Satisfaction among Olympic Medalists," 69 *Journal of Personality and Social Psychology* (1995), p. 603.

7. Norbert Schwarz and Fritz Strack, "Reports of Subjective Well-Being: Judgmental Processes and Their Methodological Implications," in Daniel Kahneman,

Ed Diener, and Norbert Schwarz (eds.), *Well-Being: The Foundations of Hedonic Psychology* (1999), p. 61.

8. Margaret W. Maitlin and David J. Stang, *The Pollyanna Principle: Selectivity in Language, Memory, and Thought* (1978). In contrast, Ruut Veenhoven has reviewed a number of studies to test the validity of happiness surveys and has concluded that there is no evidence that responses measure anything other than what they purport to measure. *Conditions of Happiness* (1984), chapter 3; Ruut Veenhoven, "Happiness as a Public Policy Aim: The Greatest Happiness Principle," in Martin E. P. Seligman, P. Alex Linley, and Stephen Joseph (eds.), *Positive Psychology in Practice* (2004), pp. 658, 665.

9. Daniel Kahneman and Jason Riis, note 3, pp. 288–89. For an interesting discussion of cultural differences, see Shigehiro Oishi, "Culture and Well-Being: Conceptual and Methodological Issues" (unpublished paper, 2008).

10. George Loewenstein and Peter A. Ubel, "Hedonic Adaptation to the Role of Decision and Experience Utility in Public Policy," 92 *Journal of Public Economics* (2008), p. 1795.

11. Ed Sandvik, Ed Diener, and Larry Seidlitz, "Subjective Well-Being: The Convergence and Stability of Self-Report and Non-Self-Report Measures," 61 *Journal of Personality* (1993), p. 317; David Watson and Lee A. Clark, "Self- Versus Peer Ratings of Specific Emotional Traits: Evidence of Convergent and Discriminant Validity," 60 *Journal of Personality and Social Psychology* (1991), p. 927. Naturally, the evaluations are much more likely to correspond with self-reports if they reflect the views of several relatives and friends rather than just one.

12. Dacher Keltner and Lee Anne Harker, "Expressions of Positive Emotion in Women's College Yearbook Pictures and Their Relationship to Personality and Life Outcomes across Adulthood," 80 *Journal of Personality and Social Psychology* (2001), p. 112.

13. Bruno S. Frey and Alois Stutzer, "What Can Economists Learn from Happiness Research?" 40 *Journal of Economic Literature* (2002), pp. 402, 406–7.

14. G. M. Devins, J. Mann, H. P. Mandin, and C. Leonard, "Psychosocial Predictors of Survival in End-Stage Renal Disease," 178 *Journal of Nervous and Mental Disease* (1990), p. 127; Sandra M. Levy, Jerry Lee, Caroline Bagley, and Marc Lippman, "Survival Hazard Analysis in First Recurrent Breast Cancer Patients: Seven Year Follow-up," 50 *Psychosomatic Medicine* (1988), p. 520.

15. See Sonja Lyubomirsky, Laura Knight, and Ed Diener, "The Benefits of Frequent Positive Affect: Does Happiness Lead to Success?" 131 *Psychological Bulletin* (2005), p. 803.

16. Daniel Gilbert, *Stumbling on Happiness* (2006).

17. William D. Nordhaus and James Tobin, "Is Growth Obsolete?" in *Economic Growth, Fiftieth Anniversary Colloquium V*, National Bureau of Economic Research (1972).

18. See, e.g., Bengt Brülde, "Happiness and the Good Life: Introduction and Conceptual Framework," 8 *Journal of Happiness Studies* (2007), pp. 10–11.

19. John Rawls, *A Theory of Justice* (1971), p. 409; Joseph Raz, *The Morality of Freedom: Essays in the Morality of Law and Politics* (1994), p. 3.

20. Slavoj Zizek, *Welcome to the Desert of the Real* (2002), p. 60.

21. Will Wilkinson, "In Pursuit of Happiness Research: Is It Reliable? What Does It Imply for Policy?" Cato Institute, Policy Analysis No. 590 (April 11, 2007), p. 27.

## Chapter 3: Should Policy-Makers Use Happiness Research?

1. In a recent survey of 10,000 people in 48 nations, Ed Diener, Shigehiro Oishi, and Richard Lucas found that happiness was rated more highly as a goal than 11 other possibilities including success, intelligence/knowledge, and material wealth. Shigehiro Oishi, Ed Diener, and Richard E. Lucas, "The Optimal Level of Well-Being: Can People Be Too Happy?" 2 *Perspectives on Psychological Science* (2007), pp. 346, 347. See also Michael Argyle, *The Psychology of Happiness* (2d ed., 2001), p. 1; David Halpern, *Social Capital* (2005), p. 80.

2. Sonja Lyubomirsky, Laura King, and Ed Diener, "The Benefits of Frequent Positive Affect: Does Happiness Lead to Success?" 131 *Psychological Bulletin* (2005), p. 803.

3. Immanuel Kant, "The Metaphysics of Morals, Part II," *The Metaphysical Principles of Virtue, Ethical Philosophy* (translated by James W. Ellington, 1983), p. 386. Kant goes on to state: "One cannot invert these and make, on the one hand, one's own happiness and, on the other, the perfection of others, ends which should be in themselves duties for the same person."

4. Quoted by Darrin M. McMahon, *Happiness: A History* (2006), p. 342.

5. See chapter 6, pp. 112–13.

6. See chapter 6, pp. 112–17.

7. Jan Narveson, *The Libertarian Idea* (1988), p. 7.

8. Aldous Huxley, *Brave New World* (1960 ed., Harper & Row).

9. Ibid., p. 184.

10. E.g., Ronald W. Dworkin, *Artificial Happiness: The Dark Side of the New Happy Class* (2006). (This author should not be confused with the philosopher Ronald Dworkin.)

11. Eric G. Wilson, *Against Happiness* (2008).

12. Sonja Lyubomirsky, Laura King, and Ed Diener, note 2, pp. 838–40.

13. Shigehiro Oishi, Ed Diener, and Richard E. Lucas, note 1, p. 346.

14. John Bartlett, *Bartlett's Familiar Quotations* (16th ed., 1992), p. 314.

15. David Lykken and Auke Tellegen, "Happiness Is a Stochastic Phenomenon," 7 *Psychological Science* (1996), p. 186.

16. Ibid.

17. Ronald Inglehart, Roberto Foa, Christopher Peterson, and Christian Welzel, "Development, Freedom, and Rising Happiness: A Global Perspective (1981–2007)," 3 *Perspectives on Psychological Science* (2008), p. 264.

18. Thomas Bulmahn, "Modernity and Happiness—The Case of Germany," 1 *Journal of Happiness Studies* (2000), p. 375; Ed Diener, Richard E. Lucas, and Christie N. Scollon, "Beyond the Hedonic Treadmill: Revising the Adaptation Theory of Well-Being," 61 *American Psychologist* (2006), pp. 305, 309.

19. See Ronald Inglehart, "Democracy and Happiness: What Causes What?" (paper presented at Notre Dame Conference on New Directions in the Study of Happiness, October 22–24, 2006).

20. Frank Fujita and Ed Diener, "Life Satisfaction Set Point: Stability and Change," 85 *Journal of Personality and Social Psychology* (2005), p. 155.

21. E.g., David Lykken, *Happiness: The Nature and Nurture of Joy and Contentment* (1999), pp. 60, 81; Felicia A. Huppert, "Positive Mental Health in Individuals and Populations," in Felicia A. Huppert, Nick Baylis, and Barry Keverne (eds.), *The Science of Well-Being* (2007 ed.), pp. 307–8.

22. See, e.g., Derek Bok, *The State of the Nation: Government and the Quest for a Better Society* (1996), p. 301.

23. Amartya Sen, *On Ethics and Economics* (1987), pp. 45–46.

24. Speech to the Electors of Bristol in Edmund Burke, *Works*, vol. 3 (1801), p. 19. More generally, on the subject of representation in a democracy, see Hannah Pitkin, *The Concept of Representation* (1967).

25. Jonathan Gruber and Sendhil Mullainathan, "Do Cigarette Taxes Make Smokers Happier?" National Bureau of Economic Research, Working Paper No. 8872 (April 2002).

26. Keith A. Bender and Natalia Jivan, "What Makes Retirees Happy? An Issue in Brief," Center for Retirement Research at Boston College, Working Paper No. 28 (February 2005).

27. Bruno S. Frey and Alois Stutzer, "Happiness Prospers in Democracy," 1 *Journal of Happiness Studies* (2000), p. 79; Frey and Stutzer, "Political Participation and Procedural Utility," 45 *European Journal of Political Research* (2006), p. 391.

28. David Dorn, Justine A. V. Fischer, Gebhard Kirchgassner, and Alfonso Sousa-Poza, "Direct Democracy and Life Satisfaction Revisited: New Evidence for Switzerland," 9 *Journal of Happiness Studies* (2008), p. 227.

### Chapter 4: The Question of Growth

1. John R. McNeil, *Something New under the Sun: An Environmental History of the Twentieth Century World* (2000), p. 336.

2. For a detailed treatment of the evolution of economic growth as a national priority, see Robert M. Collins, *More: The Politics of Economic Growth in Postwar America* (2000).

3. See, e.g., Thomas L. Friedman, *Hot, Flat, and Crowded: Why We Need a Green Revolution and How It Can Renew America* (2008). Even as committed an environmentalist as Bill McKibben seems to imply that a sensible middle ground

would be to adopt a balance between growth and the environment similar to that of Europe. *Deep Economy: The Wealth of Communities and the Durable Future* (2007), p. 7.

4. John Stuart Mill, "Principles of Political Economy," in J. M. Robson (ed.), *Collected Works of John Stuart Mill*, vol. 3 (1965), p. 755.

5. Quoted in Bill McKibben, note 3, p. 7.

6. John Maynard Keynes, "Economic Possibilities for Our Grandchildren," in *Essays in Persuasion* (Norton, 1991; originally published in 1931), p. 367.

7. N. Gregory Mankiw, *Principles of Economics* (1998), p. 489.

8. Quoted by Robert M. Collins, note 2, p. 227.

9. James G. Speth, *The Bridge at the End of the World: Capitalism, the Environment, and Crossing from Crisis to Sustainability* (2008); Bill McKibben, note 3. See also Richard Douthwaite, *The Growth Illusion: How Economic Growth Has Enriched the Few, Impoverished the Many, and Endangered the Planet* (2d ed., 1999).

10. Juliet B. Schor, *The Overspent American: Why We Want What We Don't Need* (1998).

11. Angus Deaton, "Income, Aging, Health, and Well-Being around the World: Evidence from the Gallup World Poll," National Bureau of Economic Research, Working Paper No. 13317 (August 2007).

12. Stanley Lebergott, *Pursuing Happiness: American Consumers in the Twentieth Century* (1993), p. 15.

13. Robert W. Fogel, *The Fourth Great Awakening and the Future of Egalitarianism* (2000), p. 170.

14. Benjamin M. Friedman, *The Moral Consequences of Economic Growth* (2005).

15. Ibid., p. 4.

16. See Everett Carll Ladd and Karlyn H. Bowman, *What's Wrong: A Survey of American Satisfaction and Complaint* (1998), pp. 82, 83, 99, 105, 109; Pippa Norris (ed.), *Critical Citizens: Global Support for Democratic Governance* (1999), p. 6.

17. See, e.g., Richard G. Niemi, John Mueller, and Tom W. Smith, *Trends in Public Opinion: A Compendium of Survey Data* (1989), p. 167.

18. For example, Gallup polls reveal that the percentage of Americans who approved of marriage between blacks and whites grew steadily from 29 percent in 1972 to 48 percent in 1991, 64 percent in 1997, 65 percent in 2002, and 79 percent in 2007. http://www.gallup.com/poll/1687/Race-Relations.aspx?version-print. Similarly, from 1970 to 1994, the percentage of Americans who *disagreed* with the statement that "white people have a right to keep blacks out of their neighborhood" increased from 53 to 83 percent. *Index to International Public Opinion, 1994–95* (1995), p. 443.

19. Albert H. Cantril and Susan D. Cantril, *Reading Mixed Signals: Ambivalence in American Public Opinion about Government* (1999), p. 50.

20. Everett C. Ladd, *The American Ideology: An Exploration of the Origins, Meaning, and Role of "American Values"* (1992), p. 34.

21. Fay Lomax Cook and Edith J. Barrett, *Support for the American Welfare State: The Views of Congress and the Public* (1992), p. 62. These attitudes have persisted. For example, in 2007, 77 percent of the public agreed that the federal government is doing too little for the poor, while only 5 percent felt that the government was doing too much. Alec M. Gallup and Frank Newport (eds.), *The Gallup Poll: Public Opinion 2007* (2008), p. 179.

22. For a variety of thoughtful views on some of the problems of ending growth, see the symposium titled "The No-Growth Society" in 102 *Daedalus* (Fall 1973), and Robert Heilbroner, *An Inquiry into the Human Prospect* (1980).

23. Compare Andes Hayden, "France's 35-Hour Week: Attack on Business? Win-Win Reform? Or Betrayal of Disadvantaged Workers?" 34 *Politics and Society* (2006), pp. 503, 530, with Marcello Estevao and Filipe Sà, "The 35-Hour Workweek in France: Straightjacket or Welfare Improvement" (draft paper prepared for the 46th Panel Meeting of Economic Policy in Lisbon, September 2007). Whereas Hayden highlights the creation of 350,000 new jobs, Estevao and Sà contend that the 35-hour workweek reduced employment for affected workers. For a more general discussion that is skeptical of the effects of reduced hours on employment, see Ramon Marimon and Fabrizio Zilibotti, "Employment and Distributional Effects of Restricting Working Time," 44 *European Economic Review* (2000), p. 1291.

24. See table 4, p. 28.

25. Sylvia Ann Hewlett and Carolyn B. Luce, "Extreme Jobs: The Dangerous Allure of the 70-Hour Workweek," 84 *Harvard Business Review* (December 2006), p. 49.

26. Ibid., p. 51.

27. Mark Aguiar and Erik Hurst, "Measuring Trends in Leisure: The Allocation of Time over Five Decades," 122 *Quarterly Journal of Economics* (2007), p. 969.

28. Ibid., pp. 985–86.

29. Ibid., p. 987. For a similar, more detailed account of trends in the time spent watching TV, reading, etc., see John P. Robinson and Geoffrey Godbey, *Time for Life: The Surprising Ways Americans Use Their Time* (1997), pp. 136–53.

30. For Kahneman's calculations, see chapter 1. Interestingly, Rafael Di Tella and Robert MacCulloch report that although the standard workweek in France declined by 14 percent between 1975 and 1997, average well-being in the nation did not rise. "Some Uses of Happiness Data in Economics," 20 *Journal of Economic Perspectives* (2006), pp. 25, 33.

31. Milton Friedman, *Capitalism and Freedom* (1962), introduction.

32. Harwood Group, *Yearning for Balance: Views of Americans on Consumption, Materialism, and the Environment* (1995), http://www.iisd.ca/consume/harwood.html. For similar figures, see Robert Wuthnow, *Poor Richard's Principle* (1996), p. 271.

33. John P. Robinson and Geoffrey Godbey, note 29, pp. 269, 279, 297.

34. Juliet B. Schor, note 10, p. 113.

35. Jeffrey C. Jacob and Merlin B. Brinkerhoff, "Mindfulness and Subjective Well-Being in the Sustainability Movement: A Further Elaboration of Multiple Discrepancy Theory," 46 *Social Indicators Research* (1999), p. 341; Kirk W. Brown and Tim Kasser, "Are Psychological Well-Being and Ecological Well-Being Compatible? The Role of Values, Mindfulness, and Lifestyle," 74 *Social Indicators Research* (2005), p. 349.

## Chapter 5: What to Do about Inequality

1. James K. Galbraith, *Created Unequal: The Crisis in American Pay* (1998), p. 3.

2. See table 1, p. 10.

3. Ibid.

4. Ruut Veenhoven, "Return of Inequality in Modern Society? Test by Dispersion of Life-Satisfaction across Time and Nations," 6 *Journal of Happiness Studies* (2005), pp. 457, 462; Jan Ott, "Level and Inequality of Happiness in Nations: Does Greater Happiness of a Greater Number Imply Greater Inequality in Happiness?" 6 *Journal of Happiness Studies* (2005), pp. 397, 413.

5. These figures are set forth in greater detail in Rafael Di Tella, Robert J. MacCulloch, and Andrew J. Oswald, "The Macroeconomics of Happiness," 85 *Review of Economics and Statistics* (2003), p. 809.

6. Ruut Veenhoven, "Well-Being in the Welfare State: Level Not Higher; Distribution Not More Equitable," 2 *Journal of Comparative Policy Analysis: Research and Practice* (2000), p. 91. Various scholars report that different levels of income inequality do not explain differences in average well-being among countries. E.g., Michael Argyle, *The Psychology of Happiness* (2d ed., 2001), p. 186; Ruut Veenhoven, "Sociological Theories of Well-Being," in Michael Eid and Randy J. Larsen, *The Science of Subjective Well-Being* (2008), pp. 44, 55. Bruno Frey reaches the same conclusion with respect to U.S. states; *Happiness: A Revolution in Economics* (2008), p. 57.

7. Alberto Alesina, Rafael Di Tella, and Robert MacCulloch, "Inequality and Happiness: Are Europeans and Americans Different?" 88 *Journal of Public Economics* (2004), p. 2009.

8. Jennifer Hochschild, *What's Fair: American Beliefs about Distributive Justice* (1981).

9. Ibid., p. 17.

10. Katherine S. Newman, *Chutes and Ladders: Navigating the Low-Wage Labor Market* (2006).

11. Alberto Alesina and Edward L. Glaeser, *Fighting Poverty in the U.S. and Europe: A World of Difference* (2004), p. 184.

12. Katherine S. Newman, note 10, p. 257.

13. Alberto Alesina and Edward L. Glaeser, note 11, p. 184.

14. Ibid.

15. E.g., David Miller, "Arguments for Equality," 7 *Midwest Studies in Philosophy* (1982), p. 73.

16. Robert D. Putnam, *Bowling Alone: The Collapse and Revival of American Community* (2000).

17. The classic study establishing this tendency is that of Daniel Kahneman and Amos Tversky, "Prospect Theory: An Analysis of Decision under Risk," 47 *Econometrica* (1979), p. 363. See also Richard H. Thaler and Cass Sunstein, *Nudge: Improving Decisions about Health, Wealth, and Happiness* (2008), p. 33.

18. E.g., Ichiro Kawachi and Bruce P. Kennedy, *The Health of Nations: Why Inequality Is Bad for Your Health* (2002); Richard Wilkinson, *Unhealthy Societies: The Afflictions of Inequality* (1996).

19. Angus Deaton, "Health, Inequality, and Economic Development," 41 *Journal of Economic Literature* (2003), p. 113.

20. Ibid., p. 151.

21. Donald A. Redelmeier and Sheldon M. Singh, "Survival in Academy Award–Winning Actors and Actresses," 134 *Annals of Internal Medicine* (2001), p. 955.

22. Michael G. Marmot, "Inequalities of Health," 345 *New England Journal of Medicine* (2001), p. 134; Michael G. Marmot, G. Davey Smith, Stephen Stansfield, Chandra Patel, Fiona North, and Jenny Head, "Health Inequalities among British Civil Servants: The Whitehall Study II," 337 *Lancet* (1991), p. 1387.

23. An excellent summary of philosophers' thinking about inequality can be found in Daniel M. Hausman and Michael S. McPherson, *Economic Analysis, Moral Philosophy, and Public Policy* (2006), pp. 174–97.

24. John Rawls, *A Theory of Justice* (1971). Rawls's principle of distribution is set forth on pages 60, 83.

25. See, e.g., Daniel M. Hausman and Michael S. McPherson, note 23; Elizabeth Anderson, "What Is the Point of Equality?" 109 *Ethics* (1999), p. 287.

26. Compare Gerald A. Cohen, "On the Currency of Egalitarian Justice," 99 *Ethics* (1989), p. 906, with Philippe Van Parijs, "Why Surfers Should Be Fed: The Liberal Case for an Unconditional Basic Income," 20 *Philosophy and Public Affairs* (1991), p. 101.

27. Ronald Dworkin, "What Is Equality? Part 2: Equality of Resources," 10 *Philosophy and Public Affairs* (1981), p. 283.

28. Martha Nussbaum, *Women and Human Development* (2000), especially pp. 4–14, 70–110; Amartya Sen, *Inequality Reexamined* (1992). For an interesting critique of this theory, see Leonard W. Sumner, *Welfare, Happiness, and Ethics* (1996), pp. 60–68.

29. David Miller, "Distributive Justice: What the People Think," 102 *Ethics* (1992), p. 555. As Thomas Nagel points out: "If real people find it psychologically very difficult or even impossible to live as the theory requires or to adopt

relevant institutions, that should carry some weight against the ideal." *Equality and Partiality* (1991), p. 21.

30. John Rawls, note 24, pp. 60, 83. The critical quote is as follows: "First, each person is to have an equal right to the most extensive basic liberty compatible with a similar liberty for others ... [and second,] social and economic inequalities are to be arranged so that they are both (a) to the greatest benefit of the least advantaged and (b) attached to offices and positions open to all under conditions of fair equality of opportunity."

31. Sidney Verba, Kay L. Schlozman, and Henry E. Brady, *Voice and Equality: Civic Voluntarism in American Politics* (1995), p. 190.

32. American Political Science Association Task Force Report, "American Democracy in an Age of Rising Inequality," 2 *Perspectives on Politics* (2004), pp. 651, 656.

33. Sidney Verba, Kay L. Schlozman, and Henry E. Brady, note 31, pp. 193–95.

34. Larry Bartels, *Unequal Democracy: The Political Economy of the New Gilded Age* (2008).

35. American Political Science Association Task Force Report, note 32, pp. 651, 659. See also Martin Gilens, "Inequality and Democratic Responsiveness," 69 *Public Opinion Quarterly* (2005), pp. 778, 794.

36. Larry Bartels, note 34, pp. 275–82.

37. Larry Bartels, "Inequality and Political Representation" (unpublished paper, August 25, 2005), p. 32.

38. *Federal Elections Commission v. Wisconsin Right to Life, Inc.*, 127 Sup. Ct. 2652 (2007).

39. *Buckley v. Valeo*, 424 U.S. 1 (1976).

40. *Davis v. Federal Election Commission*, 128 Sup. Ct. 2759 (2008).

41. Diana L. Rogers and John H. Rogers, "Political Competition and State Government Size: Do Tighter Elections Produce Looser Budgets?" 105 *Public Choice* (2000), p. 1; Timothy Besley and Anne Case, "Political Institutions and Policy Choices: Evidence from the United States," 41 *Journal of Economic Literature* (2003), p. 7.

42. See Janet R. Richards, "Equality of Opportunity," 10 *Ratio* (new series) (1997), p. 253.

43. Edward L. Deci and Richard M. Ryan, "Hedonia, Eudaemonia, and Well-Being: An Introduction," 9 *Journal of Happiness Studies* (2008), p. 1; Carol D. Ryff, "Happiness Is Everything, or Is It? Explorations on the Meaning of Psychological Well-Being," 57 *Journal of Personality and Social Psychology* (1989), p. 1069.

44. Amartya Sen, *On Ethics and Economics* (1987), pp. 45–46.

45. See chapter 8, pp. 149–50.

46. Ibid.

47. E.g., Paul E. Peterson (ed.), *Our Schools and Our Future: Are We Still at Risk?* (2003); Donald Boyd, Hamilton Lankford, Susanna Loeb, and James

Wyckoff, "Explaining the Short Careers of High-Achieving Teachers in Schools with Low-Performing Students," *American Economic Review* (papers and proceedings) (2005), p. 166.

48. William G. Bowen, Martin A. Kurzweil, and Eugene M. Tobin, *Equity and Excellence in American Higher Education* (2005), p. 248.

49. Anthony P. Carnevale, "A Real Analysis of *Real* Education," 94 *Liberal Education* (Fall 2008), pp. 54, 56.

50. Claudia Goldin and Lawrence F. Katz, *The Race between Education and Technology* (2008).

51. Alberto Alesina and George-Marios Angeletos, "Fairness and Redistribution," 95 *American Economic Review* (2005), pp. 960, 965. See also Alberto Alesina and Eliana La Ferrara, "Preferences for Redistribution in the Land of Opportunities," 89 *Journal of Public Economics* (2005), p. 897.

52. Alberto Alesina and Edward L. Glaeser, note 11, p. 216. "Income mobility appears to be roughly the same in the United States and Europe and, if anything, the poor are less upwardly mobile in the United States," citing several studies. See also Emily Beller and Michael Hout, "Intergenerational Social Mobility: The United States in Comparative Perspective," 16 *The Future of Children* (2006), p. 19; Gary Solon, "Cross Country Differences in Intergenerational Earnings Mobility," 16 *Journal of Economic Perspectives* (2002), p. 59.

### Chapter 6: The Threat of Financial Hardship

1. For a history of official efforts to cope with risk in the United States, see David A. Moss, *When All Else Fails: Government as the Ultimate Risk Manager* (2002).

2. Governments in Western Europe often provide pensions averaging 50 or 60 percent of prior earnings or even more. See, e.g., Axel Boersch-Supan, "European Welfare State Regimes and Their Generosity toward the Elderly," in Dimitri B. Papadimitriou (ed.), *Government Spending on the Elderly* (2007), p. 33.

3. See, e.g., Jacob S. Hacker, *The Great Risk Shift: The Assault on American Jobs, Families, Health Care, and Retirement and How You Can Fight Back* (2006). See also George P. Shultz and John B. Shoven, *Putting Our House in Order: A Guide to Social Security and Health Care Reform* (2008), p. 50.

4. Michael J. Graetz and Jerry L. Mashaw, *True Security: Rethinking American Social Insurance* (1999), p. 109.

5. For a more extended discussion, see Olivia S. Mitchell and Stephen P. Utkus, "Lessons from Behavioral Finance for Retirement Plan Design," in Olivia S. Mitchell and Stephen P. Utkus (eds.), *Pension Design and Structure: New Lessons from Behavioral Finance* (2004), pp. 3–41.

6. Alicia H. Munnell and Mauricio Soto, "What Replacement Rates Do Households Actually Experience in Retirement?" Center for Retirement Research at Boston College, Working Paper No. 2005-10 (August 2005).

7. Edward N. Wolff, Ajit Zacharias, and Hyunsub Kum, "Net Government Expenditures and the Economic Well-Being of the Elderly in the United States, 1989–2001," in Dimitri B. Papadimitriou (ed.), note 2, pp. 81, 114.

8. Keith A. Bender and Natalia Jivan, "What Makes Retirees Happy? An Issue in Brief," Center for Retirement Research at Boston College, Working Paper No. 28 (February 2005).

9. John Ameriks, Andrew Caplin, and John Leahy, "Retirement Consumption: Insights from a Survey," 89 *Review of Economics and Statistics* (2007), p. 265.

10. Ibid.

11. Keith A. Bender and Natalia Jivan, note 8.

12. Ibid.

13. E.g., Yang Yang, "Social Inequalities in Happiness in the United States, 1972 to 2004: An Age-Period-Cohort Analysis," 73 *American Sociological Review* (2008), p. 204.

14. Keith A. Bender and Natalia Jivan, note 8.

15. Alicia Munnell and Steven A. Sass, *Working Longer: The Solution to the Retirement Income Challenge* (2008), p. 3.

16. Ibid.

17. Judith Feder, Harriet L. Komisar, and Marlene Niefeld, "Long-Term Care in the United States: An Overview," 19 *Health Affairs* (2000), pp. 40, 52.

18. This subject is treated in detail by Alicia Munnell and Steven A. Sass, note 15.

19. Robert Blendon and John Benson, "How Americans Viewed Their Lives in 2005," 49 *Challenge* (May–June 2006), pp. 48, 57.

20. Jacob S. Hacker, note 3, p. 114.

21. Edward N. Wolff, *Retirement Insecurity: The Income Shortfalls Awaiting the Soon-to-Retire* (2002), p. 52.

22. See generally Damon Darlin, "A Contrarian View: Save Less and Still Retire with Enough," *New York Times* (January 27, 2007), section A, p. 1.

23. John K. Scholz, Ananth Seshadri, and Surachai Khitatrakun, "Are Americans Saving Optimally for Retirement?" 114 *Journal of Political Economy* (2006), p. 607. See also Damon Darlin, note 22.

24. Alicia H. Munnell, Anthony Webb, and Francesca Golub-Sass, "Is There Really a Retirement Savings Crisis? An NRRI Analysis," Center for Retirement Research at Boston College, Working Paper No. 7-11 (August 2007).

25. Elke U. Weber, "Who's Afraid of a Poor Old Age? Risk Perception in Risk Management Decisions," in Olivia S. Mitchell and Stephen P. Utkus (eds.), note 5, p. 53.

26. Teresa A. Sullivan, Elizabeth Warren, and Jay L. Westbrook, *The Fragile Middle Class: Americans in Debt* (2000), p. 146.

27. John Budetti, Lisa Duchon, Cathy Schoen, and Janet Shikles, *Can't Afford to Get Sick: A Reality for Millions of Working Americans* (1999), p. 2.

28. Ibid., p. 6.

29. Julius B. Richmond and Rashi Fein, *The Health Care Mess: How We Got Into It and What It Will Take to Get Out* (2005), p. 233.

30. Jacob S. Hacker, note 3, p. 142.

31. Teresa A. Sullivan, Elizabeth Warren, and Jay L. Westbrook, note 26, p.144.

32. Robert Blendon and John Benson, note 19, pp. 48, 54.

33. Ibid., p. 52.

34. One British study of the relationship between debt and well-being reported: "The evidence confirms our main hypothesis, that debt is associated with increased levels of psychological distress." Sarah Brown, Karl Taylor, and Stephen W. Price, "Debt and Distress: Evaluating the Psychological Cost of Credit," 26 *Journal of Economic Psychology* (2005), p. 642.

35. David DeWitt, George D. Lowe, Charles W. Peck, and Evans B. Curry, "The Changing Association between Age and Happiness: Emerging Trend or Methodological Artifact," 58 *Social Forces* (1980), p. 1302.

36. Louis Uchitelle, *The Disposable Americans: Layoffs and Their Consequences* (2006), p. 212. See also Henry S. Farber, *Job Loss in the United States, 1981–2001* (2003).

37. Gregory C. Murphy and James A. Athanasou, "The Effect of Unemployment on Mental Health," 72 *Journal of Occupational and Organizational Psychology* (1999), p. 83.

38. Jacob S. Hacker, note 3, p. 125.

39. Teresa Ghilarducci, *When I'm Sixty-Four: The Plot against Pensions and the Plan to Save Them* (2008), p. 137.

40. Andrew E. Clark, Yannis Georgellis, and Peter Sanfey, "Scarring: The Psychological Impact of Past Unemployment," 68 *Economica* (2001), p. 221.

41. See Kim S. Cameron, "Investigating Organizational Downsizing—Fundamental Issues," 33 *Human Resource Management* (1994), p. 183; Kenneth P. Demeuse, Paul A. Vanderheiden, and Thomas Bergmann, "Announced Layoffs: Their Effect on Corporate Financial Performance," 33 *Human Resource Management* (1994), p. 509; Ronald Henkoff, "Cost Cutting: How to Do It Right," *Fortune* (April 9, 1990), p. 17.

42. Don Sull and Nitin Nohria, "Managing Distrust: The Hidden Cost of Downsizing," 8 *Business Ethics Forum* (1995), p. 73. See also Jeffrey Pfeffer, "The Real Cost of the Virtual Workforce," 66 *Stanford Business* (March 1998), p. 21.

43. Jacob S. Hacker, note 3, p. 84.

44. Oren M. Levin-Waldman, "Plant Closings: Is WARN an Effective Response?" 56 *Review of Social Economy* (1998), p. 59; Stephen Nord and Yuan Ting, "The Impact of Advance Notice of Plant Closings on Earnings and the Probability of Unemployment," 44 *Industrial and Labor Relations Review* (1991), p. 681.

45. Paul Osterman, "Employment and Training Policies: New Directions for Less Skilled Adults" (paper prepared for Urban Institute Conference on Workforce Policies for the Next Decade and Beyond, October 2005).

46. See Derek Bok, *The State of the Nation: Government and the Quest for a Better Society* (1996), pp. 78–85.

47. Jacob S. Hacker, note 3, p. 19.

48. David G. Blanchflower and Andrew J. Oswald, "Well-Being, Insecurity, and the Decline of American Job Satisfaction" (unpublished paper, July 22, 1999).

49. Gregory C. Murphy and James A. Athanasou, note 37; Nick Kates, Barrie S. Grieff, and Duane Q. Hagen, *The Psychological Impact of Job Loss* (1990); Andrew E. Clark and Andrew J. Oswald, "Unhappiness and Unemployment," 104 *Economic Journal* (1994), p. 648. Unemployment has also been found to be strongly related to suicide. Augustine J. Kposowa, "Unemployment and Suicide: A Cohort Analysis of Social Factors Predicting Suicide in the US National Longitudinal Mortality Study," 31 *Psychological Medicine* (2001), p. 127.

50. Klaus Boehnke, Shalom H. Schwartz, Claudia Stromberg, and Lilach Sagiv, "The Structure and Dynamics of Worry: Theory Measurement and Cross-National Replications," 66 *Journal of Personality* (1998), p. 745; Shalom H. Schwartz and Gila Melech, "National Differences in Micro and Macro Worry," in Ed Diener and Eunkook M. Suh (eds.), *Culture and Subjective Well-Being* (2000), p. 219.

51. International Labor Office, *Economic Security for a Better World* (2004), p. 246. See also Hans De Witte, "Job Insecurity and Well-Being: Review of the Literature and Explanation of Some Unresolved Issues," 8 *European Journal of Work and Organizational Psychology* (1999), p. 155; Catherine A. Heaney, Barbara A. Israel, and James S. House, "Chronic Job Insecurity among Automobile Workers: Effects on Job Satisfaction and Health," 38 *Social Science Medicine* (1994), p. 1431. It should be noted, however, that David G. Blanchflower and Andrew J. Oswald, note 48, have concluded that although job insecurity is a leading cause of dissatisfaction with one's work, it has not contributed to any decline in job satisfaction.

52. Teresa A. Sullivan, Elizabeth Warren, and Jay L. Westbrook, note 26, p. 223.

53. Ibid., p. 224.

54. National Opinion Research Center survey quoted by Elizabeth Warren, "Unsafe at Any Rate," *Democracy Journal* (Summer 2007), p. 11.

55. For an extended analysis of the arguments for personal responsibility, see Alexander Brown, "If We Value Personal Responsibility, Which Policies Should We Favour?" 22 *Journal of Applied Philosophy* (2005), p. 23; see also David Schmidtz and Robert E. Gooden, *Social Welfare and Individual Responsibility* (1998).

56. See, e.g., Greg M. Shaw and Sarah E. Mysiewicz, "The Polls—Trends: Social Security and Medicare," 68 *Public Opinion Quarterly* (2004), p. 394.

57. David Hume, *A Treatise of Human Nature*, book 3, part 2, section 7, P. H. Nidditch and L. A. Selby-Bigge (eds.) (2d ed., 1978); also quoted in Avner Offer, *The Challenge of Affluence: Self-Control and Well-Being in the United States and Britain Since 1950* (2006), p. 42.

58. "Only in America," *This Week* (January 23, 2009), p. 6.

59. For an extended review of the credit card industry, see Robert D. Manning, *Credit Card Nation: The Consequences of America's Addiction to Credit* (2000).

60. There are problems in figuring out just how to devise a minimum Social Security payment, but it appears to be possible to do so in a way that will at least lower poverty rates among the elderly by two-thirds. See Melissa M. Favreault, Gordon B. T. Mermin, and C. Eugene Steuerle, "Minimum Benefits in Social Security," in Dimitri B. Papadimitriou (ed.), note 2, p. 347.

61. There is some dispute over the number of elderly persons who live in poverty. The official figure is close to 10 percent, but Bruce D. Meyer and James X. Sullivan, "Consumption and Income Poverty for Those 65 and Over," Harris School Working Paper, Series 07.21 (2007), contend that if one looks at actual consumption rather than income, poverty rates for retirees over 75 are below 4 percent, while rates for retirees aged 65–74 are just under 5 percent. Whichever figure is correct, there is much to be said for reducing the number.

62. Brigitte C. Madrian and Dennis F. Shea, "The Power of Suggestion: Inertia in 401(k) Participation and Savings Behavior," 116 *Quarterly Journal of Economics* (2001), p. 1149.

63. The arguments for placing responsibility on the employee to opt out are discussed in Richard H. Thaler and Cass R. Sunstein, "Libertarian Paternalism Is Not an Oxymoron," 70 *University of Chicago Law Review* (2003), p. 1159.

64. See David B. Lipskey, Ronald L. Seeber, and Richard D. Finch, *Emerging Systems for Managing Workplace Conflicts* (2003). A number of technical questions would have to be resolved in setting up workable procedures. For example, should employees have to assume all or part of the arbitration costs if they lose their case in order to discourage frivolous claims? Should lawyers be prohibited in order to avoid costly demands for discovery in an effort to force the employer to settle the case?

65. Stephen Nord and Yuan Ting, note 44.

66. Robert J. Landry III and Amy K. Yarbrough, "Global Lessons from Consumer Bankruptcy and Healthcare Reforms in the United States: A Struggling Social Safety Net," 16 *Michigan State Journal of International Law* (2007), p. 343. According to Teresa A. Sullivan, Elizabeth Warren, and Jay L. Westbrook, note 26, p. 75, loss of wages is the principal factor leading to bankruptcy.

67. See, e.g., Paul Osterman, note 45.

68. Amit Dor and Indermit S. Gill, "Evaluating Retraining Programs in OECD Countries: Lessons Learned," 13 *World Bank Research Observer* (1998), p. 79.

69. Lori G. Kletzer and Howard F. Rosen, "Reforming Unemployment Insurance for the Twenty-First Century Workforce," The Hamilton Project, The Brookings Institution, Discussion Paper (September 2006); Robert J. LaLonde, "The Case for Wage Insurance," Council on Foreign Relations, CSR No. 30 (September 2007), p. x.

## Chapter 7: Relieving Suffering

1. Bhavani S. Reddy, "The Epidemic of Unrelieved Chronic Pain," 27 *Journal of Legal Medicine* (2006), pp. 427, 430.

2. Walter F. Stewart, Judith A. Ricci, Elsbeth Chee, David Morganstein, and Richard Lipton, "Lost Productive Time and Cost Due to Common Pain Conditions in the U.S. Workforce," 290 *Journal of the American Medical Association* (2003), p. 2443.

3. Amy J. Dilcher, "Damned If They Do, Damned If They Don't: The Need for a Comprehensive Public Policy to Address the Inadequate Management of Pain," 13 *Annals of Health Law* (2004), pp. 81, 82.

4. Timothy E. Quill and Diane E. Meier, "The Big Chill—Inserting the DEA into End-of-Life Care," 354 *New England Journal of Medicine* (2006), p. 1.

5. Charles S. Cleeland, Rene Gonin, Alan K. Hatfield, John H. Edmonson, Ronald H. Blum, James A. Stewart, and Kishan J. Pandya, "Pain and Its Treatment in Outpatients with Metastatic Cancer," 330 *New England Journal of Medicine* (1994), p. 592.

6. Shannan W. Leelyn, "Failures in Pain Management: The Collision of Law and Medicine," 27 *Thomas Jefferson Law Review* (2004–5), pp. 133, 136.

7. Ben A. Rich, "The Politics of Pain: Rhetoric or Reform?" 8 *DePaul Journal of Health Care Law* (2004–5), pp. 519, 525.

8. Sandra H. Johnson, "The Social, Professional, and Legal Framework for the Problem of Pain Management in Emergency Medicine," *Pain Management in the Emergency Department* (Winter 2005), pp. 741, 755.

9. Shannan W. Leelyn, note 6, p. 139.

10. Amy J. Dilcher, note 3, p. 85.

11. Shannan W. Leelyn, note 6, pp. 149–50.

12. Amy J. Dilcher, note 3, p. 114.

13. Ibid., pp. 128–35.

14. Quoted in Jane E. Brody, "Let's Get Serious about Relieving Chronic Pain," *New York Times* (January 10, 2006), p. 7.

15. Institute of Medicine, *Sleep Disorders and Sleep Deprivation: An Unmet Public Health Problem* (2006), p. 1.

16. Ibid.

17. Ibid., p. 150.

18. Daniel Kahneman and Jason Riis, "Living, and Thinking About It: Two Perspectives on Life," in Felicia A. Huppert, Nick Baylis, and Barry Keverne (eds.), *The Science of Well-Being* (2007 ed.), pp. 285, 295; Daniel Kahneman, Alan B. Krueger, David A. Schkade, Norbert Schwarz, and Arthur A. Stone, "A Survey Method for Characterizing Daily Life Experience: The Day Reconstruction Method," 306 *Science* (2004), p. 1776. It should be noted that the direction of causation remains unclear. It is possible that part of this effect is due to a tendency by less happy people to have more than average trouble sleeping.

19. Gayle Green, *Insomnia* (2008), p. 1.

20. Paul Martin, *Counting Sheep: The Science and Pleasures of Sleep and Dreams* (2002), pp. 63–64.

21. Institute of Medicine, note 15.

22. Lawrence J. Epstein, *The Harvard Medical School Guide to a Good Night's Sleep* (2007), pp. 6–7.

23. Gayle Green, note 19, p. 15.

24. Institute of Medicine, note 15, p. 188.

25. Compare Lawrence J. Epstein, note 22, p. 113 ("usually advise against continued long-term use"), with William C. Dement, *The Promise of Sleep* (1999), pp. 157–66 ("taking sleeping pills to get a good night's sleep—even for extended periods—is inherently no more sinful than taking daily doses of heart medication"). The quotation appears on p. 163.

26. James K. Walsh, "Drugs Used to Treat Insomnia in 2002: Regulatory-Based Rather Than Evidence-Based Medicine," 27 *Sleep* (2004), p. 1441.

27. Institute of Medicine, note 15, p. x.

28. Ibid., p. 162.

29. Quoted by Andrew Solomon, *The Noonday Demon: An Atlas of Depression* (2001), p. 55.

30. E.g., Kay R. Jamison, *Night Falls Fast: Understanding Suicide* (1999). Jamison notes that in studies of suicide, researchers have regularly shown depression to be involved in a majority of cases; pp. 21, 245.

31. Paul E. Greenberg et al., "The Economic Burden of Depression in the United States: How Did It Change between 1990 and 2000?" 64 *Journal of Clinical Psychiatry* (2007), pp. 1465, 1469.

32. Ronald C. Kessler et al., "The Epidemiology of Major Depression Disorder," 289 *Journal of the American Medical Association* (2003), pp. 3095, 3099.

33. Ibid.

34. See Avner Offer, *The Challenge of Affluence: Self-Control and Well-Being in the United States and Britain Since 1950* (2006), pp. 347–48.

35. Ronald C. Kessler et al., "Prevalence and Treatment of Mental Disorders, 1990 to 2003," 352 *New England Journal of Medicine* (2005), p. 2515.

36. Andrew Solomon, note 29, p. 104; Patricia Ainsworth, *Understanding Depression* (2000), p. 123.

37. See generally Richard G. Frank and Sherry A. Glied, *Better but Not Well: Mental Health Policy in the United States Since 1950* (2006).

38. Cited to me in my office at Harvard University during 2007 by Dr. Ronald C. Kessler. The assertion that only one in six depressed individuals receive treatment "that meets minimal standards of adequacy" appears in Philip S. Wang, Gregory Simon, and Ronald C. Kessler, "The Economic Burden of Depression and the Cost-Effectiveness of Treatment," 12 *International Journal of Methods in Psychiatric Research* (2003), p. 22.

39. David Mechanic, *Mental Health and Social Policy* (3d ed., 1989), p. 147.

40. Joseph Glenmullen, *Prozac Backlash: Overcoming the Dangers of Prozac, Zoloft, Paxil, and Other Antidepressants with Safe, Effective Alternatives* (2000), p. 219.

41. Thomas C. Buchmueller, Philip F. Cooper, Mireille Jacobson, and Samuel H. Zuvekas, "Parity for Whom? Exemptions and the Extent of State Mental Health Parity Legislation," *Health Affairs*, web exclusives, online articles from vol. 26, nos. 4–6 (2007).

42. Claire Robb, William E. Haley, M. A. Becker, Larry A. Polivka, and H-J Chwa, "Attitudes toward Mental Health Care in Younger and Older Adults: Similarities and Differences," 7 *Aging and Mental Health* (2003), pp. 142, 149.

### Chapter 8: Marriages and Families

1. Roy F. Baumeister and Mark R. Leary, "The Need to Belong: Desire for Human Attachments as a Fundamental Human Motivation," 117 *Psychological Bulletin* (1995), pp. 497, 515.

2. Quoted by James Q. Wilson, *The Marriage Problem: How Our Culture Has Weakened Families* (2002), p. 221.

3. David G. Myers, "Close Relationships and the Quality of Life," in Daniel Kahneman, Ed Diener, and Norbert Schwarz (eds.), *Well-Being: The Foundations of Hedonic Psychology* (1999), pp. 374, 378.

4. Richard E. Lucas, Andrew E. Clark, Yannis Georgellis, and Ed Diener, "Reexamining Adaptation and the Set Model of Happiness: Reactions to Change in Marital Status," 84 *Journal of Personality and Social Psychology* (2003), pp. 527, 536.

5. Carol Gohm, Shigehiro Oishi, Janet Darlington, and Ed Diener, "Culture, Parental Conflict, Parental Marital Status, and the Subjective Well-Being of Young Adults," 60 *Journal of Marriage and the Family* (1998), p. 319.

6. Linda G. Russek and Gary E. Schwartz, "Perceptions of Parental Caring Predict Health Status in Mid-Life: A 35 Year Follow-up of the Harvard Mastery of Stress Study," 59 *Psychosomatic Medicine* (1997), p. 144.

7. Richard E. Lucas, "Time Does Not Heal All Wounds: A Longitudinal Study of Reaction and Adaptation to Divorce," 16 *Psychological Science* (2005), p. 945.

8. Sara McLanahan and Gary Sandefur, *Growing Up with a Single Parent: What Hurts, What Helps* (1994), p. 136. For a description of the adverse effects of divorce on husbands and fathers, see Sanford L. Braver, *Divorced Dads: Shattering the Myths* (1998), p. 111.

9. David M. Cutler, Edward L. Glaeser, and Karen E. Norberg, "Explaining the Rise in Youth Suicide," National Bureau of Economic Research, Working Paper No. 7713 (May 2000).

10. See, e.g., Frank Furstenberg, "Values, Policy, and the Family," in Daniel P. Moynihan, Timothy M. Smeeding, and Lee Rainwater (eds.), *The Future of the*

*Family* (2004), p. 267; Susan M. Jekielek, "Parental Conflict, Marital Disruption, and Children's Emotional Well-Being," 76 *Social Forces* (1998), p. 905.

11. Rex Forehand, Lisa Armistead, and Corinne David, "Is Adolescent Adjustment Following Parental Divorce a Function of Predivorce Adjustment?" 25 *Journal of Abnormal Child Psychology* (1997), p. 157; Paul R. Amato and Alan Booth, *A Generation at Risk: Growing Up in an Era of Family Upheaval* (1997).

12. Wade F. Horn, "Marriage, Family, and the Welfare of Children: A Call for Action," in Daniel P. Moynihan, Timothy M. Smeeding, and Lee Rainwater (eds.), note 10, p. 185.

13. James Q. Wilson, note 2, pp. 7, 8.

14. D. Lichter, *Marriage as a Public Policy*, Progressive Policy Institute (2001), available at www.ppionline.org/ppi_sub.cfm?knlgAreaID=114&subsecID=144.

15. Paul R. Amato and Rebecca A. Maynard, "Decreasing Nonmarital Births and Strengthening Marriage to Reduce Poverty," 17 *The Future of Children* (2007), p. 117.

16. See generally Harry T. Holzer, "The Labor Market and Young Black Men: Updating Moynihan's Perspectives," 621 *Annals of the American Academy of Political and Social Science* (2009), p. 47.

17. Bruce Western and Christopher Wildeman, "The Black Family and Mass Incarceration," 621 *Annals of the American Academy of Political and Social Science* (2009), p. 221.

18. Will Marshall and Isabel V. Sawhill, "Progressive Family Policy in the Twenty-First Century," in Daniel P. Moynihan, Timothy M. Smeeding, and Lee Rainwater (eds.), note 10, p. 208. More generally, see Douglas Kirby, *Emerging Answers: Research Findings on Programs to Reduce Teen Pregnancy* (2001); Maggie Gallagher, "Can Government Strengthen Marriage? Evidence from the Social Sciences," National Institute for Marriage and Public Policy, and Institute for American Values, available at http://www.marriagedebate.com/pdf/Can%20Government%20Strengthen%20Marriage.pdf.

19. Isabel V. Sawhill (ed.), *One Percent for the Kids: New Policies, Brighter Futures for America's Children* (2003), p. 68.

20. Paul R. Amato and Rebecca A. Maynard, note 15, p. 122; Scott M. Stanley, "Making a Case for Premarital Education," 50 *Family Relations* (2001), p. 272; J. S. Carroll and William J. Doherty, "Evaluating the Effectiveness of Premarital Prevention Programs: A Meta-Analysis Review of Outcome Research," 52 *Family Relations* (2003), p. 105.

21. Paul R. Amato and Rebecca A. Maynard, note 15, p. 127.

22. On the lasting effects of divorce, see Richard E. Lucas, note 7. On the subsequent well-being of unhappily married couples who decide not to divorce or separate, see Linda J. Waite, Don Browning, William J. Doherty, Maggie Gallagher, Ye Luo, and Scott M. Stanley, *Does Divorce Make People Happy? Findings from a Study of Unhappy Marriages* (2002).

23. Paul R. Amato and Rebecca A. Maynard, note 15.

24. Kathryn Edin and Joanna M. Reed, "Why Don't They Just Get Married? Barriers to Marriage among the Disadvantaged," 15 *The Future of Children* (2005), p. 117. See also Alan M. Hershey, Barbara Devaney, M. Robin Dion, and Sheena McConnell, *Building Strong Families: Guidelines for Developing Programs* (2004), p. 5.

25. Paula England and Kathryn Edin, "Unmarried Couples with Children: Hoping for Love and the White Picket Fence," in Paula England and Kathryn Edin (eds.), *Unmarried Couples with Children* (2007), p. 11.

26. Kathryn Edin and Joanna M. Reed, note 24.

27. According to Paula England and Kathryn Edin, note 25, pp. 3, 4, and 9, over 80 percent of the couples in their sample cited economic factors as a reason for not getting married, and 78 percent of the men who met the couples' economic threshold, as opposed to only 19 percent who didn't, were married to the mother of their child within the next four years. See also Alan M. Hershey, Barbara Devaney, M. Robin Dion, and Sheena McConnell, note 24.

28. See generally Ron Haskins, "Moynihan Was Right: Now What?" 621 *Annals of the American Academy of Political and Social Science* (2009), p. 281.

29. See generally David L. Kirp, *The Sandbox Experiment: The Pre-School Movement and Kids-First Politics* (2007).

30. Hirokazu Yoshikawa, Thomas S. Weisner, and Edward D. Lowe (eds.), *Making It Work: Low-Wage Employment, Family Life, and Child Development* (2006), p. 11.

31. Jane Waldfogel, "International Policies toward Parental Leave and Child Care," 11 *The Future of Children* (2001), p. 99.

32. James Q. Wilson, note 2, p. 192.

33. Anna Gassman-Pines and Hirokazu Yoshikawa, "Five-Year Effects of an Anti-Poverty Program on Marriage among Never-Married Mothers," 25 *Journal of Policy Analysis and Management* (2006), p. 11.

34. James Q. Wilson, note 2, p. 194; David L. Olds, Charles R. Henderson Jr., Harriet J. Kitzman, John J. Eckenrode, Robert E. Cole, and Robert C. Tetelbaum, "Pre-Natal and Infancy Home Visitation by Nurses: Recent Findings," 9 *The Future of Children* (1999), p. 44.

35. Gardiner Harris, "Infant Deaths Fall in U.S., Though Rate Is Still High," *New York Times* (October 16, 2008), pp. A-16–17.

36. Nancy E. Reichman, "Low Birthweight and School Readiness," 15 *The Future of Children* (2005), pp. 91, 92.

37. Norman F. Watt, Catherine Ayoub, Robert H. Bradley, Jini E. Puma, and Whitney A. Le Boef (eds.), *The Crisis in Youth Mental Health*, vol. 4, *Early Intervention Programs and Policies* (2006), pp. xxv–xxvii.

38. Betty Hart and Todd Risley, *Meaningful Differences in the Everyday Experiences of Young American Children* (1995).

39. Edward Zigler, Walter S. Gilliam, and Stephanie M. Jones, *A Vision for Preschool Education* (2007), p. 94.

40. Sandra Scarr, "American Child Care Today," 53 *American Psychologist* (1998), pp. 95, 102.

41. Nazli Baydar and Jeanne Brooks-Gunn, "Effects of Maternal Employment on Preschoolers' Cognitive and Behavioral Outcomes: Evidence from the Children of the National Longitudinal Study," 27 *Developmental Psychology* (1991), p. 932. But W. Steven Barnett and Debra J. Ackerman conclude that any negative effects on behavior do not last long. "Costs, Benefits, and Long-Term Effects of Early Care and Education Programs: Recommendations and Cautions for Community Developers," 37 *Community Development: Journal of the Community Development Society* (2006), pp. 86, 88.

42. David L. Kirp, note 29, p. 151.

43. Compare Susanna Loeb, Bruce Fuller, Sharon L. Kagan, and Bidemi Carrol, "Child Care in Poor Communities: Early Learning Effects of Type, Quality, and Stability," 75 *Child Development* (2004), pp. 47, 61; and National Institute of Child Health and Human Development, Early Child Care Research Network, "The Relation of Childcare to Cognitive and Language Development," 71 *Child Development* (2000), pp. 960, 962, with Sandra Scarr, note 40.

44. Lawrence Schweinhart, *Significant Benefits: The High/Scope Perry Preschool Study through Age 27* (1993).

45. W. Steven Barnett, "Benefit-Cost Analysis of Preschool Education: Findings from a 25-Year Follow-up," 63 *American Journal of Orthopsychiatry* (1993), p. 500.

46. Edward Zigler, Walter S. Gilliam, and Stephanie M. Jones, note 39, p. 23.

47. Compare G. J. Whitehurst and G. M. Massetti, "How Well Does Head Start Prepare Children to Learn to Read," in Edward Zigler and Sally J. Styfco (eds.), *The Head Start Debates* (2004), p. 251, with Administration for Children and Families, *Head Start Faces 2000: A Whole-Child Perspective on Program Performance* (2003).

48. W. Steven Barnett, "Long-Term Effects of Early Childhood Programs on Cognitive and School Outcomes," 5 *The Future of Children* (1995), pp. 25, 43.

49. Janet Currie and Matthew Neidell, "Getting inside the 'Black Box' of Head Start Quality: What Matters and What Doesn't," 26 *Economics of Education Review* (2007), pp. 83, 98.

50. Ibid., pp. 83, 98.

51. James Heckman, "Policies to Foster Human Capital," 54 *Research in Economics* (2000), pp. 3, 8.

52. Robert G. Lynch, *Exceptional Returns: Economic, Fiscal, and Social Benefits of Investment in Early Childhood Development* (2004), pp. 9–17.

53. Ibid., p. 12.

54. Ibid., pp. 24–32.

55. Greg Duncan and Katherine Magnuson, "Costs and Benefits from Early Investments to Promote Human Capital and Positive Behavior," in Norman F. Watt, Catherine Ayoub, Robert H. Bradley, Jini E. Puma, and Whitney A. Le Boef (eds.), note 37, pp. 27, 43.

56. William T. Gormley Jr., Ted Gayer, Deborah Phillips, and Brittany Dawson, "The Effects of Universal Pre-K on Cognitive Development," 41 *Developmental Psychology* (2005), p. 872.

### Chapter 9: Education

1. Daniel Gilbert, *Stumbling on Happiness* (2006).

2. See table 4, p. 28.

3. See chapter 1, note 45.

4. See chapter 6, pp. 102–3.

5. Lowell C. Rose and Alec M. Gallup, "The 39th Annual Phi Delta Kappa/ Gallup Poll of the Public's Attitudes toward the Public Schools," *Phi Delta Kappan* (September 2007), pp. 33, 41. Huge majorities of Americans also affirm the need for civic education in the schools; in fact, in a 1996 survey, the public supported teaching civics more strongly than any other academic subject. Margaret S. Branson, "The Role of Civic Education," Education Position Paper prepared for the Educational Policy Task Force of the Communitarian Network (1998), p. 19.

6. National Commission on Excellence in Education, *A Nation at Risk* (1983).

7. Douglas N. Harris, Michael J. Handel, and Lawrence Mishel, "Education and the Economy Revisited: How Schools Matter," 79 *Peabody Journal of Education* (2004), pp. 36, 37.

8. Bill Clinton, First State of the Union Address (January 25, 1994).

9. Statement by the President on No Child Left Behind Reauthorization (October 9, 2007).

10. "I think the big challenge that we've got on education is making sure that from kindergarten or pre-kindergarten through your 14th or 15th year of school, or 16th year of school, or 20th year of school, that you are actually learning the kinds of skills that make you competitive and productive in a modern technological economy." David Leonhardt, "After the Great Recession: An Interview with President Obama," *New York Times Magazine* (May 3, 2009), pp. 36, 39.

11. Center on Education Policy, *Instructional Time in Elementary Schools: A Closer Look at Changes for Specific Subjects* (February 2008).

12. Ibid.

13. National Center for Educational Statistics, U.S. Department of Education, *America's High School Graduates: Results from the 2005 NAEP High School Transcript Study* (2007), pp. 8–9, 12.

14. Karen D. Arnold, *Lives of Promise: What Becomes of High School Valedictorians* (1995), pp. 35, 62–64.

15. See, e.g., Sidney Verba, Kay L. Schlozman, and Henry E. Brady, *Voice and Equality: Civic Voluntarism in American Politics* (1995), p. 425.

16. See chapter 4, p. 76.

17. See, e.g., Margaret S. Branson, note 5.

18. Kenneth J. Cooper, "Most Students Have Little Understanding of Civics," *Washington Post* (November 19, 1999), p. A-16.

19. Derek Bok, *The Trouble with Government* (2001), pp. 405–6.

20. William A. Galston, "Political Knowledge, Political Engagement, and Civic Education," 4 *Annual Review of Political Science* (2001), pp. 217, 222.

21. Judith Torney-Purta, "The School's Role in Developing Civic Engagement: A Study of Adolescents in Twenty-Eight Countries," 6 *Applied Developmental Science* (2002), p. 203.

22. Compare Cliff Zukin, Scott Keeter, Molly Andolina, Krista Jenkins, and Michael X. Delli Carpini, *A New Engagement? Political Participation, Civic Life, and the Changing American Citizen* (2006), p. 145 (close to 40 percent), with Judith Torney-Purta, note 21, p. 208 (50 percent).

23. John A. Goodlad, "Toward a Place in the Curriculum for the Arts," in Bennett Rainer and Ralph A. Smith (eds.), *The Arts, Education, and Aesthetic Knowing: Ninety-First Yearbook of the National Society for the Study of Education, Part II* (1992), p. 192. According to Thomas A. Hatfield, "art education is just about anything conducted anytime, anywhere, and taught by just about anyone." "Who Teaches Art? What Is Learned?" 108 *Arts Education Policy Review* (2007), p. 7.

24. Thomas A. Hatfield, note 23.

25. E.g., Tara Parker-Pope, "With Arrival of Adolescence, a Departure of Physical Activity," *Boston Globe* (July 16, 2008), p. A-9.

26. John J. Ratey and Eric Hagerman, *Spark: The Revolutionary New Science of Exercise and the Brain* (2008).

27. Martin E. P. Seligman, "Can Happiness Be Taught?" 133 *Daedalus* (Spring 2004), p. 80; Karen Reivich, Jane Gillham, Andrew Shatte, and Martin E. P. Seligman, "A Resilience Initiative and Depression Prevention Program for Youth and Their Parents: Executive Summary" (unpublished report, October 2005).

28. See, e.g., Michael Fordyce, "A Program to Increase Happiness: Further Studies," 30 *Journal of Counseling Psychology* (1983), p. 483 (students tested 9–18 months after completing a course reported higher levels of happiness than a control group); Sonja Lyubomirsky, *The How of Happiness: A Scientific Approach to Getting the Life You Want* (2007).

29. Roger P. Weissberg, Karol L. Kumpfer, and Martin E. P. Seligman, "Prevention That Works for Children and Youth: An Introduction," 58 *American Psychologist* (2003), p. 425.

30. Mark T. Greenberg et al., "Enhancing School-Based Prevention and Youth Development through Coordinated Social, Emotional, and Academic Learning," 58 *American Psychologist* (2003), p. 466. The various articles that follow in this symposium give a useful survey of the field.

31. See Barry Schwartz, "Pitfalls on the Road to a Positive Psychology of Hope," in Jane E. Gillham (ed.), *The Science of Optimism and Hope: Essays in Honor of Martin E. P. Seligman* (2000), p. 399.

32. John H. Pryor, Sylvia Hurtado, Victor B. Saenz, Jennifer A. Lindholm, William S. Korn, and Kathryn M. Mahoney, *The American Freshman—National Norms for Fall 2005*, Higher Education Research Institute, University of California, Los Angeles (2006).

33. Ibid.

34. See, e.g., Tim Kasser and Allen D. Kanner, *Psychology and Consumer Culture: The Struggle for a Good Life in a Materialistic World* (2004).

35. Ernest T. Pascarella and Patrick T. Terenzini, *How College Affects Students*, vol. 2, *A Third Century of Research* (2005), pp. 282–83.

36. Derek Bok, *Our Underachieving Colleges: A Candid Look at How Much Students Learn and Why They Should Be Learning More* (2006), pp. 272–77.

37. Norman Nie and Sunshine Hillygus, "Education and Democratic Citizenship," in Diane Ravitch and Joseph Viteritti (eds.), *Making Good Citizens: Education and Civil Society* (2001), p. 30.

38. Ernest T. Pascarella and Patrick T. Terenzini, note 35, pp. 274–75.

39. Alexander W. Astin, Linda J. Sax, and Juan Avalos, "Long-Term Effects of Volunteerism during the Undergraduate Years," 32 *Review of Higher Education* (1999), p. 187.

40. E.g., Raymond Wolfinger and Steven J. Rosenstone, *Who Votes?* (1980). For an unusually careful study of the effects of college and volunteering on voting and other forms of civic participation, see Thomas S. Dee, *Assessing the College Contribution to Civic Engagement*, in Michael S. McPherson and Morton O. Schapiro (eds.), *Succeeding in College: What It Means and How to Make It Happen* (2008), p. 199.

41. E.g., Catherine E. Ross and Marieke Van Willigen, "Education and the Subjective Quality of Life," 38 *Journal of Health and Social Behavior* (1997), p. 275.

42. Allan Bloom, *The Closing of the American Mind: How Higher Education Has Failed Democracy and Impoverished the Souls of Today's Students* (1987).

43. Anthony T. Kronman, *Education's End: Why Our Colleges and Universities Have Given Up the Meaning of Life* (2007), p. 44.

44. Some idea of what was covered in this course is described by the instructor, Tal Ben-Shahar, in his book, *The Question of Happiness: On Finding Meaning, Pleasure, and the Ultimate Currency* (2002).

45. "Positive Psychology," Hofstra University, Department of Psychology, PSYXXX, Jeffrey Froh, Instructor (Spring 2007).

46. "Positive Psychology: Thriving and Flourishing," University of Windsor, Department of Psychology, Psych 441, Dr. Hart, Instructor (Fall 2005).

47. "The Psychology of Happiness," University of Virginia, Department of Psychology, Psychology 403, Jaime Kurtz, Instructor (Summer 2006).

48. Arthur Levine and Jeanette Cureton, *When Hope and Fear Collide: A Portrait of Today's College Students* (1998), pp. 140–41.

49. For accounts of these developments and what they imply for persons practicing law, compare Gregory Mazares, "Associate Retention of Law Firms: What Are Your Lawyers Saying about You?" 29 *Capitol University Law Review* (2002), p. 903, with Patrick Shiltz, "On Being a Happy, Healthy, and Ethical Member of an Unhappy, Unhealthy, and Unethical Profession," 52 *Vanderbilt Law Review* (1999), p. 871; and, for a much more positive view, with Charles Silver and Frank B. Cross, "What's Not to Like about Being a Lawyer?" 109 *Yale Law Journal* (1999), p. 1443.

50. Amy Delong, "Retaining Legal Talent," 29 *Capitol University Law Review* (2002), p. 893.

51. See e.g., Anthony T. Kronman, *The Lost Lawyer: Failing Ideals of the Legal Profession* (1993); Rakesh Khurana, *From Higher Aims to Hired Hands: The Social Transformation of American Business Schools and the Unfulfilled Promise of Management as a Profession* (2007); Kenneth Ludmerer, *Time to Heal: American Medical Education from the Turn of the Century to the Era of Managed Care* (1997).

52. See chapter 4, pp. 65–66.

53. This process is elaborated in much detail by James Engell and Anthony Dangerfield, *Saving Higher Education in the Age of Money* (2005).

54. Quoted by Robert Darnton, "Google and the Future of Books," *New York Review of Books* (February 12, 2009), p. 9. The words are carved in gold letters on the wall of the Trustees' Room of the New York Public Library.

### Chapter 10: The Quality of Government

1. E.g., Everett Carll Ladd and Karlyn H. Bowman, *What's Wrong: A Survey of American Satisfaction and Complaint* (1998), p. 19.

2. *CBS News/New York Times Poll* (July 2007), on file at Roper Center for Public Opinion Research, University of Connecticut; Alec M. Gallup and Frank Newport (eds.), *The Gallup Poll: Public Opinion 2007* (2008), p. 14.

3. Alec M. Gallup and Frank Newport (eds.), note 2, p. 386.

4. Ibid., pp. 7–8.

5. E.g., Karl Zinmeister, "Indicators," *American Enterprise* (March–April 1995), p. 16.

6. Derek Bok, *The Trouble with Government* (2001), pp. 22–27. The nature of the progress made in a variety of domains is discussed in greater detail in Derek Bok, *The State of the Nation: Government and the Quest for a Better Society* (1996).

7. Derek Bok, *The Trouble with Government* (2001), pp. 27–38.

8. Daniel Kaufman, Aart Kraay, and Massimo Mastruzzi, "Governance Matters VI: Aggregate and Individual Governance Indicators 1996–2006," World Bank Policy Research Working Paper 4280 (July 2007), pp. 76–93.

9. John F. Helliwell, "Well-Being and Social Capital: Does Suicide Pose a Puzzle?" 81 *Social Indicators Research* (2007), p. 455.

10. Derek Bok, note 7, pp. 30–34.

11. Ibid., pp. 123–46.

12. Ibid., pp. 147–68.

13. Ibid., pp. 169–95.

14. Fay Lomax Cook and Edith J. Barrett, *Support for the American Welfare State: The View of Congress and the Public* (1992).

15. Martin Gilens, *Why Americans Hate Welfare: Race, Media, and the Politics of Antipoverty Policy* (1999).

16. John R. Hibbing and Elizabeth Theiss-Morse, *Stealth Democracy: Americans' Beliefs about How Government Should Work* (2002), p. 102.

17. Ibid., pp. 68–82.

18. See note 6.

19. "American Public Opinion in the 1990s," 9 *The Public Perspective: A Roper Center Review of Public Opinion and Polling* (1998), p. 12.

20. Steven Kelman, *Making Public Policy* (1987), p. 272.

21. Everett Carll Ladd and Karlyn H. Bowman, note 1, p. 103.

22. Thomas E. Mann and Norman J. Ornstein (eds.), *Congress, the Press, and the Public* (1994), p. 50.

23. Harris Interactive Poll (October 2006).

24. Gary Jacobson, *The Politics of Congressional Elections* (3d ed., 1992), p. 5.

25. Pew Research Center for the People and the Press, *Deconstructing Distrust: How Americans View Government* (1998), p. 100.

26. E.g., Adam Clymer, "The Body Politic: Nonvoting Americans and Calls for Reform Are Drawn into Sharp Focus in 2000 Races," *New York Times* (January 2, 2000), pp. 1, 27.

27. Mark Rozell, "Press Coverage of Congress, 1946–92," in Thomas E. Mann and Norman J. Ornstein (eds.), note 22, p. 109.

28. Media Tenor International, *Network Coverage of President and Congress 2002–2008* (2008).

29. Doris A. Graber, *Processing Politics: Learning from Television in the Internet Age* (2001), p. 113.

30. Mark Rozell, note 27, p. 110.

31. Stephen J. Farnsworth and S. Robert Lichter, *The Nightly News Nightmare: Television's Coverage of U.S. Presidential Elections, 1986–2004* (2d ed., 2007), p. 155.

32. John R. Hibbing and Elizabeth Theiss-Morse, "The Media's Role in Public Negativity toward Congress: Distinguishing Emotional Reactions and Cognitive Evaluations," 42 *American Journal of Political Science* (1998), p. 475.

33. Joseph N. Capella and Kathleen H. Jamieson, *Spiral of Cynicism: The Press and the Public Good* (1997).

34. Ibid., pp. 139–69, especially pp. 147, 165.

35. E.g., "American Public Opinion in the 1990s," p. 43 (83 percent of Americans agreed with the statement quoted in the text).

36. Ibid., p. 31.

37. John R. Hibbing and Elizabeth Theiss-Morse, note 16.

38. John R. Hibbing and Elizabeth Theiss-Morse, *Congress as Public Enemy: Public Attitudes toward American Public Institutions* (1995).

39. Ibid., p. 147.

40. Mark Rozell, note 27, p. 112.

41. James D. Carroll, Walter D. Broadnax, Gloria Contreras, Thomas E. Mann, Norman J. Ornstein, and Judith Stiehm, *We the People: A Review of U.S. Government and Civics Textbooks* (1987), p. iv.

42. Ibid., p. vi.

43. Richard G. Niemi and Jane Junn, *Civic Education: What Makes Students Learn* (1998), pp. 71, 72.

44. See Derek Bok, *Our Underachieving Colleges: A Candid Look at How Much Students Learn and Why They Should Be Learning More* (2006), pp. 172–93.

45. U.S. Department of Education, *The New College Course Map and Transcript Files: Changes in Course-Taking and Achievement 1972–1993* (2d ed., 1999), pp. 187–89.

46. Norman Nie and Sunshine Hillygus, "Education and Citizenship," in Diane Ravitch and Joseph Viteritti (eds.), *Making Good Citizens: Education and Civil Society* (2001), p. 30.

47. Carol Schneider, "Educational Missions and Civic Responsibility," in Thomas Ehrlich (ed.), *Civic Responsibility and Higher Education* (2000), pp. 98, 120.

48. John R. Hibbing and Elizabeth Theiss-Morse, "Civics Is Not Enough: Teaching Barbarics in K–12," 29 *PS: Political Science and Politics* (1996), pp. 57, 60.

49. Cliff Zukin, Scott Keeter, Molly Andolina, Krista Jenkins, and Michael X. Delli Carpini, *A New Engagement: Political Participation, Civic Life, and the Changing American Citizen* (2006), p. 190.

50. Center for Democracy and Civil Society, *American Civic Engagement in Comparative Perspective* (2007), p. 25.

### Chapter 11: The Significance of Happiness Research

1. Heinz Welsch, "Environment and Happiness: Valuation of Air Pollution Using Life Satisfaction Data," 58 *Ecological Economics* (2001), p. 801.

2. For discussions of these issues, see Irvin Waller, *Less Law, More Order: The Truth about Reducing Crime* (2006); Michael D. Raisig and Roger B. Parks, "Community Policing and the Quality of Life," in Wesley G. Skogan (ed.),

*Community Policing: Can It Work?* (2004), p. 207; Robert C. Davis, Arthur Lurigio, and Susan Herman (eds.), *Victims of Crime* (3d ed., 2007); Marian Lieberman, *Restorative Justice: How It Works* (2007).

3. For discussions of improving the process for deciding whether to initiate war, see John Hart Ely, *War and Responsibility: Constitutional Lessons of War and Its Aftermath* (1992); *National War Powers Commission Report* (James A. Baker III and Warren Christopher, cochairs) (2008).

4. John Maynard Keynes, "Economic Possibilities for Our Grandchildren," in *Essays in Persuasion* (Norton, 1991; originally published in 1931), p. 367.

# INDEX